# International Negotiation
# in a Complex World

# International Negotiation in a Complex World

THIRD EDITION

Brigid Starkey, Mark A. Boyer,
and Jonathan Wilkenfeld

ROWMAN & LITTLEFIELD PUBLISHERS, INC.
*Lanham • Boulder • New York • Toronto • Plymouth, UK*

Published by Rowman & Littlefield Publishers, Inc.
A wholly owned subsidiary of The Rowman & Littlefield Publishing Group, Inc.
4501 Forbes Boulevard, Suite 200, Lanham, Maryland 20706
http://www.rowmanlittlefield.com

Estover Road, Plymouth PL6 7PY, United Kingdom

British Library Cataloguing in Publication Information Available

**Library of Congress Cataloging-in-Publication Data**

Starkey, Brigid, 1962–
   International negotiation in a complex world / Brigid Starkey, Mark A. Boyer,
and Jonathan Wilkenfeld.—3rd ed.
      p.   cm.—(New millennium books in international studies)
   Rev. ed. of: Negotiating a complex world. 2nd ed. c2005.
   Includes bibliographical references and index.
   ISBN 978-0-7425-6679-8 (cloth : alk. paper)—ISBN 978-0-7425-6680-4
(pbk. : alk. paper)—ISBN 978-0-7425-6681-1 (electronic)
   1. Diplomatic negotiations in international disputes.   I. Boyer, Mark A.
II. Wilkenfeld, Jonathan.   III. Starkey, Brigid, 1962– Negotiating a complex
world.   IV. Title.
JZ6045.S73   2010
327.1'7—dc22
                                                             2009043887

Printed in the United States of America

# Contents

# Illustrations

**Photos**

**Figures**

## Boxes

# Preface

Ten years have passed since the writing of this book, originally titled *Negotiating a Complex World*. This relatively short period of time in the course of international diplomacy has nevertheless been marked by events that have had a profound impact on the way nations and a host of other international actors shape their interactions. The accelerated spread of the AIDS epidemic, the September 11, 2001, attacks on the World Trade Center and the Pentagon, followed by the wars in Afghanistan and Iraq, natural disasters of unfathomable proportions in Indonesia and Thailand in 2004 and China in 2008, Israel's wars against Hezbollah in Lebanon in 2006 and Hamas in Gaza in 2008, ongoing crises over nuclear programs in North Korea and Iran, the global financial crisis of 2008–2009, the spread of international terrorism, and the reshaping of international alliances in the wake of these events, have all combined to create an international environment quite different from the one faced just before the turn of the century.

This new edition attempts to capture some of these elements of change, and to assess their impact on the practice of negotiation. In this volume, we have updated the cases that we examine in some depth to illustrate various points in our discussion of negotiation. These include an updated discussion of the Kyoto process on global climate change, and an extended case study dealing with the negotiations surrounding efforts to deal with the North Korean nuclear capability. We also discuss in some detail the Iraq case, particularly from the point of view of the contrast between the coalition pieced together through intricate negotiations in 1990–1991, in contrast to the seemingly inevitable rush to war that typified the Iraq situation in 2002–2003. We have also updated our treatment of the Israeli-Palestinian conflict, and the role that negotiation and mediation have played in that tragic region of the world.

It is not accidental that the three of us came together to author a book on international negotiation when we did. What has united us is our almost three-decade association with the ICONS project and the negotiation simulations that the project has spawned over the years. Our timing was dictated by the fast pace of developments in the electronic delivery of curricula and by our enhanced ability to conduct our business, even international negotiations, via electronic media. In some sense, the real world is catching up with ICONS, although this bold assertion requires some explanation.

In the early 1980s, the International Communication and Negotiation Simulations project (or ICONS, as it came to be called) developed an approach to the teaching of international studies and foreign languages based on the use of foreign policy simulations delivered over available computer networks. These active learning exercises, which as of 2009 have involved participants at almost 150 universities in thirty-five countries around the world, place students in the roles of national decision makers as they represent their countries in negotiations on such topics as trade, human rights, world health, the environment, nuclear proliferation, and various regional conflict arenas. The near-universal availability of Internet access has allowed ICONS to bring together in joint exercises students representing different cultural, linguistic, and ideological backgrounds through the exchange of messages and electronic real-time conferencing. The principles of negotiation remain pretty constant, as do the strategies, tactics, and approaches employed. ICONS and other pedagogical approaches involving computers and networks have allowed us both to involve larger numbers of our students in these joint exercises and, at the same time, to give our students a glimpse of the possibilities for virtual negotiation available through technology. With this volume, we inaugurate a joint ICONS/Rowman & Littlefield program in which the purchase of the book can be linked to a significant discount for classes and individuals interested in participating in ICONS exercises.

But we do not want the reader to come away with the mistaken impression that this is meant to be an ICONS supplementary text, although *International Negotiation in a Complex World* can certainly be used effectively as such. Rather, this book attempts to reach a broad audience of students and policy analysts who have a need for a more in-depth understanding of how nations and other international actors go about achieving their objectives through the give-and-take of the negotiation process. The skillful practice of negotiation can sometimes mean the difference between peace and war, and is often the only viable alternative to devolving into violence as a means of dispute resolution. In addition, in this increasingly interdependent world, strategies based more on the goal of achieving mutual benefit, rather than strict individual gain, will ultimately serve us better; effective use of the negotiation process can help us get there. This book attempts to provide the reader with some of the tools necessary to achieve this lofty objective, while drawing the reader's attention to cases in which negotiation has been used more or less effectively in recent years.

Although the three of us are the ones who put fingers to keyboard in the writing of this book, and are ultimately responsible for its content, many others over the years have contributed to the shaping of our ideas on the teaching of negotiation and the use of simulation techniques. These include Richard Brecht, Judith Torney-Purta, David Crookall, Joyce Kaufman, Leopoldo Schapira, Sarit Kraus, Robert Noel, Barry Hughes, Daniel Druckman, Kathleen Smarick, Victor Asal, James Barry, and the late Harold Guetzkow. Doreen Bass, Patty Landis, Mike Miller, Mike Butler, Natalie Florea Hudson, Kimberly Weir, Mary Caprioli, Kim Holley, Andrew Blum, Daniella Fridl, Audrey Tetteh, Beth Blake, Alex Jonas, Tim Wedig, and Rosamaria Morales, who served in various capacities over the years for Project ICONS, did much to provide the environment in which the study of negotiation could flourish. Jennifer Knerr, then political science editor at Rowman & Littlefield, believed enough in this project to provide encouragement and guidance throughout, and the late Deborah J. Gerner, New Millennium Books series editor for Rowman & Littlefield, along with her distinguished editorial board, provided important substantive input along the way. Likewise, we appreciate the continued support and guidance provided by Susan McEachern, our current editor at Rowman & Littlefield. Program assistants Virginie Grzelczyk, Nicole Powell, Jane Schmitt, and Chantal Russell offered valuable insight and extensive support for this book project at critical junctures. Betsy Kielman, former managing director of Project ICONS, guided this undertaking since its inception and helped manage the difficult task of coordinating among three authors, ever respectful of differing styles and sometimes tortured use of the English language. We gratefully acknowledge grant support from the U.S. Department of Education's Fund for the Improvement of Postsecondary Education (FIPSE), particularly for its funding of negotiation-related teaching materials, and the U.S. Institute of Peace for early funding of then daring ideas. Finally, our institutions, the University of Maryland and the University of Connecticut, have provided the intellectual environment (and of course some resources) to see this project through.

# 1

# Introduction

The desire to resolve problems amicably pervades all arenas of social organization. The function of negotiation is to provide a channel for peaceful dispute resolution. As a process, negotiation involves common and often overlapping interests. It is, after all, the recognition of a mutual interest or joint problem that produces a dialogue. The underlying mutuality of the decision to negotiate is in fact the key to the process. However, negotiation discourses can also be highly conflictual. In the international realm, this means that negotiation is often all that stands between peace and war.

*International Negotiation in a Complex World* focuses on negotiation in the international arena. In doing so, the book draws from the impressive body of academic literature on negotiation; hence, it is useful to begin with an overview of this hybrid topic. Owing to its relevance to so many different fields—including business, communication, law, political science, psychology, and conflict resolution—the academic literature on negotiation is broad and varied. Most books and articles on negotiation fall into one of four categories, as illustrated in figure 1.1. The horizontal axis plots the level of abstraction: at one end are the theoretical materials that analyze the process of negotiation; at the other are the applied materials that provide hands-on tips on how to negotiate successfully. Along the vertical axis can be plotted the value orientation or approach of the negotiation process, ranging from those that are primarily competitive in approach to those that are primarily collaborative. This range is also categorized as integrative versus distributive. The easiest way to describe the opposing sides is according to the stark split on whether negotiations result in clear winners and

**Figure 1.1   Literature on Negotiation**

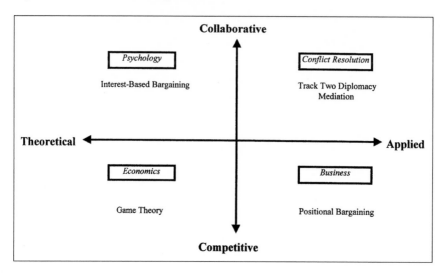

losers or whether the only negotiated settlements that last are win-win ones (Murray 1986, 180–181). As an introduction to the study of international negotiation, *International Negotiation in a Complex World* draws concepts and examples from each of the categories described in figure 1.1. More specifically, the book provides a starting point for exploration of the many factors that impact the course of international negotiations and their outcomes, including an examination of the negotiation environment or setting, the issues and actors involved, and the strategies and tactics that characterize the bargaining phase of these episodes.

## Negotiation in Broad Context

Many parallels may be drawn between the international negotiation process and the bargaining and tactics of negotiation in other forums. Newscasts often report heated disagreements between labor and management at industrial plants, usually involving issues of pay, hours, benefits, job security, and worker productivity. Work stoppages, strikes, walkouts, and lockouts can be used as instruments in serious labor disputes to apply temporal and financial pressures on the disputants. The rough equivalents of such measures in the international context include such competitive diplomatic techniques as economic embargoes, diplomatic isolation, and political sanctions (George 1997). In the legal realm, figuring out who gets what in divorce proceedings—children, property, and often blame—can also involve bargaining at its most contentious. Indeed, over time, the comparison of such troubled pairs as the Israelis and the Palestinians or Northern Ireland's Catholics and Protestants with couples involved in hotly contested divorces represents a useful analogy: all seek to split while arguing fiercely about the common property. Moreover, in the international arena, as in family disputes, third-party intervention, such as mediation or more binding arbitration, is sometimes the only way to bring parties to an agreement that will be fair and lasting.

Many popular negotiating tactics are readily recognizable from one social setting to another. Acting as the "playground bully" is one such general tack, whereby ultimatums and threats are issued and the recipient is told exactly what will happen if there is a failure to comply—"My father will beat up your father." In the international system, this can translate into "My state will invade yours." Another standard tactic is the offer-counteroffer approach, demonstrated in a car-lot transaction. Here, the salesperson normally starts off with an inflated figure for the car, so as to demonstrate flexibility when making the concession in price that the buyer will inevitably demand. An international parallel can be found in trade negotiations, when initial requests for market penetration, for example, are unreasonably high. Or consider the good cop–bad cop routine, whereby a suspect being questioned is led to believe that one of the interrogators is likely to become violent at any moment. The suspect is therefore urged to confess immediately to the nice cop before things get ugly. Aspiring member Turkey accused the European Union (EU) of using this tactic when the European Parliament very publicly encouraged Ankara's membership aspirations, while at the same time the Slovenian president of the EU canceled a planned accession conference, citing Ankara's insufficient progress toward membership goals (EurActiv 2008).

The principles that underlie successful negotiations are also recognizable from one arena to another: power, trust, equity, and status. Yet, while recognizing the very broad correspondences within varying negotiation environments, it is equally important to focus attention on the uniqueness of international negotiation. Diplomatic negotiation has particularly high stakes and tremendous visibility. Its connection to firmly established laws, standards, and practices can be much more tenuous than in these other forums. With recourse to enforcement and punishment mechanisms uncertain, the burden of responsibility on international negotiators to draft good, fair, solid agreements that all parties will respect is unmatched.

## Negotiation in International Relations

Within the realm of international relations, diplomatic negotiation is central to the functioning of the system of nation-states that has evolved over time. This type of interaction is distinguishable from transnational negotiations between non-state entities, such as those taking place between firms operating in today's global economy. For example, merger negotiations between the Dutch airline KLM and Air France represented the first cross-border airline merger among members of the European Union. Negotiations took place within the context of the global travel slowdown of the post–September 11, 2001, period. While both airlines retained their own brands, by 2007 the new group was carrying more business travelers per year than any of its competitors and ranked second in terms of total passengers carried (Eurofound 2008). These negotiations took place without involvement of either government, distinguishing them from past examples of a more hybrid nature, where governments and corporations had negotiated major deals together. For example, in the late 1980s, Chrysler CEO Lee Iacocca traveled with American president George H. W. Bush on a trade mission to Japan. In this case, Chrysler was a contributing party to diplomatic negotiations between two nation-states.

*International Negotiation in a Complex World* focuses on international diplomatic negotiation—broadly defined to take full account of nontraditional actors and issues that are changing the landscape of today's international system. While transnational issues, actors, and the "global governance" challenges they pose are increasingly important, it is still the international arena of states upon which the international relations community focuses the most attention. Despite proclamations and forecasts to the contrary, neither the nation-state nor the international system of states is dead in the new millennium. What has changed are calculations of state interest and state navigation of the international system. Both have become much more complex, owing to the increased importance of such factors as crossnational actors and forces. These topics have become central to the study of international negotiation, both as the focus of many contemporary negotiation dialogues and, in some cases, as situational factors influencing those dialogues.

Traditional definitions of diplomatic negotiation stress official state-to-state exchanges and tend to focus on the roles of important individual players—presidents, prime ministers, foreign ministers, ambassadors, and generals. Indeed, states and their leaders are still central characters in international relations and in headline-grabbing negotiations. States share the stage with a variety of other actors. Some of these others "play by the rules" in their attempts to influence outcomes in the international system. Others clearly hold these rules in disdain. With the proliferation of new states in the post–World War II period, navigating the international system has become more difficult. Some of these states are extremely weak and cannot exercise their will in meaningful ways within their regions or in the larger international system. Almost all states must endure strong pulls on their central power from increasingly vocal ethnic and other identity groups, as well as a variety of fluid international economic forces and their agents. In some cases, there are also actual rival centers of power. Some of these are sanctioned by member states, as in the case of the European Commission for European Union member states. Others are not, as exemplified by the threat posed by jihadist groups to central states in the Arab and Muslim world. Some of these rival sources of power are bigger than the central states, some smaller; but the challenges to the supremacy of central state organs are undeniable. Assumptions about uniform state motivations and responses to different situations—which are almost always oversimplified—are now more problematic than ever. The perception of the state as monolithic is no longer true. Moreover, calculations of national interest—long the guiding precept for foreign policy decisions—have been greatly complicated by a host of issues (e.g., environmental and resource concerns) that can rival traditional military-security considerations in importance to various stakeholders in the state.

Tribal, clan, religious, and linguistic identifications are just some of the factors that complicate negotiation situations for state actors. They give political voice to nonstate actors of various kinds who increasingly figure into important diplomatic situations. Clearly, U.S. dealings with Iraq over the past twenty years have been greatly complicated by uncertainties over the tribal loyalties of many of the parties, including the Kurds in northern Iraq and the many Shiite groups in the south. The U.S. military spent a great deal of time after the 2003 invasion trying to sort out the fighting between Shiite militias, some of whom were loyal to Muqtada al-Sadr (Sadrists), others of whom fought on the side of Grand Ayatollah Ali Sistani. The tribal landscape in Iraq alone involves 20–30 large tribes (Otterman 2003). A key element of General David Petraeus's 2007 "surge" in Iraq was to try to bring these key tribes into a loose alliance with the United States. Similarly, in various ongoing protracted conflicts in Africa and Asia— Somalia and Sri Lanka, for example—anomalous actors like the Bantus and the Tamil Tigers, respectively, are crucial players in any eventual peace agreements.

Looking closely at diplomatic negotiation entails the examination of some of the key processes in international relations as a whole. Negotiation highlights the extent to which foreign policy is not simply about the external relations of actors in the international system but also about their internal political situations as well. Thanks in large part to global news networks, domestic constituencies are now better informed about international developments than ever before. Calculations of group interests other than those of the state figure more prominently into unfolding negotiation scenarios. American Jody Williams, for example, won the 1998 Nobel Peace Prize for her work on the International Campaign to Ban Landmines, even though the United States was loudly condemned during those same negotiations for its lax stance on the issue. Williams, an employee of

Vietnam Veterans of America, worked on the campaign via e-mail from her farm in Vermont. That work lasted for six years and involved representing the concerns of approximately 700 humanitarian and grassroots groups on the land mine issue.

### Negotiation as a High-Stakes Game

There are many different ways to conceptualize the negotiation process, including through images of *stages*, *rounds*, and *phases*. This book offers the analogy of a board game to help organize the topic for the reader. This comparison of the international negotiation process to a game puts emphasis on the idea of strategic moves and countermoves. Key components of the process are presented as the board (the negotiation setting), the players (the negotiators), the stakes (the issues to be resolved), and the moves (the decisions the negotiators make). In fact, international negotiation can be viewed as the ultimate strategic contest. In cases of nuclear brinkmanship, such as the Cuban missile crisis of 1962, the highest possible stakes are at risk.

The game metaphor is admittedly a simple one, but it provides an entry point into a discussion of negotiation; a variety of contests can be examined in which players have different attributes and specific boards, stakes, and strategic moves available to them. A comparison of just three games—checkers, chess, and backgammon—highlights both the relationships to negotiation and the distinctions among them. Checkers is a game of attrition, suggesting a "hard negotiation" situation where the last one standing is the winner. There is only a single path to power, and that comes directly at the expense of the adversary. Difficult negotiations in protracted conflict situations, such as those between Turkish and Greek Cypriots or Ulster's Protestants and Catholics, offer a real-world equivalence. There is a sense that both sides are trying to outlast the other and finish first by simply keeping their own assets intact. In chess, however, understanding one's opponent in a strategic sense is much more important. Each side has a wide variety of tools and options available to it, and the range of correct choices is determined by the choices of one's adversary. Knowledge of an opponent's history is an important strategic asset, as is an understanding of classic strategies of the game. The Americans and the Soviets during the Cold War were often depicted as having been involved in a dangerous chess match.

Backgammon—in stark contrast to chess and checkers—introduces the element of luck to the strategy. Those who believe that fate plays an important role in negotiations favor this analogy. AbiNader (1998, C5) prefers this conception when he describes negotiating in the Middle East as a game of backgammon, or *tawla*, "in which dice and luck are significant factors in creating and closing opportunities for the opponent." This approach involves significant gambles, creating a more unpredictable negotiation process.

Winning may be defined differently in each of these games, although, as with all contests, outcomes are win-lose (zero-sum), with recognition of clear winners and losers. Negotiation in the real world is, of course, far more complicated. Collaborative approaches to negotiation are based on the assumption that it is possible to achieve win-win (non-zero-sum) outcomes, where the result is at least minimally acceptable to all involved. Moreover, real negotiation does not take place in a controlled environment, as is the case with board games. Situational factors—internal and external— have impacts on negotiations. The negotiation setting, for example, can be affected by a variety of factors, such as domestic elections, outbursts of conflict, misguided public statements, and economic and environmental crises.

## Structuring Negotiation

This book explores the topic of international negotiation by illustrating how various contextual and situational factors influence the negotiation process. In this introductory chapter, two case examples are sketched out using the game metaphor and its main components: setting (the board), actors (players), issues (stakes), and strategy (moves). Subsequent chapters will look in more detail at each of these elements. Chapter 2 describes the way the international system setting interfaces with a number of situation-specific characteristics to influence negotiations. Chapter 3 surveys the various types of international actors in negotiations and examines motivational factors leading them to behave as they do in negotiation situations. Chapter 4 explores the different ways issues play out in negotiations and develops the notion of issue saliency to account for actor responses in various circumstances. Chapter 5 examines the "game" itself, where different strategic approaches determine the outcome for all involved players. Chapter 6 summarizes the negotiation landscape and examines the role that negotiation played in the protracted Iraqi conflict.

The importance of each of these areas to an overall understanding of the negotiation process is illustrated through the two examples that follow. These provide brief sketches of how the negotiation game works in practice. These cases, the global climate talks (Kyoto and beyond) and the North Korean nuclear arms talks (six-party negotiations), illustrate the interplay of contrasting characteristics within negotiation episodes. The use of examples to highlight key elements of the diplomatic negotiation process is a central feature of this text. Various tenets of the Kyoto climate talks and the Korean nuclear crisis case are referenced in subsequent chapters to help the reader place theoretical and conceptual points into a helpful context. In addition, a number of other references are made to historical and contemporary examples, some of which are more fully developed for the reader, including the Arab-Israeli (with emphasis on the Palestinian-Israeli relationship), Northern Ireland, North American Free Trade Agreement (NAFTA), and Iraq and Iran cases.

Climate negotiations from 1992 onward represent a large, multilateral negotiation process in which nongovernmental actors play pivotal roles. The issue of climate change is a tricky one for states, as it has traditionally not been high on their list of priorities but central for some domestic and/or global constituencies. The 1997 Conference of the Parties [COP] Session 3 of the United Nations Framework Convention on Climate Change (UNFCC) was held in Kyoto, Japan, and still stands as the most productive single episode in these ongoing negotiations. As with the prior negotiations on global warming and its effects, the actual Kyoto talks were set in a very constrained time frame. Delegations were given only ten days in which to negotiate a final agreement, the main points of which were to be drawn from preliminary negotiation rounds. The range of strategies on display in Japan ran from the typical, such as stonewalling, to more sophisticated moves, such as the effort by the United States and other advanced industrial nations to shift the focus away from national accountability and implementation toward joint or collective arrangements. Although rhetoric did run high at times, the overall tone of these negotiations was collaborative, as befits a public-goods dilemma such as that posed by global warming. There was, however, tremendous pressure for quick results in Kyoto.

In contrast, the crises precipitated by North Korea's nuclear brinkmanship involve far fewer participants than the climate negotiations. Six parties have been involved to differing degrees in negotiations on North Korea from the late 1990s onward. The 2008 climate talks in Poznan, Poland, featured 186 nations! Moreover, the Korean case almost exclusively involves traditional state actors, though they have operated at times through the UN structure and talks are at times informed by intergovernmental organizations (IGOs) such as the Nuclear Non-Proliferation Treaty (NPT) and the International Atomic Energy Agency (IAEA). Taking place in the context of an unresolved fifty-year-old war and against the backdrop of possible further military confrontation, the North Korea talks are crisis negotiations. Moreover, in contrast to the climate negotiations, the North Korea negotiations are of a very traditional nature: nation-states at loggerheads over issues of national security. A notable feature of this type of negotiation case is the key roles that individuals play. Three American presidents—Clinton, Bush, and Obama—have been drawn into maneuverings with North Korean leader Kim Jong Il. Successive secretaries of state, including Madeleine Albright, Colin Powell, Condoleezza Rice, and Hillary Clinton have devoted significant energies to the cycle of crises. Special envoys, notably Christopher Hill, who had previously honed his skills in Macedonia and Kosovo, spent years trying to negotiate an agreement within the six-party negotiation framework. Counterparts in the People's Republic of China and South Korea have also played important roles on the individual level. Chinese president Hu Jintao's shuttle diplomacy and South Korean president Roh Moo-hyun's efforts to open up a bilateral channel with the Democratic People's Republic of Korea (DPRK) to the north are two important examples. The North Korean leader remains so mysterious that a cottage industry for academics and journalists has grown up around trying to predict what motivates the enigmatic Kim's behavior in Pyongyang.

Although individuals have played important roles at key points in the climate negotiations—Al Gore was even brought to Poznan in 2008 for an encore to his Kyoto performance—personalities have not been as important a factor in the climate case. Where they do play a role, it is to break deadlocks and move the delegations toward agreement, as for example during the critical endgame in Kyoto. Positions on the issues—whether to take meaningful global action on global warming or not—primarily define the camps in the climate negotiations. In stark contrast, the Korea talks have involved a more deliberate process, a negotiation dance of moves and countermoves.

Although the contrasts between the two cases are clear, several noteworthy similarities also exist. Despite the difference in stakes between the two cases—climate negotiations have been on a long-term, "slow train" for most states, while North Korea periodically produces a crisis to get itself back on the front-burner—the analogy of a game of chicken can be applied to both. In the climate negotiations, this brinkmanship has been in evidence in follow-up conferences to Kyoto (COP-4 through COP-14), where international progress has been largely stalled while states wait for each other to relent and take meaningful *national* action. With the Kyoto Treaty set to expire, this waiting game of chicken is about to reach its climax. With North Korea, the game of chicken is a somewhat more curious one, whereby Pyongyang has tried to draw attention to itself, calling on the United States to take a seat at the negotiation table "or else." Of course, after the United States relents, Pyongyang more often than not leaves the table itself, usually in a huff. Its stated position is that it does not want multilateral negotiations, but a bilateral forum with the United States. Kim Jung Il's failing health and apparent designation of his young son as his successor has further raised the sense of urgency in Pyongyang, leading to a withdrawal from the six-party forum and a threat of war against South Korea in 2009 (Herskovitz 2009).

Both cases also point to a complicated post–Cold War diplomatic era for the United States. The EU nations went after the United States and George W. Bush with unprecedented vigor when he refused to have the Americans take a seat at the Kyoto follow-up talks in Bonn (COP-6, Part 2) in 2001. His inaction became symbolic of a more general withdrawal from multilateral institutions and regimes at that time. And in Southeast Asia, Washington and Seoul had some trouble crafting a common position on the North Korean threat, despite a fifty-year partnership. Perceptions of the United States as a negotiation *obstacle* during the Bush-Cheney years pervaded both arenas, putting American credibility and resolve on trial in the diplomatic arena to a greater extent than at any other point since the end of World War II.

Moreover, neither of these cases features a clear-cut, definable endpoint. Though this chapter focuses primarily on two discrete episodes (the ten-day COP-3 talks in Kyoto in 1997 and the failure of the Beijing Accord to take hold at the 2005 six-party negotiations on North Korea), the discussion is broader by necessity. Those Kyoto talks are part of a course of action begun a decade earlier and played out long after the meeting in Japan, in what is now called the "Kyoto process" (Bondansky 2001). In fact, if the next round of negotiations is successful, the Kyoto label may well be replaced by the "Copenhagen Treaty" or process. The North Korea question and crisis goes back to the 1950s, with each negotiation attempt clearly tied to the next, creating an ongoing case that is punctuated by successive crises.

## Action in Kyoto: Global Climate Change Negotiations

*Background*

Many environmental problems are by nature transboundary in scope. This makes them classic public-goods issues, as a number of nation-states share concern over their fates and must also share the burden of finding solutions to them. Pollution and overexploitation of resources are two major collective problems that have been magnified by intense population growth, urbanization, and industrialization during the last century.

No environmental problem has engendered as much controversy as what is popularly known as the global warming debate. Although scientists had long hypothesized that emissions of greenhouse gases—such as carbon dioxide, methane, nitrous oxide, and chlorofluorocarbons—negatively affect the environment by creating a "thick blanket" that traps heat in the atmosphere, it was not until 1990 that an official international report actually endorsed the theory. Established by the UN Environment Programme and the World Meteorological Association, the Intergovernmental Panel on Climate Change (IPCC) released a report indicating that at least one group of scientists and technical experts had reached a consensus on the existence of a problem. The report asserted that emissions of greenhouse gases from such modern conveniences as automobiles, refrigerators, and air conditioners would cause rapid and harmful climate change if left unabated (Houghton, Jenkins, and Ephraums 1990, 1). The panel projected that by the year 2100 the global temperature would rise between 1 and 3.5 degrees Celsius, with potentially profound effects on water levels, food availability, and species survival.

Not surprisingly, studies questioning these predictions have been forthcoming ever since, including Thomas Gale Moore's *Climate of Fear* (1998). But the 1985 discovery of the hole in the ozone layer over Antarctica had mobilized international public opinion on environmental concerns, and despite the uncertainty surrounding the greenhouse effect, many seemed in favor of concerted international action. That action began at the 1992 Earth Summit in Rio de Janeiro. There, working on a tight deadline, 152 states and the European Union signed the Framework Convention on Climate Change. In it, they agreed that states would issue periodic reports on their national greenhouse gas emissions, share information about climate change strategies, and work toward the creation of cooperative strategies for funding and technology to combat climate change. They also agreed to accept a nonbinding commitment to take measures aimed at returning their greenhouse gas emissions to 1990 levels by the year 2000 (United Nations Framework Convention on Climate Change, or UNFCC). It was this clause—which some thought much too ambitious and others deemed not nearly ambitious enough—that would ultimately cause the most difficulty for future rounds of climate negotiations.

The working group established to follow up the Rio meeting was the Conference of the Parties, which held its first session—COP-1—in Berlin in 1995. The Berlin Mandate that came out of these meetings shocked many observers with its force. It stated that developed countries would have to do more than they had promised at Rio to reduce their greenhouse gas emissions: stabilization at 1990 levels would not be adequate (Anderson 1995, 7). The document was particularly noteworthy because it legitimized different treatment for developed and developing countries, a position that many countries in the southern hemisphere had supported. The ensuing disagreement over whether the premise was fair continued on through COP-2 in Geneva in 1996 and into the Kyoto talks of 1997. The Berlin Mandate also gave rise to a battle of percentages among the developed countries, one that defined much of the negotiations in Kyoto.

Many observers point to these twin issues—differential treatment for developed and developing countries and the lack of mechanisms to force states to realize the target goals—as the persistent weak points in the subsequent Kyoto Protocol. Indeed, Kyoto highlights the double-edged sword of two-level games. Tremendous progress is often made under pressure, but will the results stand up long-term? In the case of the international protocol agreement reached in Japan, serious domestic misgivings and conflicts over whether to pursue this level of greenhouse gas emissions nationally in the United States were swept under the carpet in the rush to find a positive outcome to the negotiations (Purvis 2003). This failure to reconcile the two-level game led directly to the United States becoming the only treaty signatory to fail to ratify. Congress was so opposed the Kyoto Protocol that neither Bill Clinton nor George W. Bush even submitted it for a ratification vote. This two-level game continues to be vexing to the pro-treaty side, as President Obama has even faced renewed skepticism from some members of Congress about the veracity of scientific claims on global warming (Fahrenthold 2009, A4). This comes despite the fact that the UN now calls the scientific community "unequivocal" in its position on the existence of climate change (Lisowski 2005, 364).

*Setup*

In December 1997 the COP held its third session (COP-3) in Kyoto. The primary goal was for the parties to the 1992 UN Framework Convention on Climate Change to agree on a legal document—a binding protocol—that would specify national targets and timetables for cuts in greenhouse gas emissions. The meeting in Kyoto represented the climax of ten years of international climate negotiations. In this way it was not an independent event but the continuation of a long process, one that is highly technical and arduous and not readily accessible to nonexperts in the science of climate change. Yet, the ongoing quest for a meaningful climate treaty has spawned a large community of people whose involvement in the issue is a full-time endeavor. Although complex, these negotiations involve a single issue, and despite the pleas for urgency voiced by many environmentalists, the negotiations are distinctly noncrisis in nature for the governments involved. Yet, time pressure put on the delegates introduced an artificial sense of crisis to the talks. One observer described this as Kyoto treating "a long-term problem as though it were a short-term crisis" (Bondansky 2001, 45). The climate talks represent negotiations with a past as well as a future. Indeed, it is important to look at what has transpired since the negotiation of this complex and ambitious protocol. The legacy factor is perhaps the defining characteristic of the Kyoto negotiations. Many participants and analysts had considered the Framework Convention on Climate Change that came out of the 1992 Rio Earth Summit to be deeply flawed. The main criticism was that it did not bind its signatories to any definite action. While some lauded the progress made in "only fifteen months" on the Rio convention, others pointed to this as the problem: such a difficult issue would take much longer to work through. They criticized the pressure that deadlines before and at Rio presented to participants. The agreement was denounced as hurried and weak, and critics repeated these criticisms about the Kyoto negotiations. It was widely argued that the ten-day deadline for Kyoto was too constraining. These talks would have to involve arduous negotiations, critics argued, because the lead-up talks in Berlin (COP-1) and Geneva (COP-2) had failed to reach consensus on the so-called Berlin Mandate—the need for the industrialized countries to sign on to more stringent and binding emissions cuts than were required for less-developed nations.

In addition to the legacy and time-factor characteristics, the difficult nature of the core issue of climate change heavily influenced the Kyoto negotiations. Questions of scientific veracity, social relevance, and political expediency were the unspoken stimuli behind the negotiation positions taken in Japan. Strong international leadership from the United States, the leader in so many other arenas, was also noticeably absent. In fact, the U.S. delegation had trouble shedding the label of world's heaviest greenhouse gas polluter and major obstructionist in the talks. Movement on the issue was made more difficult in the lead-up to Kyoto by resistance from the U.S. Congress, which had consistently questioned the need for any action, as well as the economic price that would be paid for it. Ecology interest groups were quick to point out that the purpose of the meeting for state participants seemed to be how to shift the blame and the burden onto others. The Americans kept a finger pointed at the big developing nations (e.g., China, India, Brazil) in Kyoto while trying to deflect the embarrassing scrutiny of the Europeans away from their own negotiation stance. Even a noncynical observer would probably admit that the objective at Kyoto seemed to be pleasing the "green" constituencies at home while keeping one's national business and industrial interests out of regulation's way. This quest for loopholes led Greenpeace, the well-known transnational environmental group, to declare at conference end: "[We] estimate that the agreement, when all loopholes are considered, will result in no real reductions from the 1990 levels" (Environmental News Network 1997). Despite this pessimistic postmortem, these negotiations had high drama and theatrics over the course of eleven days in Kyoto, Japan.

## The Players

The Kyoto conference hosted 2,200 official delegates from 159 nation-states. (In Copenhagen 2009, this will increase to 4,000 delegates from 186 nations, with 5,500 observers expected.) The key actors can be grouped into five clusters: the European Union—the advanced industrial countries of western Europe; the non-EU developed countries of Japan, the United States, Switzerland, Canada, Australia, Norway, and New Zealand; the transitional economies—the industrialized countries of central and eastern Europe and the former Soviet Union; the "Group of 77"—China, India, and

over 130 other so-called developing countries; and the Alliance of Small
Island States (AOSIS)—42 mainly Caribbean and Pacific island nations.

The intentions of the different groups varied tremendously along a continuum from "serious about negotiating" to "trying to stall." The undis-
puted leader of the latter group was the United States. Having criticized
George H. W. Bush's proposal at Rio to stabilize U.S. carbon dioxide emissions by the year 2000 as insufficient, the Clinton-Gore administration had
actually done much worse during its five years in office. With fuel consumption way up as a result of the booming economy and the popularity
of large recreational vehicles, the White House's negotiation stance was to
fulfill Bush's target, ten years later than originally promised (Mott 1997)!
The United States called for stabilization of emissions at 1990 levels by
2008–2012. Although disguised by a lot of confusing numbers, the target
that the Japanese proposed was basically the same—stabilization by the industrialized countries by 2012. The European Union focused its targets on
three of the six greenhouse gases, also using 1990 levels as the base, and
called for a reduction of 7.5 percent by 2005 and 15 percent by 2010. The
Group of 77 had goals close to those of the European Union, but it is vital
to note that these were goals they held for the industrialized countries only,
not for themselves. They resisted the pressure of the United States and others to bring them into the agreement, arguing that as developing nations
their economic growth and trade competitiveness would be harmed by ad-
herence to an emissions reduction regime. The AOSIS put forward the most
ambitious target by far—calling for the developed countries to agree to 20
percent reductions by 2005. In caucus sessions prior to the Kyoto summit,
it had laid the groundwork for this target by articulating its deep concerns
about increases in sea levels owing to climate change. Indeed, it argued, a
rise in the earth's temperature could be devastating to its member islands.

The conference was also noteworthy for the high-profile presence of various nongovernmental actors who tried to lobby conference participants
and court international public opinion, either for or against a protocol. The
interested parties included business and industrial groups from the energy,
electric, chemical, iron and steel, and paper and timber sectors. With the exception of nuclear energy representatives, whose industry stood to gain
from regulations on other energy providers, these groups were against a climate treaty, which they argued would negatively impact jobs and economic
growth in general. They came to be known by the acronym of BINGO (business and industrial non-governmental organizations). Also highly visible,
but on the other side of the fence, were environmental non-governmental
organizations (ENGOs) lobbying hard for a meaningful protocol. Along
with Greenpeace, hundreds of other grassroots organizations and associations were at work in Kyoto, including the German nongovernmental organization (NGO) Forum on Environment and Development, the Friends

of the Earth-UK, the Worldwide Fund for Nature, and the Japanese Kiko Forum—a coalition of more than 150 Japanese environmental NGOs mobilized on the climate change issue. These groups were creative and energetic in the mediums they used to share information, analyze events, and attempt to sway the outcome of the Kyoto talks. European NGOs sponsored a "climate train" across Europe en route to the convention to raise public awareness, and many groups used the Internet to broadcast news and analysis to Kyoto watchers around the world in the form of daily diaries and newsletters from the convention floor. The newsletter ECO gained particular notoriety among delegates for its lampooning of the slow progress and doublespeak that its authors felt were dominating the convention. Keen observers and analysts also came to Kyoto from various scientific and technical groups, such as the Union of Concerned Scientists. Together, all of these nongovernmental actors took on very high-profile roles in Kyoto as advisers to national delegations and also as independent entities.

At the individual level of analysis, only two players really stood out at the Kyoto talks: COP-3 chairman Raul Estrada-Oyuela of Argentina, who brokered the final compromise agreement, and U.S. vice president Al Gore, whose "rescue mission" to Kyoto at the one-week mark of the conference made for humorous headlines, such as "Kyoto Gets Gored" (Smith and Sheehan 1997) and "Full Gore on Kyoto" (Media Reality Check 1997). Fingered by the media in Kyoto as the main obstructionist to negotiation progress, the Clinton administration hoped Gore could promote cooperation among the United States, Japan, and the European Union, but Gore also directed international public attention to the talks and the importance of the topic at hand. His trip, his remarks, and his apparent blessing of U.S. acceptance of more substantial emissions cuts got the American delegation actively involved in bargaining and gave a much-needed boost to the process in Kyoto.

## The Stakes

Potential costs and benefits to the parties involved are of major importance to the ultimate success or failure of negotiations. Environmental treaties are particularly tricky because the benefits are often very abstract, involving notions of making the planet safer for future generations, while the costs can involve such politically unpopular and more immediate outcomes as plant closings, job losses, and new taxes. On a basic level, all states and societies have an interest in an issue such as global warming. Assuming the dire predictions concerning its advent and consequences are true, there is a general interest in controlling greenhouse gas emissions, but obviously the issue is of greater importance to some states than to others. The microstates in the AOSIS, for example, feel that global warming threatens their very physical survival. For them, this environmental issue is a life-or-death matter since these island nations could literally be underwater as a result of even modest increases in sea levels caused by melting polar ice caps. It is worth noting that the talks in Copenhagen (2009) and beyond may well benefit from increased public support for national and international action on global warming. Public opinion has notably trended in that direction in the aftermath of such events as the Asian tsunami (2004) and Hurricane Katrina (2005) and following the release of two high-profile media treatments of the stakes—Al Gore's documentary *An Inconvenient Truth* (2006) and Thomas Friedman's bestseller *Hot, Flat and Crowded* (2008).

The higher status accorded to ecological concerns on security agendas can clearly be seen in various postindustrial states—Australia, Canada, western Europe, Japan, and the United States, among them—where interest group pressure within highly mobilized civil societies makes these quality-of-life issues the business of the state. They are not popular items for these governments, however, because they involve very painful trade-offs. Estimates circulating in U.S. small-business circles prior to the Kyoto conference, for example, suggested that the Clinton administration's proposal for a carbon dioxide tax would cost the American economy $350 billion a year in reduced production of goods and services (Kerrigan 1997). Still, given the increasing dedication of resources and attention, environmental issues seem to have gained a permanent position on these countries' international agendas. For the majority of other states in the international system—newly industrialized or at various levels of development—the ecology of global warming is not high on their national political agendas. Their interests in the Kyoto negotiations were dominated by a relative-gains perspective—to get the industrialized states to commit to meaningful emissions cuts while keeping themselves out of any agreement. For these developing countries, it is imperative that the rich northern countries take responsibility for the developmental costs of the newly industrialized nations. This perspective reflects the persistent North-South divide that characterizes negotiations on many environmental and economic issues.

These states were relatively successful at keeping the spotlight off of themselves at the COP-3 talks in Kyoto, more so than Japan and the United States, which attracted a great deal of the media and public attention. Japan was under scrutiny as the host of these talks—a role that many in the international arena feel it has too often shunned since its rise to international power. For the United States, its credibility in the environmental arena was at stake in Kyoto. Washington's performance in Rio was widely condemned as obstructionist and self-serving, and many in and outside the United States were waiting to see if Clinton and Gore would redeem American environmental credentials.

Big issues and important relationships were on trial in Kyoto. Environmentalists had to face the question of whether there could be concerted international action on a matter over which the scientific community had not yet reached consensus. At issue: could something like global warming ever be adequately proven before it actually happened? Other questions included the matter of who would lead in the development of international environmental policy—the European Union, which has worked hard to build some credentials in this area, or the United States, which has not but which has such power on the world political stage that it can automatically assert itself in any forum. Also at stake were nothing less than the prevailing definitions of the terms "developing" and "transitional" in the international economic system. The economic classifications of Brazil, China, India, Mexico, and the postcommunist European states were all contentious in the debate over who would have to do what in a climate treaty. The United States and other Western states argued that such a treaty would not make sense if many big polluters—including such transitional states—were not party to it. This pressure has only increased in the years following Kyoto, during which time China has surpassed the United States as the largest carbon dioxide emitter in the world.

The Kyoto negotiations provide some classic examples of two-level games. At the same time that it is international in scope and worthy of a global summit, an environmental issue such as climate change also has an important domestic dimension. In the United States, Congress must ratify any treaty agreements the executive branch of government negotiates. In the case of the Kyoto negotiations, the U.S. Senate made its feelings clear prior to the summit when it voted 95–0 for the Byrd-Hagel resolution, a nonbinding document that spelled out the Senate's reservations about the UN-sponsored climate talks. However, the American negotiating team, led by Under Secretary of State Stuart Eizenstat, also had to respond to the domestic environmental lobby, whose profile has been very high in global environmental talks. The U.S. delegation could not afford simply to take an obstructionist position and stick to it. Two-level games were also being played out in Germany and Japan, among other countries, where highly mobilized domestic interest groups—in favor of the climate change treaty—were pressuring their respective countries via the media and public opinion to take proactive stances.

## The Moves

The end goal of improved air quality represents a public good, the achievement of which requires a cooperative effort across national boundaries. Herein lies the strategic dilemma that environmental problems present for states in the international system: pollution does not recognize national boundaries. States are unable to solve ozone depletion or acid rain problems on their own, but cooperation among states is not easy to achieve. Inherently suspicious of one another, states rely on definitions of national interest that are derived from relative gains: if you won, I must have lost. More often than not, a "tragedy of the commons" scenario develops in relation to the collaborative, long-range planning needed to combat environmental problems. In this metaphor, originally suggested by biologist Garrett Hardin, each individual herder on a medieval commons (open grazing pasture) would act in apparent self-interest and maximize his or her use of the commons by introducing as many additional cattle as possible. The outcome was the ruin, through overgrazing, of the commons and the resultant starvation of the herds (Hardin 1968).

The analogy to states in the international system, of course, is that political leaders are usually likewise unwilling to curb potentially destructive, self-interested behavior to focus instead on the collective good. There is a lack of trust between states that results, in most cases, in failure to pay the costs for benefits that will come in the longer term and are reliant on similar decisions and actions on the part of other states unwilling to implement measures unpopular at home. The need for collective action is stymied by the lack of trust among states.

**Michael De Adder, artizans.com**

Given this lack of trust, it is not surprising that positional bargaining dominated the Kyoto negotiations and continues to characterize the follow-up dialogue. This intransigence is captured in the competing percentage positions representing the degree to which greenhouse gas emissions should be reduced: the European Union offered a 15.5 percent cut, while Japan advocated a 5 percent rate, and Chairman Estrada professed at the conclusion of the talks his dream that the outcome be a 6 percent cut. Some delegations even seemed unsure of what their numbers stood for at times. The United States was pushing for stabilization of emissions at 1990 levels, which was generally perceived as a technique to achieve a zero percent solution. But in fact, for the United States to go back to 1990 levels in 2000 would necessitate a 13 percent reduction in emissions (Mott 1997)! The Japanese delegation, for its part, created confusion for others at one point on the issue of whether the base level in its proposal was 1990 or some other year.

But there were also some more sophisticated moves at the Kyoto talks. In addition to relying on a notion of stabilization in place of specific target cuts, the United States also pushed for more complex approaches to the issue of national responsibility. Among the concepts the American delegation advocated were differentiation, the sharing of a target by the developed countries, allowing them variable national rates as part of the overall effort to meet the target; flexibility, now popularly referred to as "cap and trade," wherein states may buy and sell unused emissions quota points; and joint implementation, the ability to receive national credit for emissions reductions financed in and for other countries (Anderson 1995). Critics of the U.S. position condemned these various tools as ploys developed explicitly to avoid national responsibility. For the Clinton administration, however, they represented ways to achieve congressional cooperation at the important domestic, or second-level, dimension of the negotiations.

The need for congressional approval was clearly behind the major U.S. effort in Kyoto to bring the developing countries into the agreement. Although responsible for two-thirds of past emissions and approximately 75 percent of current emissions, the United States and fellow Organization for Economic Cooperation and Development (OECD) countries have been increasingly focused on the future culpability of developing countries in the area of emissions (United Nations Environment Programme). Sensitive to political opinion at home, where the NAFTA negotiations had spurred controversy on the environmental responsibilities of Mexico and other industrialized developing states (Brazil, India, China), the U.S. delegation pushed hard on the need for those states to adhere to the rules of a climate regime.

As the deadline loomed in Kyoto, there were standoffs on these proposals for developing-country inclusion and the acceptability of protocol language that would allow states to seek and trade greenhouse gas credits. China and India were outspoken in their opposition to both ideas. The Chinese and American delegations were actually seen and heard "snarling" at one another about these provisions inside a conference room on the tenth day in Kyoto (Warrick 1997).

There was no doubt on that tenth day that the original deadline for the end of the talks was real—not simply an artificial negotiation device. Upon hearing of a one-day conference extension, many delegates panicked as they rushed to make changes to their airline tickets. Negotiations were complicated at this last minute for the Russian and Chinese delegations, both of which lost their translators when the contracts governing their translation services expired at midnight on December 10.

In the end, COP-3 chairman Estrada crafted a compromise that had the United States accepting defeat on the provision of "meaningful participation by developing nations" in return for inclusion of protocol language on the acceptability of emissions trading and related ideas as subjects for further negotiation among the parties. Even this may not have been enough to force agreement were it not for a procedural rule that allowed Estrada to decide when consensus had been reached. This he did by quickly reading the compromise language and then declaring the debate over with a bang of his gavel. Thirty-eight industrialized countries signed the protocol agreement. The deal committed them to cuts in emissions of greenhouse gases averaging 5.2 percent from 1990 levels, to be achieved during the 2008–2012 period (BBC News 1997).

*Endgame*

Under scrutiny, the Kyoto Protocol did not really represent a win for anyone involved. It was, rather, a classic compromise outcome, where no side lost too badly. The negotiators never reached the stage of collaborative problem solving. If they had done so, a postmortem piece in the influential journal *Foreign Affairs* argued, they would have moved toward framing the negotiation issue differently. Rather than national emissions targets, they would have tried to define mutually agreed-upon actions, "such as a nationally collected tax on greenhouse gas emissions"—something all signatories would agree to establish (Cooper 1998, 68). In the final analysis, the Kyoto Protocol to the Framework Convention on Climate Change may be viewed historically as an essential step in a long, arduous process. However, it will likely only be seen as such if nations do take meaningful individual action on emissions and if the international talks result in a binding agreement in the near future. Without progress on this next step, Kyoto will rather be seen as a face-saving agreement, a way around serious action on the greenhouse gas issue.

The major stumbling bloc remains the ability to manage the two-level game that has hindered progress and obscured a way forward. In the United States, it has been difficult to move beyond the blame game. It quickly became apparent after the 11 days in Kyoto that ratification by the U.S. Senate was not going to be a mere formality. In fact, when Clinton's successor, George W. Bush—a member of the Republican party—was denigrated by the environmental lobby for repudiating the Kyoto Protocol and refusing to even seek Senate ratification, Republicans cried foul. They argued that the U.S. signature on the Kyoto Protocol was always a ruse. The endgame in Japan had been a face-saving device for a Democratic president under fire, they argued. If so, the shortsightedness of the rush to agreement on Clinton's part has come at great cost to the climate negotiations. The failure of ratification in the United States and the subsequent withdrawal of the United States from participation in the U.N.-sponsored climate talks (from 2001 to 2007) was very damaging to the process. A lack of U.S. participation and/or leadership greatly weakens any possible outcome to these negotiations. The decision by Russia to use its ratification of the treaty as a bargaining chip designed to extract maximum leverage in other arenas further contributed to the perception of Kyoto as a lose-lose proposition. Lauded as one of the "most innovative and ambitious international agreements ever negotiated" (Bondansky 2001, 50), the Kyoto Protocol has been watered down considerably from its original aims. The Bush administration even attempted to redefine the purpose for international efforts on climate control—calling for a "search for new technologies that can reduce emissions" rather than an agreement to reduce emissions (Mufson and Eilperin 2007, A14).

### Copenhagen and Beyond: Prospects for a Binding Protocol

On his way out of the Kyoto conference, one delegate was heard to remark, "the hard part is over . . . but now comes the hard part" (Barr and Goodrich 1997). Developments at the subsequent two COP meetings in Buenos Aires and the Hague reinforced the veracity of this prediction. In Argentina, substantive progress on issues gave way to mere agreement on timetables for realizing the goals laid down in Kyoto. Some countries, including the United States, went ahead and signed the global warming treaty there, but without ratification from their domestic legislatures. The 2000 talks in the Netherlands, taking place as they did while the results of the Bush v. Gore presidential election were in limbo, were disastrous, prompting a high-ranking member of the Japanese delegation to remark, "To be honest, we should have made the rules first" (Reiner 2001, 42). In what would become a pattern, the most difficult questions were once again pushed back for consideration at future meetings. The Conference of Parties met regularly, at least annually from COP-4 in Buenos Aires, Argentina (1998), through COP-14 in Poznan, Poland (2008). In Poland, negotiations ended with little more than a commitment to "negotiate in earnest" with the Kyoto Treaty set to expire in 2012. A casual observer would be forgiven for asking if negotiations in the previous ten years had not been "in earnest?" But the dismal failure of the COP-13 talks in Bali (2007) had put even the degree of earnestness into question.

In fact, the "Bali Roadmap" that came out of the 2007 meeting could get no further than a restatement of the goals and conceptual framework for the negotiations. Buzz phrases included "common, but differentiated responsibilities"and mandatory rather than voluntary principles. The realization that the next round of talks (COP-14 in Poland) would come up against another election in the United States was greeted with groans all around, although there was also talk of a potentially more involved American president in the post-Bush era. Indeed, by the time COP-14 rolled around, the Bush administration was in full lame duck status and the newly elected Barack Obama sent two Democratic party heavyweights to speak for him in Poland. Al Gore and John Kerry made it clear that the next president favored domestic "cap-and-trade" legislation, a binding protocol to replace Kyoto, and more stringent emissions restrictions for the United States—"1990 levels by 2020" (Eilperin 2008, A2). It was not enough to satisfy the Europeans and it was too much for Congressional Republicans, but the signal of a new game plan had been sent.

Observers agree that the main challenges for Copenhagen are to narrow the gap between the EU and the United States on emissions targets and timetables and to bring more industrialized, developing states to the negotiation table. Contextual changes from Kyoto to Copenhagen will be noticeable. NGOs are even more involved in the actual negotiations in 2009. Some states, including Canada, Portugal, India, Indonesia and the Philippines now have NGO representation within their delegations (Lisowski 2005, 364). The Climate Action Network (see box, chapter 3) has grown to over 300 ENGOs. And, in a rather surprising development, there has been something of a split between NGOs headquartered in the developed "north" and their counterparts in the emerging economies of the "south." Lisowski describes the former as being protocol-driven, with an emphasis on emissions reductions, while the latter concentrate more attention on financial and technical transfers and requirements (2005, 368). Finally, the two-level games that are being played out in states around the globe are coming to a climax. In the United States, the fate of the so-called cap-and-trade bill, also known as the Waxman-Markey Bill, and techically titled the American Clean Energy and Security Act of 2009, will determine how quick and how deep American climate action will be on the national level. Similarly, ongoing diplomacy with the Chinese will provide an indication of whether the world's two greatest emitters of greenhouse gases will cooperate in developing and sharing carbon reduction strategies. Scientists do now agree—the stakes are very high!

## North Korean Nuclear Crisis: Cycle of Brinkmanship

*Background*

Following World War II, Northeast Asia became a main battleground in the American effort to stem the tide of communism. Due to Korea's strategic location between the two communist giants of China and the Soviet Union, the United States viewed the political status of Korea as a vital national security interest to Washington. It fought a three-year war in Korea (1950–1953) before moving the battle to Vietnam and Cambodia in Southeast Asia. Hence, the highly contentious relationship between North Korea and the United States is decades old. Long before the test of wills over Pyongyang's nuclear program and long before its inclusion in an American-targeted "axis of evil," the war on the Korean peninsula helped define a struggle between communism and capitalism that came to characterize the latter half of the twentieth century. Two of the Cold War's most enduring client states were born of the conflict in Korea—the Soviet-allied Democratic People's Republic of Korea (DPRK, also known as North Korea) and the American-sponsored Republic of Korea (ROK) to the south. Though the Korean War is now over fifty years old, it has never been resolved. With only an armistice in place, the Koreas are still technically at war, and the region stands as the most highly militarized in the world. In North Korea alone, 1.2 million out of 22 million citizens are in the military, the world's largest in per capita terms (Kleiner 2005, 205).

Following the Korean War, the DPRK, under leader Kim Il Sung, was extremely isolated from the international system. Under both the elder Kim and his son and successor, Kim Jong Il, the ruling ideology has been embedded in the concepts of *juche*, which refers to self-reliance and independence, and *songun*, a military-before-all-else policy (Oh and Hassig 2003, 45–46). In the 1990s, two factors were crucial in bringing North Korea out of the long silent period, during which time it was called the "hermit kingdom," and back to the forefront of international power politics. First, its economic system was in ruins after Cold War alliances fell apart for communist supplicants such as Pyongyang in the aftermath of the Soviet collapse. Many decades of "military first" had led to famine and starvation in the north, in sharp contrast to South Korea, which had made the list of "miracle economies," part of a group of newly industrializing countries of Asia

(NICs). The death of the elder Kim in 1994 presented both danger and op-portunity to his son. Like an unstable ship, the DPRK under Kim Jong Il has teetered on the edge of disaster—back and forth between rapproche-ment and confrontation with the United States, South Korea, and Japan. Economic destitution, coupled with an unwillingness to loosen political control, has produced a highly unpredictable North Korea. The hopes of South Korea's President Kim Dae Jung (1998–2003) for economic cooper-ation between the Koreas and possible, eventual reunification now seem more distant than ever, with another father-to-son succession reportedly in the works.

Many of the nineteen parties to the Korean war are still intensely inter-ested in the rekindled strategic standoff. However, as Cold War alliances loosened and dissolved, camps have shifted. In the new century, it has been the American hope that China and Russia would bring pressure to bear on North Korea to stop its nuclear weapons program. A multilateral effort rep-resents a last hope at this juncture, as bilateral relations between the United States and DPRK have become bogged down in a vicious cycle of bluffing, brinkmanship, and blackmail. However, the concept of deterrence, which provided an atmosphere of constraint during the Cold War, is not a prop-erly functioning mechanism in contemporary Northeast Asia. The creation of the six-party forum (DPRK, United States, South Korea, Japan, China, and Russia) was an effort to address insecurity in Pyongyang, bred by the asymmetric nature of its status vis-à-vis Washington. The principle behind the forum was that longtime North Korean patrons Moscow and Beijing could provide a check to the demands of Washington, Seoul, and Tokyo. The hope was that together, this modern-day "concert of powers" could work to create a solution to the still unresolved strategic standoff on the Ko-rean peninsula (Kissinger 2009). However, despite some modest gains, North Korea has displayed a penchant for repudiating the negotiations and walking away from the agreements. The United States, for its part, has ric-ocheted back and forth between coercion and cooptation and now is in dan-ger of losing credibility altogether.

Since George H. W. Bush's 1988 realization that North Korea was en-gaging in a nuclear program, successive American presidents and their ad-ministrations have struggled mightily to deal with Pyongyang. For the Clinton administration, movement and change in North Korea were clearly on the radar screen in the early 1990s—with the two Koreas hav-ing signed a pair of historic agreements—the first steps toward possible reconciliation. It did not take long, however, to realize that the momentum was going to take a negative turn. Pyongyang flexed its nuclear muscles and has been doing so, intermittently, ever since. What followed for Clin-ton, Bush, and now Obama has been a cycle of positioning, posturing, and testing.

## Setup

In many ways, the succession of nuclear crises that have struck American administrations can be conceptualized as part of an *iterated strategic game*. North Korea responds dramatically to challenges from the United States and its international partners, displaying an unmistakable tendency to "float concessions on a tide of threats" (Sigal 2003). It is useful to think of North Korea's motivation in terms of an *opportunity crisis*, resulting from deliberate, conscious, and calculated initiatives on their part as they anticipate a new round of bargaining with their counterparts or as they react to changing circumstances in the international system. The initiator of such a crisis anticipates specific gain from the crisis it triggers and, if it perceives threat at all, regards the danger as substantially lower than that perceived by its adversaries in the crisis situation (Ben-Yehuda 1999). When the International Atomic Energy Agency (IAEA) announced in February 1993 that the DPRK had "discrepancies in the amount of plutonium declared and produced," it requested special inspections in the north. North Korea responded to this a month later by announcing it would leave the Nuclear Non-Proliferation Treaty (NPT). From that trigger point, it took President Clinton and Secretary of State Albright only twenty-one months to start and finish negotiations on an "Agreed Framework" with North Korea. This agreement would freeze the North Korean nuclear program under way at the Yongbyon reactor, preclude any new reactors from being built, allow for IAEA inspections to resume, and reengage the north in a dialogue with South Korea. In return, the United States promised not to use nuclear weapons against North Korea and to "begin removing barriers to political and economic contacts between the two countries" (Mazarr 1995, 98).

The Agreed Framework did not prove very durable, however, with both sides failing to follow through on certain aspects in good faith and in a timely fashion. Moreover, issues that had been left for future unscheduled negotiations—such as the status of North Korea's nuclear energy program—began to cause difficulties. To some extent, the Bush administration inherited the problem of an aggressive and impatient North Korea. Reportedly, Clinton had hopes of a last-minute missile deal with North Korea before his term expired, but he ran out of time. Speculation ran high that Bush was looking for a reason to reject the "sunshine policy" cautiously embraced by his predecessor (*Boston Globe* editorial 2001). The crisis trigger for Bush came in the form of an "October surprise," when North Korean officials allegedly told American envoy James Kelly in a meeting in Pyongyang, in October 2001, that they had a uranium enrichment program under way. In response, Bush first threatened to turn to force and carry out air strikes, an economic embargo, and a naval blockade. Ultimately, however, Secretary of State Colin Powell prevailed in steering the crisis back toward the negotiation table (*Asia Report* 2003). A renewed emphasis on crisis diplomacy eventually led to the so-called six-party talks.

Powell's management of the North Koreans foreshadowed in many ways the work that would later be done by special envoys James Kelly and Christopher Hill during the eight years of the Bush administration. They faced many obstacles—some made worse by Bush's own approach, most markedly his 2002 "Axis of Evil" speech which Pyongyang interpreted as an announcement of pending invasion. American management of the ongoing crisis with North Korea was made more difficult still by the unwillingness of both traditional American allies and the four other parties to the six-party forum to take a united stand against Kim's bellicose actions (Kleiner 2005). Moreover, the timing of demands for reciprocity has always seemed deeply flawed, with North Korea looking for grandiose gestures (like a nonaggression treaty) in the wake of incredibly provocative statements and actions. A deeply suspicious and mistrustful Congress has made it clear over the years that it will not reward threats.

The establishment of the six-party negotiation channel, and the hope it produced for a real agreement—the so-called Beijing Accord of 2005—form the basis of the discussion to follow. This case looks at the flameout of that accord and finds in its failure the seeds of futility—a cycle of threats, concessions, recriminations, and revocations. Underlying all is a fundamental inability to solve the question of sequencing (Hill 2005)—who will do what, when, and with what encouragement or punishment? The mechanism of reciprocity is totally absent in this case.

### Players

The matter of who should be involved in negotiations on the future course of North Korean security has been a source of tremendous contention. The Korean War involved a full nineteen parties, those who fought with North Korea, including China and the Soviet Union, and those who defended South Korea at the request of the United Nations, including the United States and the other so-called allied nations. The Korean War represented baptism by fire for the United Nations. Its military involvement on the Korean peninsula was its first such role, coming just five years after its inception.

In more recent times, the role of the IAEA has been of central importance, sparking a crisis of confidence regarding North Korea's compliance with the Nuclear Non-Proliferation Treaty during inspections in the 1990s. From the standpoint of the DPRK, however, negotiations are not a case of "the more the merrier." Pyongyang has fought very hard over the past decade to create a bilateral negotiation forum, in which they would be seated alone with the United States at the negotiation table. This, however, is an unacceptable configuration for the United States. First, American foreign policy does not regard North Korea as separate from South Korea—after all, American troops are policing the line of demarcation! Furthermore, Washington continues to push Japan, as an allied agent, to take a lead in Asian security and is now working to achieve strategic symbiosis with the People's Republic of China (PRC) on some of these difficult issues in northern Asia, rather than trying to run counter to them.

These factors have led the United States to pursue and even, at times, insist on multilateral negotiations. Elder statesman Henry Kissinger wrote that "Pyongyang must be advised that the road to Washington goes through Seoul and not in the other direction" (Olsen 2003). Speaking to North Korea with a unified voice is a major goal of the United States, which clearly prefers a larger number of parties at the negotiation table. Indeed, a secret overture by Tokyo to Pyongyang received a cool reception in the White House in August 2002. When it failed, there was a distinct "we told you so" tone to Washington's follow-up communications. Likewise, the Seoul-Washington alliance has been under heavy pressure at times, as South Korean domestic politics have led that country's leadership to move out ahead of the United States, threatening to shift the delicate balance of power in the Korea crisis away from Washington.

Various multilateral configurations came into play as negotiation possibilities heated up in Northeast Asia. A four-way dialogue was one possibility and was tested during prenegotiations on various occasions (among the United States, China, South Korea, and the DPRK), although it never carried over into full-blown negotiations. Then, worries over the possible collapse of the negotiation channel altogether led to tripartite talks in early 2003, involving the United States, China, and North Korea. Finally, their informal dialogue on how to structure future negotiations was parlayed into an agreement on the six-party format that formed the basis of the official three-day negotiations in Beijing in 2003. The United States accepted the unofficial role that China played as arbiter of those talks, despite Beijing's close association with and empathy for the North Korean position. As long as China remains committed to a nonnuclear North Korea, the United States seems willing to accept its strong role in the negotiations. In some ways, Washington has been more critical of its allies, South Korea and Japan, on this issue. The United States has pushed them to be tougher with the DPRK and has used them as economic aid–providing proxies, preferring not to "pay" Pyongyang directly for negotiation compliance (*Hong Kong Economic Journal* 2003).

There are also important players on the individual level of analysis in these stop and start negotiations. There has been a mixture of "celebrity" envoys and the more "sweat and blood" variety. Initially, taking a gamble that part of North Korea's motivation for its behavior is to attract international attention, President Clinton sent a variety of high-profile diplomats to Pyongyang. Indeed, twice on the brink of military action against North Korea (in 1993 and 1999), missions were launched to de-escalate tensions and revive negotiations. In 1994, it was former president Jimmy Carter, who actually went less at the request of the Clinton administration than with its blessing. He instigated the activity in partnership with his personal friend, ambassador to Korea James T. Laney, the former president of Emory University in Atlanta. When Carter achieved success in opening a negotiation channel, his mission was embraced by Clinton (Sigal 2003). In late 1998, when North Korea threatened again, it was former U.S. secretary of defense William Perry who was dispatched to research the very tense situation and report back to the administration with a menu of options for how to proceed. He recommended strongly that the United States bring South Korea and Japan into any subsequent negotiations and implementation plans. From there, the six-party channel was eventually born, involving high-level diplomats from all six states on a continuing basis. From 2000 to 2008, during the George W. Bush administration, the president departed from his normal distaste for special envoys and appointed James Kelly and then Christopher Hill to work full-time on the negotiations. Both Kelly and Hill expended tremendous energies on these talks. Indeed, when President Obama signaled his intention to replace Hill with Ambassador Stephen Bosworth, who already had a full-time job as dean of Tufts University's Fletcher School of Diplomacy, an outcry ensued over whether a part-timer could handle this arduous task!

The sensitive nature of the relationship, coupled with the tedious diplomatic process, has led to extensive involvement from U.S. secretaries of state— in particular, Madeline Albright and Colin Powell, who personally led the diplomatic efforts prior to the appointments of special envoys. North Korea has also made ample use of high-level diplomats and spokespersons, often working to clarify Pyongyang's position and/or to present "new facts" on the ground in the always-shifting negotiation environment. Two of the most noteworthy have been Kim Ryong Song and Li Gun. There is still widespread speculation about the purposefulness of Li Gun's statements to U.S. envoy James Kelly in 2002—the infamous "we are enriching uranium" comment (Kessler 2004). Did he say this? Was he instructed to say it? Was deniability the reason it was said by him, in that location, and to that counterpart?

## Stakes

The values at stake in the standoff over North Korea could not be more fundamental. For North Korea, regime and state survival is clearly at risk. This danger informs the decision making of Kim Jong Il. Indeed, after listening to President George W. Bush name North Korea as a member of the triangular "axis of evil" in his January 2002 State of the Union address, the deputy director of the DPRK Foreign Ministry stated, "The United States says that after Iraq, we are next, but we have countermeasures" (Olsen 2003). Although not discussed openly in Pyongyang, the humanitarian crisis in North Korea is nevertheless a major factor there and for all of those involved in the negotiations. Estimates range from several hundred thousand to three million malnutrition deaths since 1995 (Oh and Hassig 2003, 45). This situation is closely linked to the necessity for economic reform in the north. The system is a failed one, but the political risks that would accompany true, rapid reform are too much for Kim Jong Il. It is important to note, however, that North Korea does annually receive up to $1 billion in aid from the United States, South Korea, the European Union, China, and Japan. This is a lifeline for Pyongyang's regime security and for the survival of the North Korean people at this juncture. This stark reality has prompted some to urge the United States and its cohorts to force North Korea to choose between aid and nuclear weapons. There is little doubt that Pyongyang reacted badly to the tactics of the Bush administration. They assumed that Bush's goal was to disarm them and after the January 2002 speech, they were convinced that war was going to be launched against them (Kleiner 2005). The status quo is unacceptable to North Korea and its actions can perhaps best be interpreted as designed, above all else, to change it. Those who have worked most closely with the North Koreans over time on the American side, most notably Hill, have faced accusations of Stockholm Syndrome (overidentification with the captor or "enemy") (Pletka 2009).

For the United States, North Korea threatens stability in the international system of states. Pyongyang's nuclear weapons program is seen as a direct threat to the United States and not as mere positioning in Northeast Asia. At a conceptual level, North Korea's actions from 1994 onward have threatened fundamental norms of the international system. North Korea's actions fly in the face of the doctrine of deterrence—that heavy threats, with the credibility to back them up, will deter aggressive behavior. Its failure calls into question whole notions of balance of power in the post–Cold War period, prompting one observer to assert that "mutual deterrence between vastly unequal states lacks stability and reasonable predictability. It does not exist" (Lewis 2004). Where there is some fundamental disagreement between the United States and its four partners in the talks (China, South Korea, Russia, Japan), it is over how imminent a threat the North Korean nuclear program presents and how measured a response is warranted. During the Bush administration, rumblings could be heard in Washington about a perceived lack of concern in Seoul about Pyongyang's intentions. Instead South Koreans seem more concerned about American policies in the region. A sense of alarm was evident in some of these Asian capitals about the "axis of evil" formulation, the possibility of open use of U.S. force in the region, and the stated objective of George W. Bush that Kim Jong Il's regime should be toppled (Cumings 2003). In 2009, however, the notion that the United States is driving the cycle of crisis seems to have been dismissed by its four partners in the negotiations. Pyongyang has faced unprecedented wrath from all of them, as well as from the United Nations Security Council.

Below the grand strategic standoff (i.e., at the level of the negotiations on the ground), the parties to the conflict had hoped to accomplish certain goals through the six-party negotiation forum. The stated goal of the United States and the other four parties who faced North Korea at the negotiation table was the total dismantlement of the DPRK's nuclear weapons program. There was less consensus whether North Korea should act unconditionally and unilaterally or whether it should be compensated for its cooperation. For Pyongyang, the stated goal had been for the United States to take the DPRK off its list of state sponsors of terrorism (i.e., out of the axis of evil) and to lift political, economic, and military sanctions. It further indicated that it wanted neighboring states to provide energy, including heavy fuel oil. And, it periodically toyed with notions of rapprochement (Japan) and reconciliation (South Korea). What has been less clear over time is whether Pyongyang's stated objectives are its actual goals. If actions truly do speak louder than words, then the answer to that question would seem to be no.

*Moves*

The cycle of failure in the U.S.–North Korean relationship was readily apparent by 2005. The action-reaction syndrome would start with a crisis provocation from Pyongyang and then a patterned response from Washington. First would come tough words, verbal threats of military response. Then, discussion between the two would be reframed by the sitting secretary of state, or a visiting special envoy. Usually, the North Koreans would then engage in their own war of words, answering the initial American rhetoric with bold statements and, often, dramatic moves—including violations of airspace, conduct of missile tests, and what George W. Bush referred to as the "old blackmail game" (Larkin 2003). When the threats from Washington were particulary tough, for example, with Clinton's warning that a preemptive strike might be forthcoming, Donald Rumsfeld's call for a "revision to the basic war plan for Korea" (Cumings 2003), or Bush's reference to the desire to "topple" Kim and his infamous "axis of evil" remark, the regime in Pyongyang would react very negatively to having its back to the wall.

Clearly, the setting was less than ideal for meaningful diplomacy. Breaking out of the cycle to actually engage in negotiations was a daunting task. Indeed, it surprised no one that the initial attempts at six-party agreement were very slow and disappointing. The 2003 talks never progressed past the point of pre-negotiations about the principles at stake and the process for addressing them. The 2004 talks collapsed just days after commencing. It was perhaps only due to the immense efforts of Ambassador Christopher Hill, Bush's envoy to the six-party talks, that even a tentative agreement was reached in Beijing in 2005. Coming off of a thirteen-month boycott of the six-party process, the objective was once again an agreement on principles. Hill indicated that these were the denuclearization of the Korean peninsula; movement of the DPRK back into the Nuclear Non-Proliferation Treaty (NPT); and then the quid-pro-quo for North Korea—this would become the sticking point—of the provision of a light-water reactor for Pyongyang's nuclear energy program. The sequence in which these events were to take place was clearly going to be a problem, if past experiences between the two countries were any indication. Even so, the rapidity with which the Beijing agreement fell apart was stunning. The notion that North Korea would have to abandon "first" its nuclear program (Kleiner 2005) was never accepted as a premise by the Kim regime. Moreover, the tendency for diplomacy to be conducted through a constant trading of insults (Kleiner, 215) was not a promising context either. Bluffing and blustering have characterized the North Korean approach, while for its part, the United States has clearly lost the trust and will that would underlie reciprocal talks. The collapse of the agreement mere days into its life is most attributable to the erratic behavior of the North Koreans in turning their backs on the two important principles they had insisted must be part of any deal. The first was in regard to the acceptance of the term "abandon" in relation to their nuclear weapons program. Hill commented afterward that he suspected the DPRK's negotiation team faced an almost immediate backlash on this term and concept from a powerful community inside North Korea—the scientists and technocrats working on the program (Hill 2005)! The two-level game concept, often ignored in analyses of closed societies, was perhaps a relevant factor, after all. The second principle was a "negative security assurance" from the United States. The Kim regime had long sought this public statement by Washington that it "would not attack North Korea with nuclear or conventional weaponry." Yet, after finally receiving the assurance in Beijing, they quickly dismissed it as a "mere piece of paper." In his analysis of this puzzling behavior, deputy chief of the U.S. delegation, Victor Cha, remarks that "North Korea doesn't just want the bomb. It wants to be accorded the status and prestige of a nuclear power" (Cha 2009, B3). He observes that they hoped to be treated as Washington had treated India in the wake of its nuclear empowerment. There was an agreement by

India to abide by IAEA inspections in return for Washington's passive acceptance of a "civilian nuclear energy program" that is, of course, much more. The crux of the matter, Cha argues, is that the North Koreans see the consolidation and acceptance of their nuclear weapons program as the best chance they have for regime survival. And that is what they want Washington to guarantee!

Alas, Kim's regime is a failed one in nearly every sense and it seems clear that no American president will be cajoled into guaranteeing the regime's protection. Moroever, the more Pyongyang raises the stakes in this standoff, the less likely it becomes that the White House will be able to negotiate an agreement that Congress will rubber stamp. The two-level game in Washington shows a tremendous backlash against "rewarding" North Korea for its behavior. Ambassador Hill put it all on the line to convince his boss that the DPRK's extreme insecurities, their utter fear of an invasion from Washington, needed to be dispelled with a significant move from Washington. When the negative security assurance did not cement the Beijing Accord, this approach lost its momentum. The best hope for a negotiated agreement may well have been lost. And, with Kim having suffered a stroke in 2008, and planning for the successsion of his twenty-four-year-old son in the near future, it is unlikely to be restarted anytime soon.

## Endgame

Most vexing to these successive administrations and the many diplomats they have engaged to deal with the situation is that Pyongyang's behavior seems impervious to policy changes by the United States. Clinton and Albright had high hopes for their "Agreed Framework," but the response was ultimately the same as it would be to Bush's tough talk, and then to the six-party forum—a ratcheting up of the North Korean nuclear program, complete with uranium enrichment and missile testing! With the combined rhetoric and action coming out of Pyongyang, it is clear that attempts at a negotiated settlement to this standoff are in deep peril.

Two central tenets of successful negotiations were missing in this case—mutual recognition and trust in the reciprocity of the process. Preconditions from Bush and his talk of the need for regime change (toppling Kim) were likely negotiation killers from Pyongyang's perspective at various points along the way. Perhaps they could not believe that the assurance they received in Beijing in 2005 signaled a true change in policy. It is possible that top Bush diplomat John Bolton said it best in 2003 when he stated that the United States "was prepared to talk to North Korea but not to negotiate" (Kleiner 2005, 222). The six-party channel, although promising in structure, has not matched that promise in output. That could change if North Korea agrees to return to the negotiation table, something that it is currently vowing it will never do. The silver lining in the 2009 crisis is that China, the United States, Japan, Russia, and South Korea are all speaking in unison about the need for North Korea to denuclearize.

### Postscript: Obama and North Korea

It comes as no surprise that new American president Barack Obama's first foreign policy crisis came from North Korea in February 2009 when Pyongyang conducted multiple nuclear missile tests, kicked UN inspectors out of the country, seized two Asian-American journalists, restarted a plutonium factory, directly threatened and confronted South Korea, and proclaimed that it would never return to the six-party talks. The question is whether the presidential transition in Washington, like the one in Seoul the year before, was seen as another "opportunity crisis" in the DPRK or whether some more direct actions set it off. The answer probably can be found in a combination of factors. International realities—America's continued involvement in Afghanistan and Iraq and its heated standoff with Tehran—were clearly factors. In fact, diffusion seems at work in the seizing and sentencing of the American journalists by Pyongyang—a tactic that Tehran had popularized to simultaneously threaten its diaspora community and Washington. Another factor was quite possibly Obama's "hands-off" approach to North Korea in the initial setting of his foreign policy agenda. His downgrading of the Korean crisis, using Rumsfeld's characterization of Pyongyang as a "proliferation challenge," undoubtedly caused a ruckus in North Korea. Furthermore, as the crisis played out in the spring months, Washington's success in getting Seoul to participate in the "Proliferation Security Initiative" (whereby North Korean ships can be interdicted and searched for contraband) may have been the last straw. The result has been open admission of nuclear weapons capability, direct threats to Seoul and Washington, and a level of defiance that is unprecedented, even for North Korea.

### Summary

In international relations and particularly within foreign policy analysis, negotiation is studied as a process specific to the system of states and crucial to its survival. *International Negotiation in a Complex World* utilizes a board game analogy to explain how the answers to various questions— who's involved, what's at stake, what kind of outcome is sought, and how it is sought—shape the international negotiation process. This chapter relates two case examples to highlight the phases of international negotiation and to introduce many key concepts, including mediation, public goods, negotiation legacy, hostile diplomacy, positional bargaining, and iteration. These concepts, along with many others, will be further explored in the chapters to follow.

Thematically, this book seeks to illustrate that diplomatic negotiation at the turn of this century is displaying many of the same characteristics and operating according to many of the same rules that it has since the 1700s. Much attention is also devoted, however, to new and newly prominent facets of the international arena that are having a great impact on today's international negotiations. From the new influence of nongovernmental global diplomats in the human rights and environmental areas to the much greater role domestic actors play in international affairs, state navigation of the international arena is a very complex endeavor.

# 2

# The Board

No two negotiations are the same. Even when the same actors return to the negotiation table to discuss the very same issue for a second time, both the dynamics and the results may be quite different. Identifying the particular mix of factors involved helps explain why negotiations take the twists and turns they do. This chapter first examines the international system setting in which all negotiations take place and then offers a detailed checklist of characteristics that distinguish individual negotiation situations. Taken together, the international system setting and the specific negotiation characteristics can be conceptualized as the board upon which the strategic game of negotiation is played.

This negotiation board, or the context in which the negotiations take place, must be examined from both a macro and a micro perspective. The larger picture is the international system setting in which the power relations among actors—the system configuration—and the relative stability of that configuration are particularly important. Once this overall shape has been laid out, it is possible to look in detail at individual negotiation episodes and identify their key characteristics, including such factors as the number of parties to the negotiation, the types of issues involved, and the level of commitment by the parties. An examination of the way these factors play out allows one to appreciate the strategic decisions the parties make and to understand why some negotiation strategies are more effective than others.

Consider the U.S.-Iraq situation, when on August 2, 1990, Iraqi forces invaded Kuwait and occupied the emirate within six hours. During the course of the next four months, the United States was able to negotiate the mobilization of an almost universal coalition of nations that committed to

sending troops and materiel, provided airbases and troop deployment facilities, and guaranteed financial support. In short, this coalition presented
a united world front in the face of Iraqi aggression. Six years later, the
United States was faced once again with Iraqi defiance of world opinion:
Iraq denied access to UN weapons inspectors carrying out a Security
Council mandate to search for evidence of chemical and biological warfare
preparations. This time, however, U.S. negotiators could only muster the
active support of Britain. Moreover, they were denied landing and staging
rights by virtually all of the Gulf states and received none of the financial
and moral backing that had typified the earlier confrontation. What had
changed in this relatively short time period? The answer lies in the configuration of the international system in which these two episodes occurred
and the relations among the system units—the board upon which these critical events transpired and the negotiations they fostered. (Of course, in the
2002–2003 run-up to the invasion of Iraq, the United States and Britain
faced an even more daunting task in attempting to build a coalition in support of their call for decisive action by the international community.) See
chapter 6 for a detailed discussion of the Iraq case.

## The International System

At the beginning of the twenty-first century, negotiators face an international
environment that has changed remarkably since the turn of the previous
century. The number of sovereign states has grown from fewer than 50 to
nearly 200, and myriad intergovernmental, nongovernmental, and transnational entities clutter the landscape. Citizen diplomacy, the information revolution, and the power of multinational business enterprises and financial
institutions, whose influence can exceed that of many small states, have all
combined to create a global arena wherein negotiation skills are essential.

While it is true that all of these factors and institutions have become increasingly relevant, it is still the case that the international system setting is
typically described in terms of its central units—sovereign states—and the
power relations among them. At the time of the first crisis with Iraq in
1990–1991, immediately following the end of the Cold War, the United States
was emerging as the single dominant power in the international system, the
Soviet Union having lost control over its alliance partners in central and eastern Europe. In fact, the Soviet Union itself was soon to dissolve into thirteen
independent republics. Under these conditions, the states in the international
system were scrambling to be counted among the trusted allies of what appeared to be the dominant power: the United States. By the onset of the Iraq
War in 2003, these relationships had largely sorted themselves out. While the
United States was still in a dominant position militarily, it was clear by then
that other major powers, such as France, Germany, China, and Russia, did not

necessarily need to blindly follow the U.S. lead. Even Saudi Arabia and Turkey, two of the staunchest members of the anti-Iraq coalition of 1990–1991, refused to fall into step with the United States the next time around.

## Polarity

The distribution of power among states is most commonly referred to as polarity. Both the number of poles—or centers of power—in a system and the way power is distributed among them characterize the types of international systems. Five different international systems or polar structures, along with two extremely bloody, anarchic systems corresponding to the two world wars, have characterized the twentieth century and the beginning of the twenty-first (see box).

### Polar Structures in the International System

**Balance of power** (to 1914): a relatively small number of nation-states operated in a system whereby shifting alliances kept any single state from developing a preponderance of power.

**World War I** (1914–1918): a breakdown of the balance of power, a result of the crumbling of existing alliances rather than the repeated shifting that had kept the nation-states in balance before 1914.

**Multipolarity** (1918–1939): a diffusion of military power and political decision making among a small group of relatively equal units; isolation practices among major powers.

**World War II** (1939–1945): an outgrowth of isolationism, which allowed aggressive powers to grow unchecked and become global security threats.

**Bipolarity** (1945–1962): a concentration of military power and political decision making in two relatively equal preeminent states—the United States and the USSR—and two very rigid military alliances—the North Atlantic Treaty Organization (NATO) and the Warsaw Pact.

**Polycentrism** (1963–1989): a hybrid structure, with the United States and the USSR continuing to constitute two centers of military power but with multiple centers of political decision making.

**Unipolarity** (1990– ): an overwhelming concentration of military capability in one entity—the United States clearly is the military hegemon—although political power is even more diffuse than it was under polycentrism.

One way to highlight the impact of international system structure or polarity on the negotiation process is to examine a particular long-term conflict that spans two or more of these historical systems and involves a number of negotiation episodes along the way. The Arab-Israeli conflict, stretching from the end of World War II to the present, provides such an unfortunate example. The "return" of the Jews to the Land of Israel (Palestine), beginning in the 1880s and increasing after the Holocaust, provides the backdrop for this conflict. It was, however, the November 1947 General Assembly resolution calling for the partition of Palestine into separate Arab and Jewish states, and the eventual unilateral proclamation of the State of Israel in 1948, that triggered this protracted conflict. Significant negotiation episodes produced cease-fires and disengagement agreements following each of the twenty-eight international crises that have punctuated this long-standing conflict between Israel and its Arab neighbors (Brecher and Wilkenfeld 2000).

Early Arab-Israeli negotiations occurred during the immediate post–World War II bipolar period, highlighted by the emerging strength of the Soviet Union as well as the last gasps of France and the United Kingdom as sources of power and influence. In fact, the negotiations ending both the 1948–1949 and 1956 wars found the United States and the Soviet Union working together to resolve these conflicts. However, by 1956 it was clear that the two superpowers diverged on a number of key elements in Middle East policy. Because of these disagreements, by 1970 and 1973—when Israel, Egypt, and Syria engaged in all-out military conflict —these states served as virtual proxies for the two superpowers. Finally, with the end of the Cold War and the demise of the Soviet Union, yet another transformation occurred in the structure of the international system. The shift to unipolarity has affected the Arab-Israeli conflict and, for that matter, other conflict arenas in the Middle East. The United States, for example, is extensively engaged in Israeli-Palestinian negotiations, whereas Russia and the UN are involved only marginally through the moribund efforts of the Roadmap for Peace. U.S. President Barack Obama's address to the Islamic world from Cairo in June 2009 was an attempt by that new administration to reassert a role for the United States in the resolution of that conflict after almost a decade of neglect under the previous administration.

## Crisis

Besides being affected by the existing structure of the international system, international negotiations are also characterized by the climate in which they are conducted. Of particular importance to negotiators is the impact of crisis. Since crises often act as catalysts for major system change, they represent a wild card that is capable of changing the shape of the international system and altering the outcomes of individual negotiation episodes. The extent to which national actors perceive themselves to be in a crisis can have an impact on the pace of the negotiations and the range of alternatives examined, as well as on the types of outcomes that result (treaties, interim agreements, unstable cease-fires).

From the larger system perspective, an international crisis can be defined as an increase in the intensity of hostile interactions between states. This change carries with it a heightened probability of military hostility that, in turn, destabilizes their relationship in ways that threaten the stability of a regional subsystem or the entire international system. The Berlin crisis of 1948, the Cuban missile crisis of 1962, and the 1973 Middle East War were all instances in which critical negotiations occurred in crisis environments.

From the point of view of a particular state and its decision makers, a crisis occurs when the leaders of a country perceive a threat to basic values (territory, population, economy), an awareness of finite response time (it will not go away unless some action is taken), and a heightened probability of involvement in military hostilities (Brecher and Wilkenfeld 2000). Perhaps the essence of crisis at the national level is captured by the stress levels the key decision makers experience—for example, John F. Kennedy in 1962, as he maneuvered for the removal of Soviet missiles from Cuba; Golda Meir and Anwar Sadat in 1973–1974, as they attempted to wrest maximum advantage in the negotiations that followed the October Yom Kippur War; and George W. Bush as he sought an effective response to the al-Qaeda bombing of the Twin Towers in New York and the Pentagon in Washington on September 11, 2001.

From the perspective of negotiation, the three key elements of crisis are threat, time pressure, and the accompanying stress that these engender. Neither the Kyoto environmental conference in 1997 nor the Uruguay Round of General Agreement on Tariffs and Trade (GATT) talks from 1986 to 1994 was characterized by the need for immediate resolution. Indeed, each was a stage in an ongoing and complex negotiation. This contrasts with the crisis atmosphere that has characterized negotiations involving the United States and North Korea, as explored in chapter 1. Similarly, the Iraq crisis of 2003–2004, couched in terms of weapons of mass destruction (WMD) in the hands of a regime supporting international terror, posed a serious challenge for negotiators; as deadlines approached, stress levels rose, massive troop movements took place, and the probability of military hostilities increased. Negotiations conducted in an atmosphere of threat and stress, accompanied by time pressures and deadlines, can often put decision makers in positions where they cannot fully explore options or take advantage of alternative information sources, thus leading to the possibility that less-than-optimal decisions will be made.

There are circumstances in which routine negotiations take on some of the characteristics of a crisis environment. When the delegates to the Kyoto climate change conference first gathered in 1997, after years of preparation following the Rio conference of 1992, the negotiation environment was routine. However, as the official end of the conference neared and it appeared that little in the way of an agreement would result, U.S. President Clinton dispatched Vice President Gore to Kyoto to convey an increased sense of urgency in the hope that it would spur the delegates into action. Soon, an atmosphere of crisis (nonmilitary, to be sure) gripped the participants, and both real and imagined deadlines pushed the negotiators toward the text of a treaty that would reflect at least some progress. In fact, the official end of the meeting was pushed back a day to enable the delegates to make some demonstrable progress.

Conversely, skilled negotiators, often with the help of mediators and third parties (see discussion that follows), can sometimes transform an atmosphere of crisis into a routine negotiation environment. By eliminating or at least reducing the perception of threat and limited time, thereby lowering the stress levels that these entail, the negotiation can be transformed into a positive environment more conducive to the examination of alternatives and the achievement of a mutually beneficial outcome. In late 1995, at the height of the three-year-old war in Bosnia, President Clinton invited the presidents of Bosnia, Croatia, and Serbia to a conference in Dayton, Ohio. The issues at this conference involved territory, a constitution for Bosnia, withdrawal of forces to cease-fire lines, and the deployment of a NATO peacekeeping force. Removed from the extreme crisis atmosphere of ethnic cleansing, massive civilian casualties, and severe damage to the infrastructure of Bosnia, the leaders were ultimately able to negotiate the Dayton Peace Accords under intense U.S. mediation and bring that phase of the armed conflict to a close.

---

**KEY TERM**

**Third-Party Intervention**
The introduction of an external party into a negotiation when it is apparent that progress cannot be achieved without some form of outside involvement.

---

### Third-Party Intervention

Like polarity and crisis, the intervention of a third party into particular conflicts or negotiations also represents a system-level factor that can significantly affect the progress of a specific negotiation episode. Third parties usually enter into a negotiation when it is apparent that progress cannot be achieved without some form of outside involvement. In certain crisis situations, usually when a local crisis threatens to widen dramatically, third parties intervene to defuse conflict or to prevent it from spreading and further destabilizing the region or international system. The availability of third parties to mediate in international negotiation situations can have important ramifications in terms of how the negotiations play out and their ultimate success or failure.

Major powers and small states; representatives of regional, global, or security organizations; private citizens; religious organizations; and special interest groups have all played important mediation roles in international negotiations in recent years (see box). In general, there has been a substantial increase in the proportion of international crises since the end of the Cold War that have seen significant mediation by various international actors—32 percent of international crises were mediated in the Cold War period, compared with a 48-percent mediation rate for post–Cold War crises. During the latter period, mediation was dominated by the efforts of single states or groups of states—accounting for almost 60 percent of all instances of mediation. Examples include the U.S. role in convening the Dayton, Ohio, meetings in 1995 to address the spiraling ethnic violence in Bosnia, and the

## Types of International Mediation

**Mediation by global organization:** on behalf of the UN, Count Folke Bernadotte and later UN under-secretary-general Ralph Bunche played important mediation roles in the negotiations leading to the 1948–1949 Arab-Israeli armistice agreements.

**Mediation by regional organization:** both the European Union and the African Union played key roles in mediating the conflict between the DRC and Rwanda over cross-border incursions in 2004.

**Mediation by a single state:** Libya played an important mediation role in the 2006 border crisis between Chad and Sudan.

**Mediation by a group of states:** the United States, Argentina, Brazil, and Chile, as guarantors of the 1942 Rio Protocol, played a critical mediation role in the crises involving Ecuador and Peru in 1935, 1941, 1981, 1991, and 1995.

**Mediation by private citizen:** former U.S. president Jimmy Carter conducted private mediation in negotiations surrounding the Haiti crisis of 1994 and the North Korean nuclear crisis of 1993–1994.

**Mediation by religious organization:** the Vatican played an important role in 1984 in mediating the so-called Beagle Channel dispute between Chile and Argentina.

**Mediation by special interest group:** the Ford Foundation financed a 1991 UN peace initiative to end El Salvador's civil war.

U.S./U.K. mediation effort during the 2002 crisis between India and Pakistan after a terrorist attack on Indian forces in Jammu and Kashmir. On some occasions, this third-party mediation effort can result in both a resolution of the conflict situation and a broadening of the role of the original mediating party—for example, the long-term U.S. involvement in Bosnia in the form of peacekeeping troops in the region under the terms of the Dayton Accords, or the UN-mediated cease-fires in the Middle East that have resulted in the long-term stationing of UN troops along Israel's borders with its Arab neighbors over the past sixty years, most recently in southern Lebanon following the Israel-Lebanon War of 2006. Other instances of intervention are more short-lived—for example, the very effective but limited mediation role that Algeria played in helping resolve the Iran hostage crisis of 1979–1981.

Third-party intervention—including mediation—has been defined by Young (1968, 34) as "any action taken by an actor that is not a direct party to the crisis, that is designed to reduce or remove one or more of the problems of the bargaining relationship and, therefore, to facilitate the termination of the crisis." Bobrow (1981, 188) speaks of the positive contributions of third parties as "focusing the parties on a particular termination agreement, devising a formula to avoid hard issues, providing an agenda, and manipulating timing." Third parties can also provide face-saving mechanisms for the conflicting parties by creating opportunities and excuses for what the parties would like to do anyway but might find politically difficult. Raiffa (1982, 108–109) indicates that third-party intervention can bring parties together; establish a constructive ambiance for negotiation; collect and judiciously communicate selected confidential material; help parties clarify their values; deflate unreasonable claims and loosen commitments; seek joint gains; keep negotiations going; and articulate the rationale for agreement.

A mediator, at least in theory, should be neutral across the parties involved, even though this characteristic is not always in evidence or even possible in contemporary international affairs. It should be noted that mediation is not the same as arbitration, the latter being a judicial process where the third party issues a ruling and the parties are authoritatively bound to abide by that ruling. By contrast, "mediation is a noncoercive, nonviolent, and ultimately, nonbinding form of intervention" (Bercovitch 1997, 127). Depending on the situation, however, the line between mediation and arbitration can be blurred at the bargaining table.

Mediators may adopt a variety of styles or tactics in attempting to resolve or defuse conflict. Mediators can adopt a facilitative style, whereby they attempt to bring the parties together, provide a venue for negotiations, and generally provide an environment in which a free exchange of views among the parties can occur. A formulative style is more intrusive;

the mediator in this case helps the parties formulate texts designed to move them closer to agreement. Finally, a manipulative style is used by a mediator when it appears that inducements, either in the form of carrots or sticks, are necessary to move the negotiations forward (Wilkenfeld et al. 2005).

A mediator's motives for intervening in a conflict or intractable negotiation will affect that person's ability to achieve some form of resolution. Aside from the temporal benefits of helping international actors resolve conflict, third parties get involved because on some level they have interests at stake in the negotiation and wish to facilitate peaceful resolution of the problems engendered in that negotiation (Zartman and Touval 1996). However, a closer examination of the third-party interests at stake sometimes turns up a darker side of intervention, wherein third parties intervene in negotiations in order to further their own special interests. Many of the interventions in Africa in recent history have been designed to support and strengthen one of the parties to the dispute rather than bring about a mediated settlement that is mutually beneficial. Hoping to derive ideological gain, Cuba maintained a significant military presence in Angola from the mid-1970s to the early 1990s, siding with the Marxist-oriented Popular Movement for the Liberation of Angola (MPLA) against the South African–backed National Union for the Total Independence of Angola (UNITA). In 1994, France dispatched a military force to Rwanda in a nonneutral intervention to support the Hutu-led government against the Tutsi Rwanda Patriotic Front—in this instance, to enhance France's influence in Africa in the postcolonial era. In the extreme, such interventions have resulted in territorial or economic gain for the intervening party. In the case of France in Rwanda, genocide on a scale not seen since the Holocaust followed the mishandling of this intervention.

## Negotiation Characteristics: A Checklist

Having reviewed the larger international system setting that functions as a backdrop for individual negotiations, it is now useful to examine the specific characteristics of individual negotiation episodes. Basically, one can approach a negotiation with a series of questions in hand—for example, how many actors are involved, is there linkage among negotiation issues, or is there a deadline by which the talks must conclude? The following checklist focuses on three aspects of negotiation: actor, issue, and process characteristics. Taken in combination, these factors define the structure of the episode (the board) and help determine the strategic approach that makes the most sense for the involved actors. Understanding these characteristics and how they intertwine to affect the outcomes of negotiations should prove helpful, whether one is analyzing historical negotiation episodes or developing new negotiation strategies.

## Actor Characteristics

### Number of Actors/Coalitions

It is commonplace to think of negotiations in terms of two-party interactions. Whether it is a husband and a wife, a buyer and a seller, or two nations on the verge of war, this is the model through which it is easiest to conceptualize the give and take of the negotiation process. Yet many negotiations in both the domestic and international realms involve more than two actors, and often this adds complexity far in excess of the actual number of additional players at the negotiation table.

It is important to distinguish the number of actors in the negotiation from the question of how unified a specific negotiation team is internally. It is equally important to distinguish a multiactor case from a two-actor negotiation where a third actor takes the role of mediator, as discussed earlier. This latter situation is still a variant of the two-actor negotiation model, albeit one with facilitation.

As the number of actors increases from two to many, the fundamental dynamics of the process itself are altered. Most significantly, the possibility of coalition formation between two or more of the actors means that a negotiation within a negotiation now exists. Often, the formation of a coalition has the effect of reducing the number of actors back down to two, and therefore to a more familiar and manageable model for the participants. On occasion, such coalitions are inherently unstable—take, for example, the three dominant coalitions in the United Nations during the height of the Cold War: the capitalist West, the socialist Soviet Bloc, and the Group of 77 nonaligned states. In fact, one of the first signs that the international system was evolving in the early 1960s from a bipolar to a polycentric system with looser alliance structures was the lessening of bloc voting behavior in the United Nations. The broad coalition the United States formed at the height of the 1990–1991 Gulf crisis represented a triumph of expediency and self-interest over ideology, whereas the inability of the United States to re-create that unanimity during the run-up to its invasion of Iraq in 2003 attested to a significantly changed international atmosphere. The on-again off-again six-party negotiations, which began in 2003–2004 on the issue of North Korean nuclear capability, demonstrate some of the complexities of structuring and advancing coalition objectives among parties with multiple and crosscutting interests.

Coalition ties can provide added clout by allowing an actor to rely explicitly or implicitly on the power of allies to enhance a negotiation position. However, a tight alliance structure may also restrict the maneuvering room available to negotiators by reducing the range of alternative negotiated outcomes that will be acceptable not only to them but to their coalition partners. The historical closeness of the U.S.-Israeli alliance has meant that the range of outcomes the United States has been able to explore with the Palestinians on

**KEY TERM**

---

**Coalition**   A collection of actors who band together to try to achieve common goals, at either the domestic or transnational level.

Israel's behalf has been highly restricted. Indeed, this is an area in which the Obama administration is seeking a change in the U.S. role.

Hopmann (1996) argues that multiparty or multilateral negotiations exhibit greater complexity because of the possibility of coalition formation, of crosscutting cleavages, and of group dynamics intervening in the process. At the very least, the involvement of multiple parties means an increase in the complexity of the negotiation. With each party to the negotiation seeking a different outcome, and each viewing the negotiation with a different sense of urgency, the possibilities for both delay and failure are enhanced.

### Team Cohesion

Ideally, all members of a negotiation team have reached consensus about the issue under discussion before they sit down at the table. This model of a negotiation team generally involves a leader or chief negotiator, with other members of the team possessing specific expertise (legal, economic, military). In such cases, the team leader commonly does most of the talking and seeks the advice and expertise of other delegation members, as appropriate. Under this model, one would expect the delegation as a whole to be able to present a unified position during the course of the negotiations. This can be described as a monolithic model.

**KEY TERM**

---

**Monolithic Model**   The assumption that all members of a negotiating team are working to advance the same interests and speak with one voice.

However, negotiation actors "are not only those negotiating 'across the table' (horizontally). Parties also negotiate within the team at the table or in caucus. Negotiations also occur between the 'table team members' and their respective decision makers (vertical authority), and also within the vertical authority as it attempts to decide upon directions to give the team" (Colosi 1986, 245). Thus, at the other extreme might be a model in which, although a delegation leader is still present, other individual members have status equal to the leader and possess somewhat divergent goals. Or, while the delegation head has overall authority, that person must defer to others on specific issues during the course of the negotiation; this is different from simply seeking advice and expertise in the monolithic model described previously. In fact, the delegation might reflect the types of cleavages present in the government itself or in the society as a whole. We may even find instances where there is some uncertainty about who the actual negotiating partner is: during the complex negotiations over the U.S. Embassy hostages held in Iran from 1979 to 1981, the United States was not certain that the group with which it was negotiating did in fact represent those who were actually holding the hostages. Such delegations often reflect the failure of one of the teams to reach a consensus position prior to departure for the negotiation session. While this phenomenon is most common to countries with a highly bureaucratic foreign policy apparatus—the United States, for example—it also occurs in more centralized systems, where the interests of competing elites must be attended to. This is the heterogeneous model.

---

**KEY TERM**

**Heterogeneous Model**   The assumption that the different members of a negotiating team hold different interests, which may be in conflict with one another.

---

Even more complicated is the maintenance of a team approach to negotiation when the members of the team are in fact themselves sovereign nation-states, as is the case with the loose coalition that includes the United States, China, Russia, South Korea, and Japan in the periodic negotiations concerning the North Korean nuclear capability. In this instance, there is no real team "leader" setting overall goals and strategy, and in fact there is only a nominal agreement on some of the very basic overall objectives of the negotiation. For example, the United States and China strongly disagree over the possibility that force might ultimately be used in this situation—with China unwilling to consider such measures against what is at least a nominal communist ally. In such situations, it may be possible for the more unified negotiation team—in this case North Korea—to exploit such divisions for its own advantage. The resumption by North Korea of nuclear and missile tests in 2009 resulted in the first strong and united stand at the United Nations on the part of all five parties to the negotiation.

These two models represent extremes, and most often negotiation teams include elements of both. There may be issues on which there is broad team consensus and on which the delegation can act in a unified manner, as well as issues on which there is sharp disagreement within the team. In the case of Israel's complex negotiations with the Palestinians, no member of an Israeli government delegation would be willing to make territorial concessions involving a radical change in the status of Jerusalem. At the same time, there might be differences within the delegation over the size and timing of

Israeli withdrawals from occupied territory in the West Bank, reflecting the deep cleavages in Israel's government and population that successive elections have not been able to resolve. This same dynamic was evident in the case of successive American delegations to the Strategic Arms Limitation Talks (SALT). Delegations were composed of specialists from the Departments of State and Defense, and while they agreed on the need to reduce arms, they often reflected the sharp differences within the government itself over the political and military aspects of U.S. relations with the Soviet Union during the height of the Cold War.

### Actor Capabilities

The first part of chapter 2 illustrates the ways that power relations at the international system level (bipolarity, multipolarity, etc.) define the larger setting in which the negotiations take place and impact the options available to the actors in the negotiation. This section discusses how the relative capabilities of individual actors affect the course of the negotiation and its ultimate outcome. Since it is rare that all parties to a negotiation have equal power, conventional wisdom assumes that stronger actors will drive the better bargain and end up with the lion's share; conversely, weaker actors have less clout and therefore get the shorter end of the negotiation stick. However, strength is often a matter of perception, as evidenced by the fact that power relations are among the murkier concepts in social science. In international relations, not only is there great difficulty in reaching consensus on what constitutes national capability, but the problem is further confounded by discussion of measurement issues. In the increasingly complex international environment of the twenty-first century, different elements of power will come to the fore under varying circumstances—military, economic, political, territorial, demographic. The issue is how and when the various aspects of power impact the course and ultimate outcome of a negotiation.

### Limits to Power

Power is situational. To understand this, one need only think back to the horrifying pictures of U.S. Marines removing the bodies of over 200 dead comrades after a 1983 suicide bombing destroyed their barracks in Beirut; the sight of an American troop carrier under siege in the harbor of Port-au-Prince, Haiti, in 1994; the helplessness of the world's five declared nuclear powers as first India and then Pakistan detonated underground nuclear devices in 1998; the inability of the United States and its allies to deal effectively with worldwide terror organizations such as al Qaeda in the wake of the September 11, 2001, bombings; the difficulties the United States faces in trying to stabilize Iraq long after it had achieved a military "victory" in

May 2003; or the apparent lack of options available for dealing with the ongoing North Korean nuclear issue. The mere possession of overwhelming military power does not necessarily mean that it can be effectively and fully exercised in the pursuit of national goals.

At the negotiation table, power intertwines with commitment and opportunity to create unique, and sometimes unexpected, dynamics. The Paris Peace Agreements, under which the United States formalized its withdrawal from Vietnam, represent a classic case of commitment and resolve winning out over "objective" power. The stark pictures of U.S. helicopters plucking the last of the American staff and their South Vietnamese collaborators from the rooftop of the U.S. Embassy in Saigon, while those left behind clamored desperately to get inside the embassy compound, pointed to the final humiliation in a decade-long struggle the United States had conducted with itself over the disconnect of power, commitment, and resolve.

History shows that preponderant power cannot always be effectively exercised during negotiations. For example, the possession of nuclear weapons does not necessarily afford a means of achieving advantage in a negotiation. Only if a nuclear power can actually convince the other side that such weapons will be used in pursuit of the objectives under negotiation will such capability make a difference. North Vietnam did not believe the United States would use tactical nuclear weapons on the battlefield, largely because of the impact of such a decision on the Soviet Union's position in the conflict. In fact, the deployment of U.S. long-range bombers to flatten significant portions of North Vietnam had the unintended effect of hardening the resolve of the north and making it even less flexible at the negotiating table. Hence, the United States was effectively stripped of its nuclear capability at the Paris negotiations—its credibility was hopelessly compromised—and the gap in power between the United States and North Vietnam was thereby narrowed dramatically. The United States learned a costly lesson in Vietnam about the limits to power.

### Actor Norms

National negotiation teams differ widely in terms of the norms they bring to the table. As will be apparent in chapter 3, some cultures stress the need for clear-cut victory, while others value the achievement of consensus and a mutually beneficial outcome. U.S. negotiators, for example, are known for a laissez-faire attitude toward planning, "cowboy" shoot-out techniques, demands for rapid action, and even excessive legalism. Their sense of independence, desire for individual achievement, and personal drive for success are all reflected in their behavior in the negotiation setting. Japanese and other East Asian cultures, evolving from the general beliefs and social structures of the Confucian system, tend to bring a different set of values

Mobs of South Vietnamese try to scale the fourteen-foot wall of the U.S. Embassy in Saigon, April 29, 1975. AP Photo/Neil Ulevich

and norms to the negotiation setting: dependence, trust, reticence, hierarchy, obligation, loyalty, and harmony. It should be obvious that these two very different approaches translate into very different styles of negotiation.

These two approaches can be differentiated by labeling them low-context (individualistic) and high-context (relationship-oriented) negotiating styles (R. Cohen 1997). Under this generalized rubric, Americans—representing a classic low-context culture—exhibit a style grounded in a belief that a person can "freely manipulate his environment for his own purposes" (Mushakoji 1976, 45-46, as cited in R. Cohen). Results, rather than relationships, are the key. On the other hand, the Japanese—representing a classic high-context culture—exhibit an adaptive style. Negotiation is not an end in itself but an episode in a long-term relationship to be built between the parties. The clash of low-context and high-context cultures at the bargaining table can create serious problems in communication and, ultimately, in negotiators' ability to reach agreements.

Clearly, as states acquire more information about the negotiation styles of others, they will adapt their approaches where possible. This, in turn, is leading to what many students of negotiation are calling a culture of negotiation, which entails a language, style, and approach that nations share while negotiating, and which washes out many aspects of individual cultural tendencies.

### *Actor Commitment*

Actors involved in a negotiation may also differ in terms of their commitment to the issues under discussion. Just as on the playing field or battlefield, where differences in the degree of commitment of the parties can sometimes make up for more objectively measured power differentials, so, too, can variations in commitment strengthen or weaken hands at the negotiation table. These differences, of course, can be real or perceived. During the protracted Vietnam conflict, it was clear from the outset that the relative commitments of the United States and North Vietnam were heavily influenced by the differences in the conflict's immediacy for the populations of the two countries. The U.S. administration was never able to effectively convey the strategic importance of South Vietnam to the American people to the same degree that the North Vietnamese government was able to for its own population. The North Vietnamese negotiators in Paris certainly took the growing domestic dissent in the United States and the erosion of public support for the American role in Vietnam as signs of weakening U.S. commitment to its negotiating positions and hence were encouraged to hold out for larger concessions.

While the Vietnam War and its negotiated termination offer an example of the impact of both the limits to power and a weakening American commitment, the behavior of the United States in the tense negotiations surrounding the Cuban missile crisis shows a much different pattern. In that 1962 crisis, the United States was able to demonstrate a credible threat to use the ultimate in force at its disposal and to couple that threat with a demonstrable commitment to the particular conflict issue. Ultimately, the Soviet Union backed off, unwilling to exercise the necessary power and unable to demonstrate an overwhelming commitment to the issue in dispute.

A key player in the Kyoto climate negotiations, the AOSIS offered another example of how intense commitment can provide a compelling substitute for actual power in influencing a negotiation outcome. This coalition of forty-two small island nations from around the world was formed in 1994 to ensure that the needs of its members would be heard amid the clamor from the vastly more powerful states in the climate negotiations. Working in conjunction with two NGOs—Earth Kind and Counterpart International—AOSIS crafted a program of action for Kyoto and achieved prominence at the negotiations with its argument that rising sea levels would spell disaster and death for island populations around the world if concerted action were not taken soon (Alliance of Small Island States 1997).

An important factor to bear in mind is that, over a period of time, the same adversaries may face off across a negotiating table over different issues (see discussion of legacy later in the chapter), and power and commitment levels do not necessarily remain constant across issue areas. Six years before the Cuban missile crisis, the United States failed to demonstrate sufficient resolve as Soviet troops and armor rolled into Hungary; nor did it keep the Soviets from similar action in Czechoslovakia in the Prague Spring crisis of 1968. More recently, the United States again passed on an opportunity to thwart Russia's assertion of regional power as it overwhelmed Georgia in the summer of 2008 in that country's dispute over the breakaway region of South Ossetia.

## Issue Characteristics

### Number of Issues/Bargaining Dimensions

Besides the variations attributable to the number of actors involved, negotiations can be characterized by the number of issues in contention among those actors. Like the addition of actors to a negotiation, an increase in the number of issues clearly expands the complexity of the negotiation. However, an increase in issues can also enhance the probability of a successful outcome to the negotiations since the number of combinations of favorable outcomes for each of the actors to consider is increased. In effect, as the number of issues increases, the situation has the potential to change from one where a single actor wins and the other loses (zero-sum) to a more mutually beneficial one that offers opportunities for each actor to win something (positive sum).

The zero-sum case is characterized by a single issue in contention, such as territory, where the two actors have strictly opposing interests. The more one actor gets, the less the other gets (Raiffa 1982, 133). Another variant involves one actor's holding all of a territory in dispute, while the other has no access to it at all. Many of the most intractable international conflicts can be seen as zero-sum bargaining cases over territory: India and Pakistan over Kashmir; Ethiopia and Eritrea over a disputed border region; the Israelis and the Palestinians over the West Bank. The apparent simplicity of the winner-takes-all bargaining situation is also its inherent weakness when it comes to negotiating a resolution. With only one issue in contention, one actor will always win, while the other will always lose.

---

**KEY TERM**

**Zero-Sum**   A situation where one player can gain only at the expense of the other player—when one player wins, the other necessarily loses.

---

By contrast, if there are several issues to negotiate, the two parties can often move into a non-zero-sum environment. Now they are no longer strict competitors. As Raiffa notes, "It is no longer true that if one party gets more, the other necessarily has to get less: they can both get more. They can cooperate in order to change the pie that they eventually will have to divide" (1982, 131). In the fall of 1962, the United States and the Soviet Union were locked in what was ultimately the most dangerous superpower confrontation of the Cold War—over the issue of Soviet installation of nuclear missiles in Cuba, only ninety miles from the U.S. mainland. Initially, the confrontation involved the single issue of American insistence on the immediate withdrawal of the missiles. As the crisis continued, and military action seemed inevitable, the United States gradually expanded the issue set to include the status of U.S. missiles stationed in Turkey and targeted at the Soviet Union, as well as the question of an American invasion of the island of Cuba itself. This expansion of the issue set had the effect of allowing the Soviet Union to commit to the withdrawal of the missiles from Cuba and, nevertheless, to be able to claim victory on the latter two issues. In essence, both parties emerged from the negotiation with some degree of victory.

---

**KEY TERM**

**Non-Zero-Sum**   A situation where it is possible for all players to be " winners"; the possibility of mutual gains.

---

Skilled negotiators, often with the help of mediators, can transform a winner-takes-all bargaining situation into one with opportunities for mutual benefit. Once this happens, it is possible for both actors to come away from the negotiation feeling that they won on at least some issues. In 1996–1997, Israel and the Palestinian Authority were locked in a seemingly unresolvable dispute over Israel's pullout from Hebron on the West Bank, the last major Arab city from which Israel was to withdraw as part of the Oslo Accords of 1993. U.S. mediators were able to expand the issue set from a narrow focus on territory to one that encompassed additional issues, such as security arrangements and access to holy places, so that it was possible for both parties to see benefit and thereby move toward an eventual agreement. However, this apparent diplomatic success was subsequently overturned, with the reoccupation in September 2000 by Israel of Hebron and the entire West Bank in response to the second intifada—or uprising—by the Palestinians.

*Issue Linkage*

Related to the number of issues is the question of whether there are linkage effects. One manifestation of linkage occurs when a negotiation that a nation conducts with an actor is tied to other negotiations it is also conducting with that actor. For example, in 1998, as President Clinton prepared to make the first presidential visit to China since that country's government's violent repression of prodemocracy student demonstrations in Tiananmen Square in 1989, it was clear that the standards to which the United States was holding China in the area of human rights were not the same as those it was applying to other nations with which it was then negotiating. While human rights groups and others cried foul, the United States was following a policy of expediency, wherein it applied standards in a differential manner, depending on overall American foreign policy objectives. In this case, the U.S. position on human rights violations in China appeared to be linked (some would say held hostage) to the U.S. economic desire to capitalize on the vast Chinese markets.

But linkage and the U.S.-China case can be looked at from a second perspective, one that is perhaps more generous to the United States. The United States, of course, is pursuing multiple goals simultaneously as it interacts with the Chinese government. While the U.S. government is interested in moving China toward a more acceptable standard of human rights practices in its society, it has important economic and strategic interests vis-a-vis China as well. By attempting to create linkages among these issues, the United States hopes to move policy in a favorable direction for both countries. Indeed, this second aspect of linkages brings us back to our discussion of the mutually beneficial bargaining perspective—and to the means nations have at their

> **KEY TERM**
>
> **Linkage** The inclusion of additional issues not directly related to the issue under negotiation.

disposal to transform difficult and even deadlocked negotiations into ones with the possibility of mutually beneficial outcomes for all.

*Time Frame*

In the earlier discussion of the international system setting, the time factor was explored as one of the distinguishing characteristics of a crisis, in that the actors in a crisis negotiation often perceive a finite or limited time for response. In international crises involving military-security issues, time is often coupled with the possibility of violence, in the sense that as real or perceived deadlines approach, resorting to violence is increasingly seen as the only available alternative. But even in routine situations, and in instances where the alternative to not achieving agreement in some time frame need not be violence, time pressures nevertheless exert their own influences on the negotiation process.

The time factor does not necessarily affect all negotiation actors equally. Consider, for example, the drawn-out on-again, off-again Israeli-Palestinian negotiations involving the conditions under which Israel would undertake a pullback from territories it has occupied in the West Bank since 1967, perhaps as part of a so-called two-state solution. Assuming there is value to Israel from continued occupation of these territories, Israel has no particular incentive to move quickly in these negotiations, even though it continues to pay a heavy price in terms of violence against its own citizens and in the court of world public opinion. In fact, withdrawal from the occupied territories might appear as a retreat under fire in the context of ongoing violence in these areas. The Palestinians, on the other hand, given the context of the power struggle between the Palestinian Authority (PA) and more militant Palestinian movements, most notably Hamas, feel pressure to bring this matter to a hasty and successful conclusion—or else the PA risks losing power to Hamas on the West Bank, in a manner similar to its electoral defeat and ultimate expulsion from Gaza in 2006. From this perspective, the incentives for Israel are to move slowly; for the PA, they are to move quickly.

However, for Israel, there is a modest incentive to strengthen the Palestinian Authority because the alternative prospect of negotiating with Hamas is not appealing. Thus, Israel may be inclined to speed things up under these circumstances. On the other hand, slowing down allows Israel to continue to create "facts on the ground" in the form of settlement expansion and increased settler population, making it more and more difficult to make extensive territorial concessions to the Palestinians. So not only does time function differently for the two parties, but even within a single negotiation party there are often conflicting perceptions of the role that time plays.

Time, in the form of deadlines, may be real or artificial. Real deadlines exist in hostage situations, when treaties are about to expire, and when actual or impending natural disasters require concerted effort on the part of members of the international community. Deadlines are more artificial or flexible when all that is at stake is the changing of travel plans or the rescheduling of meetings between important leaders (the eleventh day in Kyoto). There is a maxim to the effect that 90 percent of a negotiation takes place in the last 10 percent of the time allowed, emphasizing the importance of mutually credible deadlines (Colosi 1986).

It is critical for negotiators to gain an accurate understanding of the different ways in which time impacts the parties to the negotiation. In some instances, time can be bundled as part of the negotiated outcome, so that the ultimate agreement reflects one party's need for a time-sensitive resolution, while the party with less time pressure may be able to gain other types of concessions. For example, in negotiations in the late 1990s, Israel saw considerable value in what has been termed a phased pullback in the West Bank, under which it could periodically check on the Palestinians' compliance with their end of the bargain before making further concessions. The Palestinians, for their part, would be able to demonstrate to their constituency that through the negotiation process, some tangible gains had been made in terms of the restoration of territory. In this instance, time and security are being bundled as part of a mutually beneficial bargaining process, thus creating the potential for each party to come away from the negotiation in a position to point to positive gains. Another well-known instance in which time had differential value for the adversaries was the Cuban missile crisis of 1962, where it was clearly in the interest of the United States to move toward an early resolution, while the Soviet Union would have liked to have dragged out the negotiations so as to allow time to fully assemble the missile batteries. In the Vietnam peace negotiations in Paris in 1973, the North Vietnamese were able to exploit the U.S. administration's political need for an early resolution and thereby gain concessions. In the unfolding North Korean nuclear crisis, North Korea would appear to have time on its side, while the United States, China, South Korea, Japan, and Russia clearly need the crisis to move toward resolution as expeditiously as possible so that North Korea will not be able to extract yet more nuclear weapons-grade materiel. And in the case of the Iranian nuclear program, clearly Iran has an interest in delaying negotiations.

## Process Characteristics

### Public or Private Forum

Another way in which negotiations can be characterized has to do with whether they are conducted in private or public forums. In actual fact, we almost never see pure cases of either, although some come pretty close.

When U.S. secretary of state Henry Kissinger held his famous news conference in Beijing in 1971, announcing that the United States and the People's Republic of China (PRC) had just negotiated the opening of relations between the two countries, it was clear that this negotiation had taken place virtually in complete secrecy. This was also the case with the negotiations conducted by the United Kingdom and the United States with the Libyan government that resulted in Libya's admission in 2003 that it had been secretly developing a nuclear weapons program, which it subsequently agreed to dismantle. Similarly, instances of track-two—or unofficial—diplomacy, such as the negotiations in Oslo, Norway, that resulted in the Oslo Accords of 1993 between Israel and the Palestine Liberation Organization (discussed in chapter 5), usually require that completely private negotiations take place, lest the parties be subjected to insurmountable internal pressures from extreme elements within their societies.

Other negotiations, however, are very public in nature. For example, the various negotiations on the environment and climate change or the negotiations on the Law of the Sea or the Universal Declaration of Human Rights take place squarely in public view. While this does not mean that private negotiations do not take place among delegates in the corridors of the main halls, the venue is largely public, with interested parties watching.

Sometimes the line between private and public is intentionally crossed when, in an effort to scuttle the negotiations, parties leak details that, by themselves, could be seen back home as threatening to one or more of the parties. In other instances, the parties may use selective public leaks from what is largely a private negotiation in order to test the waters or to otherwise put some public pressure on the other parties in the negotiation. The more public a negotiation becomes, the less it resembles a negotiation and the more it takes on aspects of a public meeting, like the UN General Assembly, where speeches intended for domestic consumption, or for the benefit of alliance partners, often replace hard bargaining. But depending on the nature of the issue, and how much is already known, it may not always be possible or even desirable to keep the negotiations under wraps.

*Outcome*

Negotiations also differ according to whether or not agreements are mandatory. Some negotiations, particularly those that take place under crisis conditions, require some sort of agreement for the crisis to end. This does not mean that the crisis will be resolved quickly, even if negotiations are ongoing. Consider, for example, the yearlong negotiation to resolve the Iran hostage crisis of 1979–1981 or the multiyear negotiations that led to the end of the Vietnam War in 1973. But in these and other similar instances, both actors perceived (although perhaps not with equal strength) that an agreement had to emerge no matter how long it took.

Many other international negotiations take place in an atmosphere in which the actors have the option of walking away—perhaps with an understanding to meet again at a set time, perhaps not—and in which the only consequence is delay and possibly failure. In a noncrisis atmosphere, while the stakes may be high for some or all of the actors, the lack of urgency dampens the need to reach agreements quickly. So, for example, the Law of the Sea treaty took fourteen years to negotiate, the SALT agreements ten years, the Uruguay Round seven and a half years, and the Kyoto agreement thirteen years and counting.

There are also instances where what began as a negotiation that did not require an agreement is transformed into one that does because of a sudden change in circumstances. The prospect of a transfer in the national leadership of one of the parties to the negotiation may transform what was a leisurely approach to a negotiation into one that suddenly takes on some urgency and may even become a crisis for the actors. The underground nuclear tests conducted first by India and immediately thereafter by Pakistan in the spring of 1998 had the effect of adding urgency to the virtually nonexistent negotiations between the two countries over the status of Kashmir and other outstanding issues. At the extreme, the Soviet threat to move tactical nuclear weapons to the eastern Mediterranean during the 1973 Middle East War raised the stakes in that crisis to a new level and created an extreme sense of urgency among those involved in attempting to negotiate a ceasefire between Israel and Egypt. Similarly, North Korean tests of long-range missiles in 2006, followed closely by the underground testing of nuclear devices, added urgency to the multiparty talks and resulted in strong action by the UN Security Council.

As noted earlier, the actors may differ in terms of their respective need to reach an agreement in a timely manner or even over whether an agreement is necessary at all. The actor that needs the agreement more may find itself at a disadvantage in the negotiation since it may have to make significant concessions to attain its goals. The United States appeared to need an agreement to end its involvement in the Vietnam War with greater urgency than did North Vietnam, and so the north was able to extract concessions from its more powerful opponent. Under the threat of continued atomic bombing of the population centers on its mainland in World War II, the Japanese were compelled to make concessions involving some of the most central institutions of their culture, among them the status and authority of the emperor.

### Ratification Issues

When actors operate under different ratification rules and expectations, negotiations can often fail, owing to incomplete understanding of the domestic constraints under which each party operates. Thus, it is important to know whether negotiation teams can reach a final and formal agreement or whether further decision-making bodies need to ratify the agreement. During the long series of talks between the United States and the Soviet Union leading to the SALT agreements, it was clear that the actors differed substantially in terms of ratification requirements. Agreements reached by the American team, representing the president of the United States and therefore the executive branch, had to be ratified by Congress before they became official U.S. policy. By contrast, the Soviet negotiators had more authority to negotiate final agreements, subject to the approval of a small group of advisers appointed by the Soviet leadership. In this latter case, while approval was not automatic, it was far more predictable than it was for the U.S. negotiators on that same issue.

Perhaps the classic example of this phenomenon is Woodrow Wilson's dramatic failure to secure U.S. Senate ratification of the treaty establishing the League of Nations in 1920. He might have been able to win ratification if he had pushed for alterations in the League charter, especially in one article that seemed to imply that the League could force the United States into war. Not only was the ratification defeat a significant embarrassment to Wilson and the U.S. negotiators, but the practical consequence of the absence of the United States from League of Nations deliberations was a serious impediment to the ability of that organization to perform its peacemaking functions. This failure ultimately contributed to the League's inability to act decisively as the storm clouds of war gathered over Europe in the late 1930s.

In a negotiation, such constraints can be exploited by an adversary, who might indicate that despite the "obvious" reasonableness of a particular formula for agreement, it would never survive the ratification process back home and hence needs to be modified. At the extreme, negotiators might threaten that were they to agree to a particular outcome, it would almost certainly mean the fall of their government, with the less attractive possibility of a group with an even harder negotiation stance coming to power. Clever manipulation of both public opinion and political coalitions back home can often strengthen the hand of the negotiators at the table. In the early 1990s, Israeli prime minister Yitzhak Rabin noted that while he was in favor of the return of the Golan Heights to the Syrians, such a position was a complete nonstarter insofar as the majority of the Israeli population was concerned at the time, and hence could not be considered as part of the complex negotiation then under way through various intermediaries.

A related issue has to do with how binding a negotiated agreement is on the actors concerned. Were the Oslo Accords of 1993, negotiated by persons close to the somewhat "dovish" Israeli Labor government of Rabin and Shimon Peres, binding on the more "hawkish" Likud government, which won the subsequent election in 1996 under Benjamin Netanyahu? And how might the actors make adjustments to a negotiated agreement as circumstances change? Is Cuba forever bound by agreements negotiated by previous governments involving the leasing of Guantanamo Bay to the United States, especially in light of vastly changed circumstances in the last third of the twentieth century?

Suspicions about how binding particular agreements might be on one's adversary in a negotiation can have a serious impact on the types of agreements that may be reached. Not unlike the issue of ratification, these suspicions can lead to a minimalist approach to the negotiations, whereby an actor is willing to make only minor and nonrisky concessions, so that a possible later renunciation of the agreement by the other actor would have limited negative impact. Or consider the elaborate inspection and verification procedures built into the SALT agreements, designed to make sure that the actors continue to live up to their ends of the bargain. Various confidence-building measures designed to increase the level of trust between the actors may be built into an agreement. Lacking this trust, such provisions can at least make defection from a negotiated agreement costly for the defector in some tangible way.

## Legacy

In the international system, it is generally the case that the actors in one negotiation will meet again across the negotiation table. In many instances, they may be dealing with an aspect of the same issue, as is the case with a violent outbreak during an ongoing, protracted conflict. For example, Israel and Syria negotiated—with U.S. mediation—a cease-fire agreement ending their 1973 war, but they have negotiated on other related issues over the years since then, including missile placement in the Beka'a Valley in Lebanon in 1986, the Lebanon War itself in 1989, and, most recently, the future status of the Golan Heights under mediation efforts by the prime minister of Turkey. In other instances, the actors may meet again over issues seemingly unrelated to the first negotiation. Consider, for example, the myriad issues currently under negotiation between the United States and Russia, ranging from economics, security, and the environment to nuclear proliferation in Iran and North Korea. Finally, actors may find themselves adversaries in one negotiation and allies in another—for example, the United States and Japan in the economic and security arenas, respectively.

In all such cases, the repetition in negotiations produces a legacy that carries over from one negotiation episode to the next. Thus, tactics that have been used in one instance will be remembered the next time around. If an actor has employed bluffing, or at least been suspected of its use in an earlier episode, it will be much

> **KEY TERM**
>
> **Legacy** A repetition in negotiations; a carryover from one negotiation episode to the next.

more difficult for that actor to establish a credible bottom line in a future negotiation episode, even if the issues have changed. Similarly, if an actor drove a particularly hard bargain earlier, perhaps to the point where the other party to the previous negotiation views the outcome as a serious defeat and even a loss of face, then aspects of that perception will carry over into a future round of negotiations, perhaps engendering a "never again" attitude on the part of the previously humiliated actor. At the very least, it can make the climate at the negotiation table extremely strained.

In the heat of a serious negotiation, it may not always be possible to keep the issue of repetition in mind. While it may be tempting to extract maximum concessions now, the prospect of facing a very hostile adversary in a future round is unappealing. Negotiating in a way that allows the other actor to emerge with some degree of self-respect is more likely to result in a positive atmosphere over the long term. In its study of crises in the twentieth century, the International Crisis Behavior Project (www.cidcm.umd.edu/icb) found that 44 percent of all crises terminated in such a way that the same actors were again involved in a crisis within five years. A more positive negotiation atmosphere, coupled perhaps with a win-win approach to the outcome, may mean that future issues arising between these actors will not need to be dealt with in a crisis environment. The harsh conditions imposed on Germany as a result of the negotiations ending World War I created a negative climate in which the seeds of Nazism and World War II were sown. On the other hand, despite exceedingly hard bargaining and brinkmanship, the Cuban missile crisis ended in such a way that the Soviet Union avoided complete humiliation by being able to claim it had extracted some concessions from the United States in the form of the removal of American missiles from Turkey.

## Summary

Every international negotiation episode takes place in context. Two dimensions of this context are of particular importance: the international system setting, which provides a framework for negotiation, and the individual characteristics that mark each specific negotiation episode. At the system level, negotiations take place within one of many historical power configurations—on a continuum from unipolar to multipolar, indicating the way power is distributed among states at any point in time. The presence of a crisis, with the increased sense of threat and urgency it invokes, significantly impacts the receptivity of the parties to particular negotiation opportunities and the dynamics of any ensuing talks. Another system-level factor that can define a negotiation is the presence of third-party intervention—sometimes in the negative form of pressure or interference from outside the negotiation sphere, other times in a positive form, with an external party suggesting ways to move beyond the stalemate.

After establishing the climate in which the negotiations take place, the next step involves identifying the particular conditions of the negotiation episode in question, whether historical or current. To facilitate that step, a checklist of actor, issue, and process factors is presented. Together they determine the uniqueness of one negotiation as compared with another. This list of characteristics—from the number of actors involved to the extent to which ratification of an agreement is required at home—presents an image of a negotiation situation that may be quite simple and straightforward or multilayered and complex.

Chapters 3 and 4 will further develop a number of these negotiation factors in relation to the actors and issues that are central to most international negotiations; chapter 5 will describe their dynamic properties or strategic interactions. Finally, chapter 6 will reflect on important trends in diplomatic negotiation.

\* \* \*

*For a list of related web resources for this chapter, consult*
*www.icons.umd.edu/negotiating/links.htm.*

# 3

# The Players

The structure of negotiation in the international system is nuanced and complex. Diplomatic representatives of states, coalitions of states, and international organizations continue to play high-profile roles in the world of negotiation, as they have since the founding of the state system with the Peace of Westphalia treaty in 1648. Over the last several decades, however, they have had to make room for the many nongovernmental and anomalous actors that have crowded onto the world stage. These have risen to prominence largely in response to a multitude of newly internationalized issues such as the environment, health, human rights, democratization, narcotics, and crime.

Whereas diplomatic negotiation was once solely the domain of official state representatives, the trend has moved toward what Kennan described as "diplomacy without diplomats" (1997, 198). Instead of being professionals with years of resident, personal experience in specific regions or states, specialists these days are more likely to be issue experts. This shift can result in a new type of negotiation team, such as those assembled to deal with global financial governance in the contemporary era. Indeed, the frontline Group of Twenty Finance Ministers and Central Bank Governors (G-20) teams heads of government with their finance ministers, central bank governors, and private interest representatives to collaborate in the policy design process. In recent Brazilian trade negotiations with the United States and the EU, agribusiness representatives sat side-by-side with government officials in São Paulo, pushing for aggressive market access strategies (Viega 2005, 109). This trend has also given birth to a new kind of negotiator—the global diplomat—whose primary attachment is not to a nation-state but, rather, to a transnational issue or cause. Some of these citizen diplomats are mobilized by the cause to take action; others are part of a recognized group of experts on a specific issue, an epistemic community, defined by Haas (1992, 3) as a "network of professionals with recognized expertise and competence in a particular domain." These individuals and the nongovernmental groups they often represent have made significant inroads into the diplomatic negotiation arena. Their expertise is often requested at the fact-gathering stage of the multilateral negotiation process and then entered into the negotiation record to substantiate the nature of the problem under consideration. They later enhance the transparency of dialogues by calling attention to the actions of states in the diplomatic process and their accountability to constituents. They are involved with consultation, advocacy, and implementation and enhance accountability to stakeholders across the "transnational civil society" (Florini 2001, 29).

> **KEY TERM**
>
> **Epistemic Community**
> A "network of professionals with recognized expertise and competence in a particular domain" (Haas 1992, 3).

The contemporary period has also seen a rise in two alternative arenas for diplomacy—track-two settings and global governance milieus. Second Track or unofficial negotiations are those in which nationals not closely affiliated with governments are deliberately chosen as negotiators. The most famous application of this approach was at the Oslo negotiations between the Israelis and the Palestinians in the early 1990s, where many of the representatives at initial meetings came from academic rather than governmental circles. Since then, the approach has been applied to many other very difficult negotiations, giving rise to "peace zones" in the Philippines and committees on reconciliation in many different troubled areas, from South Africa to Rwanda, Nepal to Croatia. *Global* forums used to be unwieldy and largely for show, aimed at exposing an issue to increased international attention. Now, however, large multilateral forums on single issues—climate, trade, and trafficking, to name a few—feature actual bargaining and concrete outcomes. Who negotiates is increasingly dependent on the issue at hand and the context in which the dialogue takes place. Track-two forums, as

> **KEY TERM**
>
> **Track-Two Diplomacy**
> Unofficial negotiations, wherein nationals not closely affiliated with the government are deliberately chosen as negotiators.

well as single-issue, multilateral negotiations, tend to feature high levels of participation from various nontraditional actors (Davies and Kaufman 2002). Pigman refers to the array of possible actors (private or "for profit" interest groups, as well as nonprofit or cause-based groups) as the "organs of global governance" (Pigman 2005). Their functions, as seen in the Kyoto case study, center around consultation and knowledge-generation.

The first part of this chapter looks at the expanded list of diplomatic actors that are increasingly impacting international negotiations. The second half looks beyond these characterizations to identify what motivates actors to approach negotiations in the ways they do. While traditional assumptions of territorial allegiance are still valid for states, other sources of identity play increasingly important roles for state and nonstate actors alike, at both individual and group levels. Such factors as culture, ethnicity, and religion, as well as gender and status, can shed much light on negotiation dynamics.

## Sovereign States as Negotiators

Representatives of states—governmental actors—are clearly still significant players in the international negotiation arena, despite the fact that they increasingly share the diplomatic stage with other actors. Much of the routine diplomatic work of states is handled by professional diplomats, usually operating from embassies or through groupings of states, such as the United Nations. Their work is often augmented by that of top-level national leaders during times of crisis or intense media focus. And more and more in the international system, important matters are being negotiated by states, but in collaboration with private actors—nonstate or substate actors of various types.

### The Diplomatic Corps

In the international system of states, negotiation has traditionally been the domain of diplomats formally assigned to serve their countries in foreign capitals. Diplomacy is a very old profession full of tradition and symbolism. To some, it is a professional fraternity (R. Cohen 1997, 20) with great emphasis placed on titles, hierarchy, and protocol. For example, when one country wishes to "slap" another for a perceived wrong, it works through the continuum of actions available to it—ranging from pulling some diplomatic personnel out of the host country, or downgrading its diplomatic mission there, to breaking off diplomatic relations. It has always been the great hope of international diplomacy that open or violent conflict can be avoided through this system of conventions, whereby responses ranging from trust to anger can be conveyed to other nations. The signals sent through diplomacy can be loud and clear, or they can be quietly symbolic. As part of its efforts to normalize relations with the Chinese in 1978, for example, the United States recognized the People's Republic of China (PRC) as the "sole legal government of China" but added language stating that "within this context, the people of the United States will maintain cultural, commercial, and other unofficial relations with the people of Taiwan" (Bernstein 1995, 11). This seemingly innocuous statement was meant to inform Taiwan that it would continue to be afforded special diplomatic status, despite the return of an American ambassador to Beijing. More recently, in an effort to persuade leaders in the PRC to take a more active role against North Korean nuclear development, the United States sent some reverse signals. It vacillated on Taipei's bid to join the World Health Organization, jeopardizing an important aspect of the Taiwan Relations Act—the backing of Taiwanese participation in international organizations (Tkacik 2004).

Much of the work of the diplomatic corps is routine. The overriding duty is to gauge political developments in the host country from a resident vantage point. The specific duties of the diplomat are many, including assessing, estimating, reassuring, and verifying incoming and outgoing information (Freeman 1997, 121). The diplomat's mission is, most importantly, to try to preserve a peaceful balance in the relations between states and to lay the groundwork for negotiation possibilities in the event of tensions. In the contemporary era, accusations abound that diplomatic bureacracies are bloated and out-of-touch with the rapidly developing global agenda. The European Union employs 40,000 diplomatic staff members, working at more than 1,500 diplomatic missions (Kuekeleire 2003, 38). This is an astounding number by any standard! Yet the survival of a traditional diplomatic corps is threatened by new forms of direct communication between political leaders and citizens around the world. President Obama's 2009 video message to the Iranian people on the occasion of the Persian New Year bypassed traditional diplomatic channels and was received and disseminated directly to the Iranian people via numerous channels, including YouTube, Facebook, Radio Farda, and satellite television from such regional neighbors as Qatar and India.

Yet, the mundane nature of the day-to-day functions of the diplomatic mission should not detract from the very important role it needs to play in sensitive situations. Iran is instructive in this regard, as well, albeit prerevolutionary Iran. In 1979, the U.S. State Department failed to interpret the changing political environment in the country, with disastrous results for long-term foreign policy goals and strategy. U.S. diplomats and embassy personnel found themselves at the center of a revolutionary storm when Iranian students took over their building and took them hostage. The occupation of the American Embassy represented a dramatic breach of widely accepted international diplomatic protocol, but it also highlighted a significant weakness in American-style country expertise. It turned out that the U.S. mission lacked contacts with persons outside of the royal court and the Western-educated elite. It also had very few officials who could speak Farsi at this very sensitive political time, which undoubtedly contributed to the misreading of events on the ground (Sick 1985, 77). The shah's abdication of his throne in early 1979 shocked the Carter administration. Caught off guard, the United States did not respond well to the volatile situation. The intelligence and diplomatic fiasco reached its climax when personnel from the American Embassy were taken hostage. Negotiations for their release did not even take place until almost a year later, when Algerian officials were finally able to mediate a de-escalation of tensions by focusing some much-needed attention on the cultural issues inherent in the process. Today, it seems clear that *bloggers* and *twitterers* from inside Iran greatly aid efforts to gauge public opinion in the midst of political tumult. However, the information is still only as helpful or good as those assigned to interpret its policy implications. Too much information, in the age of the Internet, is a danger as well.

## Political Leaders

Much of the work that political leaders do in the negotiation realm takes place at a symbolic level. Major summits are usually the pinnacle of lower-level negotiations that have been ongoing, in some cases, for many months or even years. In certain cases, however, arduous negotiations are actually conducted from the top. As national security adviser and secretary of state in the Nixon and Ford administrations, Henry Kissinger became famous for his personal diplomacy. During Kissinger's tenure as America's top diplomat, U.S. negotiations were more tightly controlled from the top than at perhaps any other time in recent history. Kissinger spent years shuttling from capital to capital on bilateral negotiation missions, trying to establish a basis for broad multilateral consensus on Egyptian-Israeli disengagement agreements and working to reopen relations between the People's Republic of China and the United States. Negotiating on behalf of a superpower, Kissinger found the corridors of power open to him. The approach was a very traditional one—part of what is called the "great man" approach to international relations—as he negotiated one-on-one with the world's key leaders. This personal diplomacy, laborious but direct, also characterized Jimmy Carter's mediation of the 1978 Camp David Accord, where Carter guided the contentious negotiations by utilizing a so-called one-text procedure. Retaining control over the document that was to become the agreement, he personally negotiated with both leaders on important questions of wording and meaning, keeping the negotiators quite literally on the same page (Carter 1982, 396–397). Two decades later, Bill Clinton attempted to replicate Carter's success with Palestinians and Israelis at the Wye River and Camp David II negotiations. Despite dropping most other state business from his agenda and devoting enormous personal attention to the efforts, Clinton was not successful.

Indeed, as more issues have risen in importance on the international agenda, this kind of control at the very highest level has been difficult to maintain for such powerful nations as the United States. The modern-day version of shuttle diplomacy has a troubleshooter or special envoy rather than the president or a cabinet member sent to work on difficult conflict situations. Christopher Hill led the efforts of the George W. Bush administration's efforts in North Korea and Barack Obama is looking to three successful envoys from the Clinton administration, Richard Holbrooke, George Mitchell, and Dennis Ross to redouble American efforts in the Middle East and South Asia.

In smaller countries whose foreign policy agendas are likewise more narrow in scope, it is not unusual for top political leaders to handle much of

### Richard Holbrooke: The Balkans' Bulldozer*

Richard Holbrooke may someday go down as one of the most distinguished American diplomats never to have held the office of Secretary of State. In fact, despite his decades of high-profile work, Mr. Holbrooke's only cabinet-level position has been as U.S. Ambassador to the United Nations under Bill Clinton. His most memorable work to date may have been his strong-arming Serb leader Slobodan Milosevic to sign on to the Dayton Peace Accord in 1995, ostensibly after imbibing with him at a local establishment (Holbrooke 1999, 235). Holbrooke's initial work to end the genocidal war in Bosnia was done in his capacity as Assistant Secretary of State for European and Canadian Affairs. He returned to the region to deal with Milosevic once again in 1999, as a special envoy, at the request of President Clinton. In 2009 he agreed to reprise that role as Special American Envoy to Afghanistan-Pakistan, where he reports directly to Secretary of State Hillary Clinton and President Obama on the administration's military and diplomatic efforts. The latter includes highly sensitive overtures to the Islamic Republic of Iran, part of a reported effort to re-engage with a country where the United States has had no diplomatic outpost for more than thirty years. Ambassador Holbrooke's work illustrates the benefits to be gained from having a full-time envoy on the ground when negotiations are sure to be long and laborious. His one-month visit to Afghanistan in 2007 could never be duplicated by a secretary of state, but yielded the insight and contacts that may just make the difference to U.S. efforts.

---

* The term "Balkans' bulldozer" is from BBC News 1999.

the official diplomatic workload themselves. For these states, foreign policy is more easily managed, and the ties between domestic and international policy are often very close. Issues that would likely be handled by government bureaucracies in large countries can receive executive-level attention in smaller states. Calculations of national interest (the stakes) are also different in small states. For the Nordic nation of Norway, for example, the highly contentious issue of international restrictions on whaling goes to the very heart of the national economy and has become an issue of sovereignty. The Norwegian decision to defy the International Whaling Commission's 1986 moratorium and resume commercial hunting came from the highest levels of national government. Norway even has a cabinet-level minister of fisheries, who works full-time to arbitrate among different domestic constituency groups, as well as between Norway and the world community (Official Documentation and Information from Norway).

This type of high-level involvement can at times be advantageous to negotiations, speeding them up and bringing a higher sense of purpose and commitment. But it can also work against them. Brought to the brink of peace by the track-two-negotiated Oslo Accords, the Israelis and the Palestinians subsequently reverted to the more traditional "top down" negotiations. This change has resulted in intransigence and worse, with the outcome on every issue a matter of personal ego for the respective leaders of the two societies. Ultimately, those Clinton-mediated negotiations between Israeli prime minister Ehud Barak and Palestine Liberation Organization (PLO) chairman Yasir Arafat in 2000, broke up without an agreement on Palestinian statehood. Unrest and lack of progress on the diplomatic front has plagued the region ever since, while both sides struggle with who should be at the proverbial negotiation table. Tension over this issue was heightened after the Palestinian militant group Hamas won the 2006 elections in Gaza. President Obama now seems to be leaning toward a negotiation structure that would bring the neighboring Arab states back into American-sponsored Middle East peace talks, ostensibly on the basis of the common regional threat posed by the Iranian nuclear program.

## Groups of States

Individual states have varying levels of diplomatic leverage. Some are relatively powerless to affect a situation in which others far outweigh their clout. It can therefore be to the benefit of the weaker state to join with others—either formally, through intergovernmental organizations or alliances, or temporarily, through coalitions—for the duration of the negotiations. Moreover, some problems require collective solutions—no state working alone can control the issue of ozone depletion, for example. Transboundary pollution and financial market instability respects neither state sovereignty nor national borders. For these reasons, it is not unusual for states to use organizational forums for negotiations. As part of these various interstate groupings, they attempt to pool their sovereignty in order to affect the outcome of the negotiations to the greatest extent possible. Certain groupings of sovereign states—NATO and the World Trade Organization (WTO), for example—very often act as single, independent actors in negotiations, at least after their internal member discussions have produced a consensus. They have the authority and credibility to speak on behalf of their member states in most cases. Hence, the media broadcast such pronouncements as "NATO is urging Russia to re-engage in talks with the Georgians" and "the WTO is establishing new anti-piracy provisions for intellectual property."

As states have proliferated and their dealings with one another have become more complex, these official bodies have come to play very important roles in the diplomatic negotiation process. They not only function as clearinghouses for information, which can be of a highly technical nature, they also provide guidelines for international behavior. When well established, these guidelines become the norms and rules, or soft laws, that negotiators look to for an objective standard of fairness (discussed in detail in chapter 5).

Other intergovernmental actors also play more complex roles in negotiations. At the United Nations, the secretary-general, the Security Council, and the General Assembly—not to mention all of the various agencies—can play very different roles in the same negotiation episode. It is not unusual for them to play contrasting roles or to act as separate actors in the same situation. For example, in the late 1990s, there was much international contention over how to handle Saddam Hussein's repeated arms control violations. The UN General Assembly voiced its displeasure with American plans to try to bomb Saddam Hussein into submission. In this body where every member state has an equal vote, less economically and militarily powerful countries often tend to side with the underdog in battles with great powers. At the Security Council, which has limited membership and stronger representation of the most powerful states in the system, a tougher stance was adopted toward Iraq in 1997–1998, although it still fell far short of what the United States and Britain had hoped for. Ultimately, it was the secretary-general himself who visited Iraq and mediated the crisis. Even as he went to Baghdad as a representative of the UN, Kofi Annan apparently carried with him explicit instructions from the United States on the acceptable parameters for the negotiations. It is difficult, therefore, to talk of a single UN role in this situation.

Similarly, the International Monetary Fund (IMF) has been a central player in economic negotiations around the world, especially in trying to combat monetary crises from Russia to Asia and Latin America, and ultimately globally, during the last decade. The IMF is generally thought of as an independent actor—requiring austerity measures for states in economic crisis in exchange for monetary relief—but it is actually an intermediary between the "will of the majority of its membership" and the individual member states that seek its financial help (Driscoll 1997). Its board of governors has been given the latitude to make decisions about payment policies, but it is clear that because of the fund's membership quota system—based on the amount of money each member contributes upon joining—the United States, Germany, Japan, Britain, and France have a disproportionate amount of power within the organization. In reality, the IMF does not act independently of sovereign states in the international system; rather, it is supposed to act to represent their best interests—a sort of commissioner of baseball for the world of international finance. It is essential to the effectiveness of the IMF, however, that member states be able to appear unrelated to the organization when it must play the role of the "heavy" in difficult negotiations.

The notion of pooled sovereignty also has a potentially negative side. At times, states lament the erosion of their sovereignty by international governmental organizations. Led by the EU, there has been movement toward supranationalism or extraterritorial allegiance within some institutions in Europe. In practice, this means that individual states are not always able to opt out of decisions with which they do not agree (Taylor 1984, 3). Debate still rages in some European capitals over whether the powerful EU Commission is a beneficial negotiation channel for its member states or whether it has effectively neutered them in certain arenas, most notably on monetary issues. The post-2002 "eurozone" of twelve European Union (EU) countries that surrendered their individual currencies in favor of the euro is the most extreme example of supranationalism to date. Public opinion polls show something of a backlash against the common currency and the European Central Bank that administers it, with some voters complaining that it is too independent, disregards the individual economic needs of EU member nations, and has led to weak exports and offshoring of jobs (*EU Digest* 2007). Movement toward labor market integration among the states involved in the North American Free Trade Agreement (NAFTA) engendered similar sentiments, and has yet to make it off the ground.

### Transnational Actors

Increasingly, negotiation situations feature actors that are neither sovereign states nor reliant on those states for membership and direction. This book considers various nongovernmental actors that exert significant impact on diplomatic negotiations in the state arena. Many international business textbooks look at yet another phenomenon: episodes in which private entities negotiate transnationally with other private parties. Although negotiations in that private arena can impact or spill over into the state realm—for example, the negotiations between Boeing and Airbus in the civil aviation field—it is, for the most part, outside the purview of this text.

It has been hypothesized that nongovernmental actors tend to gain more prominence in policy areas where there has been a significant state failure to perform (Skocpol 1988, 293). This does ring true for a variety of endeavors, such as the pursuit of private economic interest, the protection of the environment, and the protection of individual and group rights. A broad array of nongovernmental actors are at work in the international arena, performing a variety of functions. Some are stand-ins for states or rivals to them; others work to influence the global diplomatic agenda. The following section looks at these types of nongovernmental actors and the important roles they play in the contemporary international arena.

### Substates (Cross-Regional Actors)

Regionalism at the substate level is a noticeable trend that has resulted in erosion of central governmental control over foreign policy. Numerous manifestations of this phenomenon—what one analyst called "cross-frontier regional organizations"—occur in different areas of the world (Langhorne 1997, 7). In the United States, for example, individual states have developed close ties of their own to regions of special geographic and ethnic importance to them—California to East Asia and Mexico, and Florida to the Caribbean and South America. California has its own Office of California-Mexico Affairs, along with many foreign trade offices in Africa, Asia, and Europe. The state of Florida has been influential in negotiations over the establishment of a Free Trade Area of the Americas (FTAA), going so far as to release position papers that urge not only the government of the United States but also those of South American countries to adopt certain stances (Ponce 1997; Drezner 2003; Summit of the Americas Center 2005).

In the post–Cold War era, many substate actors have behaved in a manner independent of their national leadership to establish strong cross-border ties. Various länder (states) in Germany led the charge to reestablish a long-dormant "Baltic identity." They linked themselves to Russian Baltic port cities and to the now independent states of Estonia, Latvia, and Lithuania, as well as

| KEY TERM |
| --- |
| **Cross-Frontier Regional Organizations** Manifestations of regionalism at the substate level; can result in erosion of the central governmental authority over foreign policy. |

the Nordic states (Lehti and Smith 2003). Special economic zones started in Canton Province, China, have served a similar purpose. Explicitly linking Canton to neighboring Macau and Hong Kong provided the Chinese with an important test case of the "one country, two systems" policy that defines their post-1998 relationship with Hong Kong. The linkage has also led to an integrated Pearl River Delta region, where economic complementarities and competition offer the Chinese exposure to the complex workings of free-market economies. Many cities have also made substantive gains in international reach. Some are embarking to a greater degree on the formulation of their own diplomacy. Lyon, the center of France's Rhône-Alpes region, has its own embassies in Germany, Switzerland, and Italy (Matthews 1997, 62). In the United States, California governor Arnold Schwarzenegger hosted a "world summit on climate change" in Beverly Hills in 2006 and signed an emission declaration with government officials from Canada, Mexico, Brazil, Indonesia, India, and China. Lamented the governor, "we as a state are forced to create [environmental] policy on our own" (CBS News 2008). Some observers refer to regional and substate identities—some newly formed, some rediscovered—as the third level of international policy making (Jeffrey 1997, 1). Traditionally confined to cultural negotiations only, regional entities have begun to negotiate in policy areas previously reserved for national governments, including security and economics. The proliferation of interstate groupings and the growth of diplomatic actors at the substate level have complicated the formulation of negotiation strategies and the conduct of negotiations for state actors. The simultaneous but contradictory forces of integration and devolution encroach on state sovereignty from different directions, complicating the calculus of national interest so traditionally important to the negotiation process.

## State Rivals and "Substitute States"

A number of entities serve as stand-ins for nation-states in the negotiation arena, in essence acting as substitute states. Although very different in legitimacy and scope, these entities perform similar negotiation functions, acting in the place of national governments. The need for articulation and representation of the economic, security, and political interests of such stateless groups as the Palestinians and the Kurds, for example, led to the formation of the rebel groups known as the PLO and the Kurdish Workers' Party (PKK). In Sierra Leone and some other West African countries, the penetration of the state system by foreign firms and global business interests is seen by some observers as so advanced that it has created new, elite networks with more power than national governments (Reno 1996). In Freetown, for example, an Iranian-backed Palestinian group was allowed to establish an embassy in return for a promise of private access to Iranian oil on easy credit terms. The establishment of a shadow state—a virtual buyout of the state—puts a price on legitimacy and establishes the values of the free market as superior to those of sovereignty and territoriality.

In some other countries, private interests are so highly structured that they rival the central state for authority over international matters, including negotiations. Sometimes, these forces lack political legitimacy and authority but nevertheless challenge state sovereignty. Currency speculators have not yet taken a seat at the negotiation table; nonetheless, they exercise great importance in the international financial market. Currency speculation made up about 20 percent of foreign exchange transactions in the mid-1970s, but

> ### KEY TERM
>
> **Substitute States** Entities that replace or rival the authority of the nation-state and its diplomatic capacity.

had risen to over 95 percent twenty-years later. By 2007, daily turnover in these markets was charted at $3.2 trillion. This leaves national economies extremely vulnerable to currency crises, which in turn directly impact poverty and unemployment. Indonesia, South Africa, Brazil, South Korea, and Mexico are among the states that have experienced this phenomenon firsthand in the last fifteen years (Debt and Development Coalition Ireland).

Various transnational forces and movements can also rival the state in legitimacy and authority, ultimately affecting negotiations on a variety of issues. The so-called Islamic movement is one such example. Political Islam actually has many different faces and rarely speaks with one voice, but many predominantly Muslim nations did find a common position during the height of the Bosnian conflict in the 1990s, when there was widespread, open support for the arming of the Bosnian Muslims in their struggle against the Serbs. Some Muslim groups even managed to funnel weapons to them. More recently, as the United States has waged its "Global War on Terror" (GWOT), intelligence efforts have focused much attention on the connections between various militant Islamic groups and the extent to which they coordinate with one another and with the states that sponsor their transnational activities. Connections between such groups as Hezbollah, Hamas, Taliban, and al-Qaeda, and possible ties that they have to states such as Iran, Syria, and Pakistan remain question marks. Elsewhere, in the Central American country of El Salvador, vast family networks tend to represent subregional economic interests. In Mexico, drug trafficking is an estimated $50 billion a year business, the loss of which would shrink Mexico's economy by 63 percent (Hazard 2008). In Colombia, the influence of illegal drug cartels has been known to rival or surpass that of the regional governments in the areas they penetrate and control. Their wealth and influence allows them to penetrate almost every aspect of Colombian political and social life (Krauss 2009). In post–Cold War Russia, vast criminal networks rival the central state for control over economic resources, owing

primarily to underground economic activity, such as drugs and prostitu-
tion (Satter 2003). The overriding question in relation to these groups is
whether their influence warrants their presence at the negotiation table. The
hope would be that to engage them as stakeholders would benefit the larger
populations, but it is a risky endeavor (Herzog 2006). In other examples,
private interests have carved out a legitimate place at the negotiation table,
working in tandem with traditional state representatives. At World Health
Organization negotiations on tobacco in 2003, Japan Tobacco International
(JTI) was represented on the official Japanese delegation to the Framework
Convention on Tobacco Control (FCTC) by staff from the Ministry of Finance, which owns a two-thirds share of the company. Their influence on
the positions of the Japanese delegation in the negotiations was profound
and was responsible for Japan's unbending opposition to such measures as
a ban on misleading descriptors and comprehensive restrictions on ciga-
rette advertising. Indeed, at certain points in the negotiations, Japanese delegates suggested that the treaty be "balanced" by including recognition of
the positive aspects of tobacco use, such as stress reduction. This type of
"NGO-government collaboration" is becoming more commonplace in the
new century (Edwards 2001, 3).

## Nongovernmental Organizations (NGOs)

A vast number of NGOs exert an impact in the diplomatic negotiation
arena. In environmental politics, the influence of these so-called environmental nongovernmental organizations (ENGOs) has greatly contributed
to the 100 percent growth in the number of multilateral treaties signed over
roughly the last two decades (Lisowski 2005). In the area of human rights,
Amnesty International has formed a vast cross-border network of citizen
groups that, through write-in campaigns and other tactics, routinely exert
pressure on states that violate human rights. Not only does it act as an international lobbyist in this area, but Amnesty International also provides
expert witnesses to shed light on certain situations for which little information is otherwise available to states. Langhorne writes that Amnesty International and Save the Children have both "upgraded" the representation
of their organizations at the United Nations and have offices in both New
York and Geneva now, with many more professional staff members running those outposts (Langhorne 2005, 338).

In the past, states have tended to dismiss NGOs with reputations as
protest groups. The influence attained by the environmental NGO Greenpeace at the international level and as an electoral presence in many individual countries, however, probably did more than any other single factor
to change this perception. Increasingly, NGOs represent their issue-based
constituencies at international negotiations or join with state delegations
to bring their perspectives in approach and opinion. Their enhanced

## The New Negotiators: Global Diplomats

As certain issues have ascended to global status in the international arena, a new kind of negotiation actor has grown in importance. On the individual level, this is the citizen diplomat working on issues related to the environment, human rights, population, development, and other social concerns, often as part of an authoritative community of experts. The allegiance of this global diplomat is to an area of transnational concern. The work arena is the vast NGO network.

Rather than the personal power that serves as the main negotiating tool of traditional diplomats, the global diplomat uses scientific evidence or other in-depth knowledge of the issue area to impact negotiations. Personal anonymity is the unspoken rule. Global diplomats spur states on to negotiate in areas that are not always high on their national agendas. They do this by creating frameworks and forums into which state actors can easily be integrated. These NGO networks are adept at finding creative ways to influence negotiations. The Climate Action Network (CAN) produced the influential ECO newsletter in Kyoto, which reportedly became a "must read" for all on-site participants and was also disseminated over the Internet to interested observers outside of Japan. It then developed a confidential mailing system—called "CAN-Talk"—and serves as an umbrella group for over 300 NGOs in over 180 countries (Lisowski 2005, 367). It has eight regional launching points: Africa, South Asia, Southeast Asia, Latin America, central and eastern Europe, Europe, the United Kingdom, and the United States. One of its main functions is to organize the tremendous amount of information that exists on climate change. This means that CAN must stay on top of the huge amount of data that exists on the national, regional, and international dimensions of this issue. CAN also formulates policy positions, which it explains in position papers that it distributes. Finally, it serves as a channel for collaboration among NGOs working on this issue as they enter the policy arena. CAN is now considered a formidable player in negotiations on climate-related issues. It counts among its member organizations the transnational Greenpeace, Friends of the Earth, and World Wildlife Fund, as well as numerous national and regional environmental action groups.

Global diplomatic actors—whether individual scientists or activists, vast networks of NGOs, or other "private actors"—including corporations and cross-border associations—represent a new force in the international negotiation arena. Their ability to mobilize public opinion and political action is unprecedented and closely tied to the information revolution of the late twentieth century. Cable news and the Internet represent potent tools in NGO campaigns to educate and organize people around the world in areas where governments have been slow to respond.

respectability and roles have led to the formation of an entirely new type of negotiation actor: the global diplomat (see box). This force in the diplomatic arena promises new levels of "efficiency and responsiveness" in comparison to states (Langhorne 2005, 332).

## Actor Dynamics

Many factors determine how players will behave in negotiation situations. Subsequent chapters will discuss such major elements as issue intensity (stakes) and strategic decision making (moves). Each of these explanatory approaches is based, to some extent, on the assumption that negotiation actors react similarly in certain situations. In contrast, the remainder of this chapter will consider the factors that differentiate actors' motivations. The relationship of negotiators to identifiable rules of the game or international norms is an important reference point for this discussion, tempered by culture and identity. When such sources of meaning and understanding are in conflict, "othering" is often the result—the politicization of cultural differences between negotiation parties.

> **KEY TERM**
>
> **Othering**  The politicization of cultural differences between negotiation parties.

## The Rules of the Game

Although a system in only a conceptual sense, a prevailing international order exists, defined by such key principles as state sovereignty and territoriality. Critics lament this system's lack of punitive power and enforceable law, but great strides have been taken in the post–World War II period to create a set of norms that govern state behavior. Many of these concepts have been spawned by Western institutions—such as the Bretton Woods monetary system—and are therefore controversial for some non-Western states. For better or worse, however, these institutions have defined the rules of the game in the international system.

The relationship of actors to this system and its norms is an important factor in negotiation and has many different dimensions. At the broadest level, it is necessary to establish whether the actors in the negotiation under examination are in good standing in the system. In other words, are they considered good neighbors? Evidence of positive standing includes active participation in international organizations, international regimes—informal institutions organized around "sets of mutual expectations" (Ruggie 1975, 570)—and other collective institutions. Negative indications involve nonparticipation in the defining institutions of the system and aggression against other states, including certain expansionist and irredentist policies designed to unilaterally extend national borders. At the extreme negative end are so-called rogue states, which deliberately reject prevailing norms in a broad array of areas—most notably security—and which often refuse negotiation as an option for conflict resolution.

However, between those predominantly Western states that define many of the rules of the game and those few who deride them are the majority of members of the international system. Many are classified as economically developing and politically democratizing. They have not been readily welcomed into the many clubs—including the Group of 12, the OECD, and that most exclusive of bodies, the acknowledged nuclear powers—that define the rules of the game. This leads to angry complaints about the existence of an international hierarchy and Western-contrived definitions of values. Indeed, one step down from generally accepted norms such as sovereignty is another layer that is highly controversial, including such value-laden areas as human rights. In defending its "one couple, one child" policy against criticism from Western states, for example, the Chinese government charges the West with cultural imperialism. The United States has also been charged with hypocrisy in relation to its own policies at times. International outcries over U.S. treatment of detainees (Abu Ghraib prison and Guantanamo Bay, Cuba) focused renewed attention on accepted standards of human rights and, in particular, on the Geneva Convention and the rules governing war. The implications for ignoring common standards are more damaging with today's far-reaching and instant media coverage of news. Former UN Secretary General Kofi Annan talked of a "new diplomacy," characterized by a more common, global governance, whereby the "rules, norms, and institutions that govern public and private behavior across national boundaries—are changing in new and important ways" (Edwards 2001, 3). Other commonly heard terms in today's diplomatic lexicon, such as "soft power" and "complex multilateralism," speak to the vast networks of people-to-people contact. Yet, Edwards (2001, 1) laments that these global institutions are "still the prisoners of a state-based system of international negotiation."

It is also premature to claim universal standards when talking about behavior in the international system. Fundamental disagreements about norms still abound, with research showing that negotiation actors are more likely to negotiate successfully with states like them (Druckman and Broome 1991, 571). In other words, negotiation has a better chance when cultural misinterpretation is at a minimum. The next section on culture and identity will explore how different appearances, assumptions, languages, roles, and values can affect the course of negotiations.

## Power and Identity

Diplomacy is not just about bargaining. There is a human dimension to the negotiation game that should not be ignored. The process of reaching negotiated settlements to problems relies on the willingness of all actors involved to sit down together and look for common solutions. Peaceful coexistence in the system of states rests on a notion of mutual recognition. Often, when negotiation has proven futile over a long period of time, it is likely that diplomatic recognition and, indeed, basic group recognition did not exist. This had been true, to various degrees, of the Northern Ireland conflict for over thirty years. Progress was only achieved after some of the key actors were afforded "seats" at the negotiation table, including Sinn Fein, considered by many to be the political wing of the Irish Republican Army, and the Ulster Volunteer Force, their Protestant counterpart.

Are nations' cultures really so different from one another? The main reference points are the same across most lands—family, community, authority, and religion—but Lewis asserts in *When Cultures Collide* that these concepts are viewed from different perspectives (2000, 2). It is this different angle of vision that leads to culturally grounded misunderstandings in international relations (see Barber 1995).

In the negotiation realm, culture is operationalized mainly through different styles of communication. Different verbal and nonverbal patterns of expression, ways of organizing information, and relationships to time and space are major elements. Differences along these dimensions can translate into discordant definitions of such concepts as timetables, fairness, and closure. As well, problems often arise with very specific notions such as reciprocity, which many Western negotiators consider crucial to successful negotiation processes. This idea—that both sides should make equal concessions as they move toward agreement—places a high premium on compromise. Crosscultural analysis shows us, however, that compromise is not valued equally—or even at all—in some cultures. It can, in fact, connote a bad agreement—one that neither side really wanted, thereby suggesting a lose-lose outcome (R. Cohen 1997). There is also much cultural misunderstanding surrounding the notion of issue discreteness in negotiations. Some states focus on the larger relationships they have with their negotiation partners when they sit down to negotiate, ensuring the establishment of a broad context for the talks. Other states do not see the utility of this approach and prefer to devote attention only to the issue at hand. The misunderstanding and even bickering that ensue can stall negotiations before they even have a chance of success. Many misunderstandings and

Delegates at the Fourth World Conference on Women put their collective strength and will on display during eleven days of deliberations. UN/DPI Photo

incompatibilities that occur at the negotiation table are due to these different interpretations of key reference points (R. Cohen 1997). Skillful negotiators can often move around them by understanding their counterparts' cultures (McDonald 1996). However, even if negotiators successfully maneuver through this labyrinth, they must then manage the challenge that comes from competing identities, from the national level on down.

Where the interests of negotiation players are very different or even competing, elements of individual and group identity can become dangerously politicized. Identity is about the self in relation to others. Since resources are scarce the world over, anything that differentiates people from one another—including ethnicity, gender, language, race, and religion—can become a potential source of conflict. Identities are easily perceived as competing, giving rise to "us versus them" or "othering" scenarios: Jews and Arabs, men and women, French and English, whites and blacks. Such simplified images of the "other" prevent negotiators from engaging in the kind of problem-solving discussions that could lead to mutually beneficial agreements (Druckman 1994).

Many contentious negotiation situations involve competing identity groups. Moving beyond obvious differences to engage in a joint process such as negotiation may not come easily. When racial, ethnic, and religious differences are involved, contrasting appearances, roles, and rituals often block the abilities of negotiators and the broader societies they represent to find what they share—some common values in addition to their competing ones. In the old city of Jerusalem at the Temple Mount, for example, Jews revere the Wailing Wall and Muslims the Dome of the Rock. Their dual presence on this site makes it one of the holiest in the world to these ethnic groups. But because they are unable to settle their competing claims to the land on which the site is found, the Temple Mount has been the site of bloody confrontations between followers of the two faiths. Several hundred meters away, tradition has Jews holding the keys to the Church of the Holy Sepulchre, revered by Christians as the spot where Jesus was crucified and buried, to minimize the possibility of clashes among various Christian sects.

It is also the case with identity politics that the international system sometimes acts as more of a reference point for action than does the nation-state. Such is the case with "women's issues" in international relations (see box). Here, gender identification cuts across national lines as women's interests coalesce around certain issues they feel disproportionately affect them worldwide.

## Competing Identities

Deep cultural misunderstandings or disconnects can impede the mutual understanding that is so important to negotiation; so, too, can competing identities, where resources and legitimacy are deemed scarce. But the most dangerous obstacle to meaningful negotiation is the invocation of these differences to demonize the "other," thereby putting cooperation out of reach.

Why do culture and identity matter in negotiations? After all, it is the problem between two or more actors that is supposed to be the focus, not the actors themselves. However, research on negotiation patterns reveals a predisposition to negotiate with and negotiate successfully with those who are most like oneself, as opposed to those designated as the "other." Huntington (1993, 35) talked about this phenomenon in terms of "kin-country syndrome" replacing political ideology as the main determinant of cooperation. It does seem logical that where there are commonalities in, for example, history and language, there would be a greater basis for trust and understanding. The successful contemporary relationship between the United States and Britain would seem to bear this out, even though the shared history involves a violent revolution. But what of other pairs, such as India and Pakistan, Ethiopia and Eritrea, Cambodia and Vietnam, and Greece and Turkey? In these relationships, various commonalities are overridden by highly charged sources of differentiation (religious, ethnic,

## Women and International Negotiation

Underrepresented in national leadership roles, women have long wielded more influence in local politics and increasingly in nongovernmental organizations. With emphasis placed on health, nutrition, peace, and environmentally safe and technologically appropriate development strategies, women have argued strenuously for greater state and international accountability to ordinary citizens. As the relative power of NGOs has grown over the past two decades, so has the global influence of women. Their work has been focused on agenda setting in the international arena—trying to bring peace, ecology, and other similar concerns to the forefront of national agendas. They have also argued forcefully for a focus on stakeholders in development and conflict arenas, a "bottom-up" focus in place of the traditional "elite-down" perspective.

Their work has been centralized and legitimized to an even greater degree by UN Security Council Resolution 1325 on "Women, Peace and Security"(October 31, 2000). This document and its call to action recognize the damage done to international negotiations in which women are expressly left out of the decision-making process. The involvement of women's groups in peacemaking and peacebuilding has been facilitated by the proliferation of groups working in the field. The "NGO Webring" of women's groups coordinated by PeaceWomen is testament to the breadth and scope of coordinated work in this area (www.peacewomen.org/webring.html). The many women's groups active in the international arena—such as the Organization of Women in International Trade, the Mongolian Women's NGO Coalition, and the Women's International League for Peace and Freedom—are working to change perceptions of issues and goals. They are also working to persuade states to embrace different strategies in their struggles with one another. Women's groups' struggle against war has been central for many decades. Recent efforts have focused on crucial sub-issues such as "children and armed struggle" and "sexual violence and conflict." Women's participation in Sudan's Abuja negotiations broadened the scope of the 2006 Darfur Peace Agreement substantially, troubled as its subsequent implementation has been. Moreover, the influence of females in international negotiations is not confined to special women's groups. Women are also playing stronger and more active roles in traditionally male-dominated NGOs, such as the global climate negotiations (Villagrasa 2002).

territorial) that have, for the most part, made meaningful negotiation dialogue impossible.

The key point here is that culture and identity are dynamic, interactive forces. When they are not invoked and "othering" is not a factor, then the negotiation relationship is usually based on the issues at hand. This was true of Americans and Soviets during the détente period of the Cold War during the 1970s, after the initial hysteria over competing ideologies had died down and before Ronald Reagan ushered in a new, highly confrontational era of cultural "othering" with his use of the "evil empire" image. In more recent times, George W. Bush's formulation of an "axis of evil," comprising Saddam Hussein's Iraq, Iran, and North Korea, created a similar negative construct through which all communications between the United States and these governments then passed.

Sometimes cultural differences are not understood and are instead an implicit factor defeating cooperation between parties. This has been true of the relationship between the United States and Japan, where crosscultural understanding has been slow to come at times and disdain for each other's culture has often been professed instead. And then there are the situations where identification vis-à-vis the "other" is so intense that meaningful dialogue is effectively blocked. This has been true of the Greek and Turkish Cypriots, as well as the Israelis and the Palestinians. "Othering" can therefore be visualized as purposeful and tactical in its invocation or little understood and at times confusing in its influence on negotiations. The following three brief examples illustrate how "othering" plays out in various contexts.

### Deterrence and Dangerous Trust: The Cold War

One of the lessons learned from the forty-five-year Cold War between the United States and the Soviet Union is that even states with seemingly opposed values can successfully negotiate with one another. The explanation for this apparent inconsistency lies in the dynamic nature of culture and identity as forces in the international system. Cultural differences are not always invoked as reasons to avoid negotiation. Trust can be built regardless of these many differences when objectives are shared. The Americans and the Soviets shared a belief in the strategic doctrine of deterrence—the principle that their mutual willingness to destroy each other was a basis for cooperation. This mutual fear led to a shared value: the need for survival in the face of possible annihilation. This fear is what guided their behavior in such negotiations as SALT and the Strategic Arms Reduction Talks (START). It also led to placing great importance on open communication lines and active negotiation agendas. Indeed, out of their most dangerous confrontation—the Cuban missile crisis of 1962—came the hot-line agreement that guaranteed a direct Teletype channel between the Kremlin and the White House. In the latter half of the twentieth century, the United States and the Soviet Union dominated international politics with their strategic showdown, but they also revealed an important negotiation principle: shared norms can emerge out of repeated (iterated) bargaining situations (Kratochwil 1984, 350). Negotiations can produce a laboratory-like setting in which enemies can become partners and cooperation, once learned, can be transformed from one arena to another when their common interest is great enough—for example, preventing nuclear war.

The development of norms, even in contentious relationships, is something that has carried over into "deterrent"situations in the new century. India and Pakistan set off alarms in the international community with their twin nuclear tests in 1990 and 1998. But an "existential deterrent" has forced a certain amount of restraint in the relationship (Ganguly and Hagerty 2006, 191), most recently seen following the 2008 terrorist attacks in Mumbai. Under intense domestic pressure to blame the Pakistani government for the actions of Lashkar-e-taiba, India instead opted for a rather cooperative approach, implicity accepting the notion that it would be better to work *with* Pakistan to ascertain who was involved and to what extent. Likewise, despite significant strategic differences in the post–Cold War international system, the United States and China have worked successfully thus far to keep the lines of communication open on thorny issues such as North Korea and Iran's nuclear programs.

### Moving Beyond Cultural Differences: The U.S.-Japan Case

The United States and Japan have a unique relationship, born of the role America played in reshaping Japanese politics after that country's defeat in World War II. The ensuing friendship was one of patron and client, or as some had characterized it, parent and child. In the new century, however, Tokyo and Washington are deepening their strategic partnership, even as they weather disputes that are rooted in their fundamentally different cultures. Younger Japanese think it anachronistic to talk about deference to the United States, and they have pressured Tokyo to grow into its role as a world leader and reject a junior status vis-à-vis the United States. For their part, many Americans continue to complain that the Japanese only selectively play by the rules of the international economic system. They feel that the free trade that is supposed to underlie the friendship is a sham and that Washington has long been taken advantage of by a Japan that welcomes American security protection but deceives the United States in economic matters.

The most serious disputes have involved trade and monetary policies, and have brought Japanese corporate culture, so different from its American counterpart, into focus. At the fore have been questions of market access, governmental protectionism, and currency valuation. The automobile sector has, over time, served as a microcosm of the troubles the two countries have had, but also, ultimately, of the spirit of cooperation that underlies this relationship. Throughout the 1980s, CEOs of the traditional American "Big Three" auto companies—Ford, General Motors, and Chrysler—complained bitterly that Japanese manufacturers—Honda, Toyota, Nissan, and others—were fully able to penetrate the U.S. market but resisted the reciprocation of this access. They accused the Japanese government of colluding with corporate conglomerates in its country to keep American cars and car parts out of its domestic market. The Japanese retorted that U.S.-manufactured products were often inferior and that American manufacturers had not even bothered to make their cars usable for, let alone attractive to, Japanese consumers. As evidence, they pointed to a dearth of right-hand-drive American automobiles available in Japan. The relationship hit trouble spots with great frequency, with the mutual recriminations almost always the same: the U.S. government accusing its Japanese counterpart of not doing enough to make things right in the area of trade, to which Tokyo would respond that the American view of capitalism is too narrow. What is instructive about these exchanges is that the Americans frame the problems as economic and structural, while the Japanese respond by pointing to political factors. It has been up to academics and others in the social realm to point out that the major source of misunderstanding in this relationship is cultural (Oka 1992, 18A).

Also instructive is that all of this bickering has not stopped the United States and Japan from negotiating. In fact, private-sector negotiations between companies such as Toyota and General Motors resulted in new hybrid Japanese-designed, U.S.-manufactured automobiles in the 1990s. This type of cooperation led Japanese automobile companies to invest $28 billion in the American manufacturing sector and create 170,000 jobs for American workers. For its part, Japan has been America's largest export market (Carnegie Endowment for International Peace 2007). A U.S.-Japan Automotive Agreement in 2001 set up a hybrid of its own, a public-private "Automotive Consultative Group" (ACG) to foster long-term cooperation within the industry. The resulting interdependence is very clear in the wake of the 2008 global financial crisis. American companies teeter on the brink of collapse, while Toyota has posted its first annual loss in over 70 years. However, the response has not been nationalistic, but rather in the spirit of cooperation, as behooves these truly multinational corporations. The outlook is a more global one now, with talks of mergers in full force and all companies looking to new markets in India and elsewhere in the developing world as a possible next frontier.

Most objective analysts of U.S.-Japanese disputes agree there is merit to the positions both sides take. The Japanese have benefited tremendously from their access to many sectors of the American economy. However, they do have a fundamentally different style of doing business. The producer, not the consumer, is revered in Japan. Moreover, networks of businesses work together closely to design, manufacture, and market. The resulting *keiretsu* system (loose conglomerates) does offend the tradition of antitrust sentiment in the free-trade lexicon, but it is an inherent part of the Japanese business culture, dating back to the pre–World War II *zaibatsu* (tight, family-controlled conglomerates). Across the board—from the relationship of business to government, to that of the state to its people—the Japanese emphasis on winning market shares as distinct from the U.S. emphasis on profit complicates this important international relationship. But as long as trust in the goodwill and good intentions of the "other" endure, the Americans and the Japanese will likely continue a successful negotiation partnership.

*Mirror Imaging in Societal-Level Conflicts: The Northern Ireland Case*

The Anglo-Irish Treaty of 1921 granted independence to the twenty-six southern counties of Ireland—the Republic of Ireland—while preserving British governmental rule over Northern Ireland. It was in this northern

Billboard suggesting a brighter future for Northern Ireland if voters approve the Good Friday Peace Amendment, 1998. <http://cain.ulst.ac.uk>

area, often referred to as Ulster, that the minority Catholic population waged a protest against British rule for the remainder of the century. Discontent with what they deem as inequalities vis-à-vis the majority Protestant population, Catholics used a variety of means, both violent and nonviolent, to try to affect the situation. From 1969 onward, Northern Ireland was deeply impacted by the sectarian violence of paramilitary groups, most notably the IRA, but also the Ulster Volunteer Force (UVF) and others on the Protestant side. At times, IRA violence was directed at the British through attacks on political figures and civilians in London. But the day-to-day conflict was fought in the streets of Belfast, Derry, and other cities of Northern Ireland, where the "Troubles"—as the Irish characterize the bloody, protracted conflict—resulted in over 3,200 deaths and over 20,000 injuries.

The conflict in Northern Ireland pits Republicans, or nationalists (the Catholic minority that favors unification with the independent Republic of Ireland to the south) against Unionists, or loyalists (the majority Protestants who favor continued union with the United Kingdom). Every aspect of competing group identities between the two sides has been politicized over the decades, with fault lines along class, national identity, and religious affiliation. Widespread segregation in housing and schools and allegations of discrimination in employment practices and the legal system provide the most obvious manifestations of "othering." Its more insidious outlets come through the symbolism of colors—green for the Republicans and orange for the Unionists; derogatory terms that children learn early on—fenians for the Catholics and orangies for the Protestants; and the various holidays and days of remembrance that each side regularly celebrates with emotionally charged parades (Robinson 1992; Jarman 1997).

Negotiations aimed at reconciliation of the many parties to this conflict (the Republicans and the Unionists are both split into various groups, and the United Kingdom and Irish Republic are central actors as well) failed to make any substantive progress until the 1997–1998 All-Party Talks. These talks came about as a direct result of the extreme frustration all sides felt when the paramilitary cease-fires of 1994 broke down in early 1996. The IRA resumed violence at that time, citing a lack of good faith on the part of then British prime minister John Major. This perception of British intransigence was reinforced by then prime minister of the Republic of Ireland, John Bruton, who stated, "Britain has [shown] less courage, generosity and decisiveness since the paramilitary ceasefires last year than [have] many people in Ireland" (Brams and Togman 1998, 35). Not long afterward, the Unionist cease-fire collapsed as well, and it was widely feared that the peace process had reached a dead end.

Several factors helped move the negotiations out of gridlock and back on track in 1997. One was the May election of Tony Blair as prime minister of

Britain. Like his predecessor Major, Blair insisted that the IRA cease-fire be reinstated before peace negotiations could resume. However, he followed the lead of International Commission chairman George Mitchell (a former U.S. senator) in recognizing that IRA willingness to repeat the cease-fire move would not be likely unless the British promised to reciprocate quickly this time around. To this end, three weeks after his election, Blair went to Belfast to promise that if the Republican groups would take a conciliatory stance, "I will not be slow in my response" (Brams and Togman 1998, 37). Indeed, he did much to move the process forward by agreeing to Mitchell's proposal that the thorny issue of paramilitary disarmament be handled at the peace talks, rather than as a precursor to them. This promise of reciprocity and the personal attention and energy that Blair devoted to the situation moved all the parties forward once again. With cease-fires back in place and the parties finally at the negotiation table, Mitchell imposed a deadline of April 9, 1998, on the talks.

One day after the deadline, at Stormont Castle in Belfast, an announcement was made that an agreement had been reached. Dubbed the Good Friday Agreement, it outlined proposals for a Northern Ireland Assembly, political structures connecting the north and south of Ireland, new human rights legislation, normalization of security forces and policing practices, and a planned decommissioning of all paramilitary groups within two years after the endorsement of the agreement (Ingraham 1999, 11). In the first "all-Ireland" vote in the contemporary period, the agreement was approved in joint referenda in Northern Ireland and the Republic of Ireland on May 22, 1998. In the north, nearly 97 percent of Catholics voted yes in support of the agreement, along with 51 to 53 percent of Protestants. There have been great challenges to the will of the Irish people to stay with the agreement—notably the violent activity of IRA splinter groups such as the Provisional Irish Republican Army (PIRA) and the Continuity Irish Republican Army (CIRA), which picked up in intensity once again during the summer of 2008 (Northern Ireland Monitoring Commission 2009). Yet, the referendum illustrates a crucial point about cultural conflicts and negotiations to end them: it is not enough for political leaders to sign on to peace agreements. When conflicts are so entrenched at the societal and cultural levels, it is ultimately the people who must decide to reconcile, take steps toward trust, and choose the path of negotiated peace over sectarian violence and hatred. Moreover, as the sometimes rocky aftermath to this peace agreement has further illustrated, conflicts entrenched at the societal level must be constantly tended to avoid slippage.

Lessons learned from the Northern Ireland case have been applied to negotiations in other regions. One such example is Nepal, where in 2002, the internal parties were able to work out a framework by rejecting externally generated solutions and looking deeply into their own societal needs. The framework for "participatory governance" that came out of the Nepali peace process relied heavily on the creation of institutions that could guarantee the "substantive political participation" of minorities at both the local and national level. It was an agreement that sought to ensure that basic services would be available to everyone in that society, regardless of ethnic identification and that the nation would move on in a direction that rejected the "exclusion or marginalization of particular communites for short-term political gain by certain elements of the leadership" (Kumar 2004, 106 and 114).

## Summary

The diplomatic landscape has changed from the heyday of "great man" personal diplomacy. It continues to change as a result of the diffusion of power from centralized national governments to superstates, substates, shadow states, and a host of other entities. These anomalous players can heavily impact the foreign policies of states and, in some cases, even practice their own versions of foreign policy.

NGOs, the citizen diplomats who work from within them, and the vast networks they often form around issues such as health, the environment, and human rights can now mobilize tremendous power. The information revolution has brought with it a greater understanding of global problems and avenues of action for those experts and activists who work to coordinate international and transnational efforts in these areas.

The proliferation of issues on the proverbial negotiation table and the actors that bring them there have transformed the negotiation landscape. Identity politics has found its way into diplomacy, bringing new attention to old notions such as peace. From Burma to Iran, we see the operationalization of gender as women's groups mobilize in the name of both reconciliation and change. The impact of these women's groups on the international agendas of states is just one of the many influences on the changing rules of the game in the international negotiation arena.

Yet, despite these many dynamic elements, cultural "othering"—the villainization of the adversary—still blocks progress in many conflict situations. Despite what traditional diplomats have long professed, negotiations and negotiated agreements are always extremely tenuous when they come from the top down. Reconciliation, it seems, must be accepted by those down below.

*   *   *

*For a list of related web resources for this chapter, consult*
*www.icons.umd.edu/negotiating/links.htm.*

# 4

# The Stakes

The North Korean crisis negotiations and the environmental negotiations begun at Kyoto have been used throughout this book to highlight many important dimensions of the negotiation process. They can also illustrate the stakes for negotiators, or using the term that will be developed throughout this chapter, the issue salience—the importance of a negotiation issue to the actors involved. The crisis with North Korea represents an example of what has traditionally been termed a high-politics issue, with a focus on nuclear proliferation and other military-security concerns of the states involved in the recurrent crises. In contrast, the concern with climate change in the Kyoto negotiations presents what has traditionally been viewed as a low-politics issue—of less urgency to states and of lesser salience than a military-security matter. The aim of this chapter is to illustrate how the issues involved in particular negotiations shape the negotiations themselves. This discussion focuses on what gets discussed in international negotiations and how the issues determine which actors get involved, the dynamics among the issues, and the types of outcomes that result from the negotiation process. The chapter begins with an examination of the traditional way issues have been viewed—the high politics versus low politics dichotomy—and then moves on to a more complex framework, shaped around the concept of issue salience.

## The Traditional Issue Framework

The traditional way to think about issues in international relations is to classify them as high politics (e.g., security and survival issues) or low politics (e.g., economics, human rights, and just about everything else). Such dichotomous frameworks are admittedly limited because they cannot deal effectively with extremely complex or fluid situations. They represent a useful starting point, however, for organizing the analysis of a given event or problem. As explained later, one of the reasons these terms have been used is that high-politics issues are traditionally thought to exhibit larger degrees of participation on the part of top-level officials, thus accounting for their higher profiles. Low-politics issues, in contrast, have traditionally been viewed as the domains of lower-level governmental officials. The following sections lay out in more detail the actors and issues associated with each domain of international activity.

## High Politics

High-politics issues have traditionally been seen as ones that threaten the survival of the state and thus demand the attention of its highest officials (Mansbach 1997). For example, in the United States during the Cold War period, military-security issues around the globe consistently required the attention of the president and other high-level officials. In the contemporary international system, however, military-security challenges are reappearing in many different forms and sometimes in unexpected places. For instance, of the 26 armed conflicts in the world in 2008, all except two (Iraq and Afghanistan) were subnational is nature (Hewitt et al. 2009, 28). In all security-related situations, it is clear that today's military-security threats are new and different, requiring governmental security strategies that are yet evolving.

Comments by leaders of European Union countries also indicate the degree to which the boundaries between traditional conceptions of high and low politics are blurred, and at times completely illusory. At the May 2004 announcement that the European Union was expanding from fifteen to twenty-five countries, then German chancellor Gerhard Schroeder put it this way: "Who would have thought, sixty years ago, that there could be a day like today when Europe is united and we all have the chance to make Europe a place of lasting peace and prosperity?" ("Celebrations as EU Grows to 25," 06/14/04, cnn.com). As this suggests, economic prosperity, peace, and security have increasingly become intertwined in the contemporary world system, rendering the traditional distinction between high and low politics obsolete in contemporary international politics.

## Low Politics

If high-politics issues have traditionally monopolized the attention of high-level officials in the foreign policy and negotiation arenas, then low-politics issues—such as the environment, human rights, economic development, foreign aid, and health—have usually been perceived as the purview of lower-level career officials often buried deep within faceless bureaucracies. Negotiations over the disbursement of foreign aid, for example, are routinely conducted and overseen by legislative committees or special departments within governments. In humanitarian crises—as opposed to military-security ones—the dialogue about a proper response is often managed by international development agencies, the U.S. Agency for International Development (AID) or the Swedish International Development Agency (SIDA), for example, and by NGOs, such as the International Red Cross or Doctors Without Borders.

Part of the problem with this issue dichotomy, however, is that many issues blur the line between high and low politics. In addition, what may be high politics in the eyes of some international leaders or individuals on the ground may not be as important to others. The recurrent violence in the Democratic Republic of the Congo, for example, illustrates this case. To many leaders in the West, Congolese violence presents a humanitarian concern, but not one that threatens their own security. Thus, what is perceived as low politics in the West might easily be viewed as high politics within the Congo and by its neighboring countries. So even though the United Nations continues to have a peacekeeping presence in that region, direct involvement by the more powerful Western countries has been slow to develop, even as violence flared in late 2008, forcing many to recall the lack of international action regarding the Rwandan genocide of the mid-1990s.

Returning to Mansbach's definition, then, because low-politics issues are not perceived as threatening the territorial integrity of the state, they are not viewed in the same light as security issues. In the past, this has meant that high-level decision makers are not usually involved in negotiations dealing with these issues. The officials who manage them are much less likely to receive significant public attention or media scrutiny during their negotiations on these matters. Even while invoking these differences, however, it is not always so easy to distinguish high politics from low, as the following sections will explain.

### New Approaches to Issues

There have long been objections to the high/low politics framework described earlier, in part because it is an outgrowth of state-centered models of international relations and does not adequately describe the variety of forces present in the international system. The usefulness of the distinction began to undergo serious questioning as early as the 1960s, when interdependence among the main units in the system—the nation-states—began to increase greatly as a result of the growth of world trade and finance, developments in transportation, and the rapid pace of change in communications. This interdependence led to the globalization of many once local activities, such as those related to the environment. The impact of individual states' decisions on environmental action was now clearly seen as important to neighbors near and sometimes even far away. Visible linkage of high- to low-politics issues was also apparent during this time, with the Americans, Soviets, and others using foreign aid disbursements as a tool of foreign policy. High correlations, for example, were found between anti-Soviet sentiment and receipt of American foreign aid monies (Hook 1995). It was also clear that strategic concerns motivated the aid policies others adopted, including Japan, France, and Sweden.

It is important to understand that these so-called low-politics issues have always been crucial to the majority of people around the world. From natural environmental disasters that have long disproportionately affected the southern hemisphere to the HIV/AIDS epidemic spinning out of control in parts of Africa and Asia, social issues have increasingly become hot political issues. Moreover, issues such as the AIDS epidemic are increasingly threatening the capacity of states to govern because of the degree to which they drain governmental resources and the working-age population, thus creating serious security concerns for those states and their neighbors (Price-Smith 2002). Recently, concerns about avian and swine flu pandemics have demonstrated the need for national capacity to cope with these threats and for international cooperation to manage their potential spread.

As a result, it is important to explore the extent to which average citizens agree with their leaders about what constitutes high politics as opposed to low. This point is well illustrated in figure 4.1, which displays public opin-

**Figure 4.1   U.S. Public Attitudes toward Environmental and Defense Spending.
National Opinion Research Center**

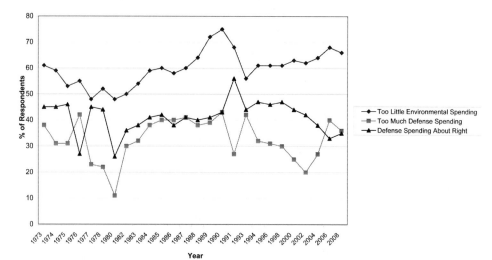

ion on U.S. government spending on the environment and military defense over time. As this figure shows, from 1973 to 2006, a significant portion of the American public has consistently viewed spending on the environment as too low and defense spending as either about right or too high. Even post-9/11, these public views changed very little, with the environment remaining a priority that is underfunded in the eyes of the public, while defense is perceived as generally well maintained.

Public sentiments about policy priorities have been an important factor in moving problems once relegated to various bureaucracies to center stage in international negotiations, including cross-border environment, health, and narcotics issues. Certainly the evolving U.S. climate change policy under the Obama administration is a case in point. As has been discussed in chapter 1, the United States has been a primary resistor of climate change initiatives at the international level over the past decade. But the 2008 presidential campaign signaled a change, as both candidates McCain and Obama advocated more progressive climate change policies than those espoused by the Bush administration. It is clear that however the U.S. stance on climate change now evolves, it will have broader public support than did the Bush policy on climate change.

On an institutional level, this gradual rise in importance of low-politics issues has led to the negotiation of numerous international protocols and agreements, including, in the environmental area, the Law of the Sea, the Montreal Protocol on the protection of the ozone layer, and the Kyoto Protocol, among many others. Moreover, the increase in attention afforded formerly low-politics issues has grown in the post–Cold War international arena. Although military-security concerns have certainly not disappeared, the ability of many states to shift some of their attention to other issues has allowed more negotiations to focus on the broadening and deepening of economic ties among states. The EU movement toward monetary union, the creation of NAFTA in the early 1990s, and the prospective broadening of free trade to more countries in the Western hemisphere provide three such examples. More than ever before, ordinary citizens and their political leaders cannot fail to note that successes and failures of others are related to their own economic well-being.

This rise in the importance of economic issues and the connections among economics, politics, and security have been abundantly evident during the global financial crisis that began in 2008. European Commission President Jose Manuel Barroso stated early in the crisis that "[w]e need more and better long term coordination [among countries], to ensure transparency and confidence in the market. In order to cushion the impact of financial crisis on the real economy, we also need to sustain domestic demand, and to further promote international trade" ("Barosso: Interdependence and Reform Are Needed to Solve Global Financial Crisis,"

10/24/08, http://english.cri.cn). His statement clearly argues that the interconnections among countries' domestic economies and global financial stability require greater coordination among decision makers worldwide. And as many people throughout the world have undoubtedly realized since the economic downturn began, security—especially at a personal level—is based on employment and financial stability. Moreover, as Nobel laureate Mohamed elBaradei argues, "The modern age demands that we think in terms of human security . . . a concept that acknowledges the inherent linkages between economic development, respect for human rights, and peace. . . . Until we understand and act accordingly we will not have either national or international security (University of Maryland, "Sadat Lecture for Peace," 10/24/06, http://sadat.umd.edu).

### Issue Salience in a Changing International System

One step that can move the discussion beyond the high/low politics approach is to introduce the concept of issue salience when considering the impact of issues on the negotiation process (Boyer 2000; Butler and Boyer 2003, 2009). Issue salience is the importance given to an issue by a particular actor or set of actors—the perceived stakes of the issue. An example of a highly salient issue area for a broad cross section of political actors is international trade. The stakes perceived to be at risk—jobs, prosperity, and even environmental integrity—appeal to a wide array of actors and affect fundamental values for those actors. In essence, it is not the issue itself that generates stakes for the actors involved, but rather the interests that underlie the issues for each and every actor involved (Sebenius 2002). In other words, what an actor values most highly will define which issues are of high or low importance.

> **KEY TERM**
>
> **Issue Salience** The importance a particular actor or set of actors gives to an issue— the perceived stakes.

This section of the chapter develops a framework based on issue salience as synonymous with perceived stakes.

　　Understanding variations in issue salience for the actors involved in international negotiations is an important step in the effort to build a more complex understanding of the ways issues affect negotiations. For example, even though environmental issues may be traditionally viewed as low politics, the stakes in cross-border environmental negotiations are very high for businesses that will confront rising energy costs, for groups that work to enhance environmental quality, and for those companies that stand to gain financially by providing technology for cleaner energy sources. Because the perceived stakes for these groups are so high, they will work very hard within their home political systems—and often internationally—to achieve their goals. This case makes it clear that the high/low approach overly simplifies the stakes for the interested parties by ignoring variations in salience. Focusing on salience gives more insight into why the same issue might at one point in time be very important but at other times of seemingly little consequence for the various stakeholders.

Sometimes, issues are highly salient for one group but less so for others. In U.S. politics, for example, Middle East peace negotiations are very important to members of the Arab American and Jewish American communities, but somewhat less so to others in the U.S. political system. In some cases, issues do not seem salient for many at the domestic political level at all. Efforts to get the Brazilian government to focus on the global impact of environmental issues—such as the destruction of the Amazon rain forest, for example—have not always been successful. With the exception of some "green" groups in Brazil, most domestic constituency groups have been much more concerned with improving economic growth and stability in that country than with environmental quality.

To understand how issue salience can be so changeable for state actors, it is necessary to recognize the extent to which national interest has become complicated. Put simply, the determination of national interest is no longer an easy calculus for states to make, nor is it the only kind of interest that counts on the world stage. Increasingly, ethnic, corporate, transnational, and global interests—among many others—must be taken into account. The presence of such pressures at the domestic level is a particularly important factor in determining issue salience for state actors.

Although it is convenient to regard nation-states as monolithic entities, the reality of policy making is that many actors within countries vie for control of and influence over the outcomes of international negotiations. Members of legislatures with opinions on international affairs that differ from those of the head of state, bureaucrats who work on specialized problems, and interest groups who champion certain causes often hold more narrow views on the desirability of certain policies. As a result, they work within the political system (and sometimes outside of it) to produce foreign policy decisions that will change the negotiations.

Of course, the fact that domestic constituencies participate in the negotiation game does not mean that they will all be happy with the outcome. At the conclusion of the Kyoto talks in 1997, many business groups ultimately opposed the signing of the Framework Convention on Climate Change because they did not want to have regulations imposed on them that would raise production costs. Referring to U.S. negotiators, Bill O'-Keefe, chairman of the pro-business Global Climate Coalition that opposed the Kyoto pact, argued, "We gave the store away. . . . We conceded everything. We got nothing. . . . There's no practical way we can reduce energy consumption in this country by over 30 percent in 12 years" (CNN Interactive 1997). Clearly, the fact that a company's home government signs an international agreement does not mean that everyone agrees with the position of the negotiators who—in theory at least—represented the national interest at the bargaining table.

Even if an issue is highly salient for domestic groups in one party to a negotiation, it is not necessarily very salient for those on the other side. As discussed earlier regarding multilateral decisions on humanitarian intervention, it is often the case that conflict-ridden countries and their neighbors perceive intervention as much more salient than do those countries that are most likely to provide the peacekeepers or other intervening troops. This is one reason why developing a globally accepted strategy for conflict resolution in Darfur, Rwanda, and the Democratic Republic of Congo has been so difficult to achieve. From an international negotiation perspective, when such situations occur, the flexibility and strategies of the negotiators from opposing sides will be different, even though they are discussing the exact same issue.

Because international negotiations have become so complex, it will be helpful to consider four factors that influence issue salience: (1) the distribution of costs and benefits among domestic (substate) actors (which is essentially the controversy over the domestic stakes); (2) the commitment of key individuals and groups to the negotiation issue; (3) the urgency that the presence of a crisis situation adds; and (4) the level of media attention focused on the negotiations.

## Controversial Domestic Stakes

Perceptions about the fairness of negotiated international agreements affect who gets involved in the negotiation process at the domestic level, as well as the salience of the issue for those actors. In fact, one scholar has argued that issues of fairness and justice are routinely factored into negotiations, especially when the negotiators wish to craft stable and durable agreements (Albin 2001). Put simply, the degree to which any negotiation party feels that it is being unfairly burdened or that others are being unfairly rewarded will increase the intensity of that group's efforts to change policy course (Zimmerman 1973). Policies that impact society symmetrically are often less divisive and intense than policies that impact society asymmetrically, with some groups and individuals emerging as winners and others as losers. For instance, during the NAFTA negotiations in the early 1990s (see the NAFTA box later in the chapter), Thomas Donahue (1991, 91), then secretary treasurer of the American Federation of Labor and Congress of Industrial Organizations (AFL-CIO), wrote, "Among those who would suffer most from NAFTA are industrial workers in the United States. It would pave the way for tens of thousands of their jobs to be exported to Mexico, and it would bump hundreds of thousands down the economic ladder to under-employment and low wages." Fear of losing jobs to the Mexican market pushed narrow sectors of the American public and interest groups to argue against the signing of NAFTA by President George H. W. Bush. Once it was signed, those same interest groups urged President Clinton to negotiate and sign the three side-agreements to NAFTA and lobbied against approval of NAFTA by Congress, even though they ultimately lost their political battle. The vociferous opposition to NAFTA that labor unions put forth was motivated by their perception that the potentially high costs would be absorbed almost exclusively by American industrial workers.

Consideration of the perceived distribution of costs and benefits is also affected by short-term versus long-term calculations, as illustrated in the Kyoto case. Business interests looked at the short-term costs of meeting the emissions restrictions the Kyoto Protocol imposed and focused on the impact this would have on production costs and, by extension, corporate profits in the short term. On the other hand, environmental groups looked at the long-term costs associated with global warming and tried to make the case for fast action—not an easy task—as they struggled against popular perceptions of a lack of immediacy. Thus, differences among the negotiation parties on short-term and long-term perspectives on who pays the costs and who derives the benefits may exacerbate conflict in the negotiation process.

Finally, it is also interesting to note in the Kyoto case that both business and environmental groups viewed the issue as highly salient, but for very different reasons: business because of Kyoto's potential negative impact on commercial competitiveness, and environmental groups because of the potential positive impact the accords might have on the control of global warming and its potentially catastrophic environmental effects. Perceptions of stakes create incentives for interested parties to sway public opinion on an issue. As discussed in chapter 1, these perceptions have kept the basic components of the Kyoto Protocol in political play to the present day without conclusive findings about the real impact of the agreement.

### Commitment to the Issue

Another factor that affects the salience of a negotiation issue is the level of commitment to the resolution of the problem by top leaders and other key domestic groups. High commitment can result from national pride, ethnic ties, deeply held political ideologies, perceived offenses, the personal interests and temperaments of the negotiators, and other causes. For example, the emotional legacy of anticommunist sentiment during the Cold War, particularly among older Americans and western Europeans, at times translates into wary support for constructive relations with Russia. In addition, that anticommunist legacy also plays a role in the evolving U.S.-Chinese relationship, especially as the wave of democratization spreads around the world. Similarly, American involvement in the Muslim world has also received lukewarm support in the post-9/11 context, where Muslims have been perceived in overly general terms as anti-American. Moreover, the emotional impact of the revelations in the 2004 Iraqi prison abuse scandal have stoked the fires of anti-American emotions among Iraqi citizens and others in the Muslim world.

The impact of commitment on how issues are perceived in international negotiations can be both positive and negative. On the positive side, a personal stake on the part of negotiators may motivate them to work harder for an agreement, whether that agreement is ultimately a compromise or a perceived victory for their cause. King Hussein of Jordan had such a connection to the success of decades-long Arab-Israeli negotiations. His son has also worked to carry on that legacy of personal involvement and many hope will continue to be a moderating influence in those negotiations. Personal interventions and the ability of negotiators to capitalize on established relationships with other negotiators may mean the difference between success and failure. The first President Bush's tendency to take to the phone with other world leaders during times of crisis—his "Rolodex diplomacy"—added an individualized and extremely timely element to international negotiations during his presidency. These relationships paid off for him in 1990, when he had to build the anti-Iraq coalition in a very short amount of time.

Intense commitment, however, can also lead to emotional involvement that can create a negative impact on the negotiations. Emotion may cloud the objectivity of the negotiators and lead them to choices that are not well advised. Some commentators have argued that one of the factors that contributed to the hard stance taken by President Bush toward Iraq in the 1990–1991 Gulf War was his being dubbed a wimp by *Newsweek* magazine during the 1988 presidential campaign. They contend that Bush's minimal use of the negotiation channel in favor of military force against Iraq can be interpreted at least partly as an effort to reduce his wimp image with the American public. Similar arguments have been made about Bill Clinton's actions during the Iraqi weapons inspections crises, especially the Desert Fox operation in the winter of 1998–1999: that, facing impeachment and removal from office at home, he eschewed the negotiation channel in favor of air strikes on Iraq. And many have argued that President George W. Bush waged war in Iraq to complete what has been perceived as his father's unfinished business. At least one memoir, that of former Bush secretary of the treasury Paul O'Neill, provides testimony to support this reading of the son's motivations in formulating Iraqi policy (Suskind 2004).

The injection of ethnicity into the mix of negotiation variables can also significantly impact the commitments parties have to particular negotiations and their outcomes. In fact, many of the negotiations described in this book and studied over the years have focused on the resolution of ethnic conflicts and the accompanying claims for resources and legitimacy. The post–Cold War period has seen a variety of long-simmering hostilities— such as those among Croats, Muslims, and Serbs and between Serbs and ethnic Albanians in the Balkans, and between the Shiites and Sunnis in several Middle Eastern countries including Iraq—come openly and violently to the fore. Besides its long-standing negotiation efforts in Northern Ireland and the Middle East, the international community is also attempting to continue or expand mediation efforts in Bosnia, Chechnya, East Timor, and Rwanda. In these places and many others, legacies of ethnic hatred and conflict produce perceptual roadblocks to negotiated settlements because of a lack of trust and often a record of bad faith among the parties. In some instances, these legacies are the result of ethnic animosity that dates back hundreds of years. The Balkan conflicts, for example, can be traced back to medieval times.

The potential for misunderstanding is rife when relationships are rooted in emotional perceptions of the "other." Communication in such situations often seems trapped in a negative cycle, with symbolism and innuendo carrying enormous weight. In 1988, when the British tightened controls over the press in Northern Ireland and asked Catholics to "support the law, the British government, and your Queen," the message that Catholics interpreted was closer to "indicate that you are ready to betray friends and neighbors by ceasing to tolerate violent protest by the IRA because loyalty to the crown is important and violence is wrong" (Fisher et al. 1997, 75, 77). Conflicts laced with ethnic threads can raise perceived stakes for the actors involved and increase the likelihood that misperceptions or differing perceptions of the same phenomena will occur and create obstacles to successful negotiations.

As these examples illustrate, when issue involvement becomes emotionally charged at the domestic level, it will complicate the international dimension of the negotiations. Even in policy arenas traditionally considered low politics, controversy can develop as more domestic actors become involved in the process and push hard for negotiated solutions that are favorable to their own particular interests.

## The Effect of Crisis

A key factor affecting perceived issue salience in the negotiation arena is the existence of a crisis atmosphere in the decision-making and negotiating environment. Discussed in chapter 2 as a feature of the international system, the impact of crisis on issues is worth mentioning here as well.

When core national values are at stake, a situation that often occurs during crises, domestic infighting becomes less important. Crisis situations also tend to focus decision-making attention on a country's chief executive and narrow circle of advisers.

Crisis situations create perceptions of high levels of potential costs to a nation-state. Because crises threaten basic national and societal values, they raise the interest of all policy actors, even if that attention may largely be of only a supportive nature from those outside the executive circle. The North Korea case offers an excellent illustration of the ways a crisis atmosphere shapes the course of international negotiations and limits the number of actors involved in them. As detailed in chapter 1, the primary actors each time the North Korean problem flared to crisis proportions were the U.S. president (Bill Clinton in the early 1990s, George W. Bush in the early 2000s, and Barack Obama since 2009), the U.S. secretaries of state, the secretive North Korean leaders, UN officials and inspectors, and several other high-profile actors, including former U.S. president Jimmy Carter, who attempted mediation. During the various crisis points, diplomatic overtures and, more often, hostile rhetoric characterized the interactions that took place among the actors. But throughout the crises, high-level interactions occurred, including the six-party negotiations in August 2003 and the continuing interactions over the problem. The immediate attention to this recurrent crisis by President Obama was also well noted by the international community in the wake of North Korea's spring 2009 weapons tests.

This type of high-level political involvement resulted from the perception that the issues at stake in these crises threatened the core values of the actors. For the United States, those values included international political influence in the region and the threat posed to other countries in the region by a potentially nuclear North Korea. Although difficult to discern directly because of the closed nature of the regime, North Korea was concerned with obtaining increased security guarantees about nonaggression from the south and other powers in the region. And Japan, China, and others were focused on the threat posed directly to them by a North Korea in possession of nuclear weapons and how that might adversely affect the balance of military power in the region. In the wake of the spring 2009 North Korean missile tests, the North Korean news agency stated that "[o]ur army and people are fully ready for battle . . . against any reckless U.S. attempt for a pre-emptive attack." The United States and other countries in the region viewed the test as innately aggressive and escalatory, but also recognized the difficulty posed by the North Korean action. U.S. ambassador to the United Nations, Susan Rice, echoed this sentiment when she stated that negotiations within the UN Security Council were going well, but that "[w]e are thinking through complicated issues that require very careful consideration"("N. Korea 'Defiant' Amid Warnings, 5/27/09, bbc.co.uk).

## Media Attention

Issue salience can also be affected by the level of domestic and international attention afforded a negotiation issue. Research shows that when visibility increases, negotiators become less flexible, leading often to impasses (Druckman and Druckman 1996). As established earlier in this chapter, sometimes this attention is focused as a result of perceived subgroup stakes in an issue area. At other times, such as in crisis situations, there is a tendency for the whole group to rally behind the responses of top leadership. Nonetheless, perceptions of stakes can be greatly swayed by national and international media reporting on an issue. The importance of the media has grown in this era of CNN and the Internet. The press now reaches out to people through a variety of different media and fulfills key roles in setting the agendas for top policy officials, providing information on and analyses of international events, often shaping the opinions held by elites and the public in countries throughout the world (see box).

### The Press: Uninvited Negotiators?

The press is not usually invited as a player in international negotiations; nonetheless, it often influences negotiation outcomes. The role played by CNN in the events surrounding the Gulf War of 1991 has been well documented, and many vivid images of CNN reporting during the war remain icons of the press's role in world affairs. A recent example of the press's international influence was seen in the aftermath of the June 2009 Iranian presidential election. In the end, the role played by the press, and the news-gathering skills of many independent individuals for that matter, ultimately constrained the Obama administration's ability to negotiate with the Iranian regime over a host of issues ranging from its nuclear program to its role in Middle East affairs. The publicity surrounding the disputed elections, as will be shown briefly below, changed many opinions about the willingness of the Iranian regime to engage in good faith dialogue on these issues.

To summarize the June 2009 events, two hours after the polls closed in Iran on June 12, the Iranian election authority declared President Mahmoud Ahmadinejad the winner, garnering almost 63 percent of the votes cast. Immediately, supporters of the primary challenger, Mir Hossain Moussavi, began to question the validity of the announced result. First, many questioned whether 39 million votes could accurately be tallied in two hours. Moreover, pre-election polls predicted a much closer election result. These and other apparent problems with the announcement helped to mobilize Moussavi supporters shortly after the election (see "Iran 101: Understanding the Unrest," 6/18/09, cnn.com).

Within days, pro-Moussavi supporters flooded the streets of Tehran and other cities and towns to protest the announced result and argue for fresh elections. These protests were immediately met with harsh suppression techniques by Iranian security forces and pleas from Ahmadinejad and supreme leader Ayatollah Ali Khamenei to refrain from the protests and accept the outcome. Nonetheless, the protests continued to receive widespread international press coverage until June 16, when the Iranian regime banned international journalists from covering the protest rallies.

But in the Internet age, the ban on foreign journalists did not end the world's access to the protests. Some might even argue that it only intensfied the unrest and efforts to broadcast the events worldwide. CNN's i-reporters began to send in graphic cell phone videos of the violence in waves. Foreign leaders, including U.S. President Obama, became more outspoken with questions about the possibility that the election results were fraudulent and urged negotiation between opposition forces and the regime currently in power.

In this way, the press—and its use of individuals to feed voice and video from the protests even after the press ban took place—became a major player in the tacit, indirect international negotiations that took place among the Ahmadinejad regime, the protesters, and countries around the world arguing for free and fair elections in the Islamic republic.

An example of media impact can be found in the Clinton administration's last-minute decision to send Vice President Gore to Kyoto in 1997, as documented in chapter 1. American and international media sources were targeting Bill Clinton and Al Gore as having sold out on the environmental credentials they so carefully crafted during the 1992 election campaign. The Clinton team was clearly in a "put up or shut up" situation in Japan. This made the apparent American negotiation strategy—stall and obstruct—very hard to maintain in the face of media scrutiny. This high level of attention and criticism was a major factor in the decision to dispatch Gore to Kyoto, a trip he had not planned to make.

Media watchers have long debated whether the media represent a check on political power or are manipulated by the powers that be for their own political goals (Rourke, Carter, and Boyer 1996). Refining this dichotomy further, Eytan Gilboa (2001) argues that the press can take one of three roles in political affairs. First, the press faclitates "public diplomacy" by providing the conduit through which governments and individuals can get their points heard, particularly in foreign countries. Second, officials sometimes undertake "media diplomacy" in an effort to communicate with actors and to promote conflict resolution that might be prevented otherwise. And third, "media-brokered diplomacy" emerges when the media assume the role of mediator or facilitator in negotiations for periods of time. This third role is similar to the concept of "dual-track diplomacy" that is discussed in more detail in chapter 5.

Along these lines, journalists are at times manipulated by political leaders to further the politicians' goals, but at other times journalists blow the whistle on situations about which they feel the public would be interested to hear. In fact, recent diplomatic history provides evidence of both portrayals. The role of the press following the Tiananmen Square massacre in Beijing, China, in 1989 supports the watchdog characterization. In May and June of that year, pro-democracy student protests took place in Tiananmen Square; the protesters were kept informed through links with other students and peers around the globe. The world community was stunned in June when the Chinese government rolled tanks and troops into the square, killing many protesters and reestablishing firm control over domestic politics. Human rights groups worldwide led the cry for sanctions against the Chinese government and lobbied many governments to link trade with China to political reforms and an improved human rights record in that country.

Largely out of fear of losing access to the immense Chinese market, however, President George H. W. Bush sent National Security Adviser Brent Scowcroft and Deputy Secretary of State Lawrence Eagleburger on a secret mission just weeks after the massacre to smooth over the harsh rhetoric both countries had been using since the onset of the crisis. When the press got wind of this mission and reported on it, human rights groups and, more generally, the Democratic Party in the U.S. Congress widely took the Bush administration to task. It seemed at the time that the president was out of sync with the wishes of the American people regarding these secret diplomatic negotiations and that the press was serving the public interest in making the events public knowledge. Thus, when the media are in watchdog mode, their attention does increase the visibility of the negotiation, thereby increasing its salience. Of course, the case can also be made that the media are subject to manipulation by decision makers.

At times, the media are used by high-level leaders to achieve their goals in international negotiations, serving as a kind of lapdog. For example, most international trips world leaders take are media events of a high order. These events are staged to influence officials and constituents in their own countries and those of their negotiating partners. When Palestinian leader Yasir Arafat and Israeli prime minister Yitzhak Rabin were photographed shaking hands in the White House Rose Garden in 1994 with President Clinton by their sides, this photo opportunity was staged at least partly to send a signal to all the parties—domestic and international—with a stake in the Arab-Israeli conflict that the two leaders had learned to get along and put many of their differences behind them and that the United States sanctioned this progress made toward peace.

The Clinton administration provides another example of the connection of media attention to manipulation of international public opinion. In 1997, President Clinton invited the leader of Northern Ireland's Sinn Fein (viewed as the political wing of the IRA) to the White House. This was an astounding turnaround for the United States, which up until that point had refused formal contact with officials associated with the IRA, and Britain immediately registered a strong diplomatic protest over this event. But the media swarmed in to capture Sinn Fein's Gerry Adams shaking hands with a smiling Bill Clinton—his green tie visible on St. Patrick's Day in Washington. On the negotiation front, the chance afforded Adams to show that he was a responsible leader paid off for Clinton. Not long afterward, British prime minister Tony Blair decided that perhaps it was time to allow Sinn Fein a chance to sit at the negotiation table in the Northern Ireland talks. Many credit this change in the negotiation setting for the eventual progress made in the peace talks. It is also worth noting the impact that twittering and cell phone video had on the aftermath of the disputed June 2009 Iranian presidential elections. Even though the media were significantly constrained by the Iranian regime working to hold power, the regime was unable to prevent the much more independent use of electronic media that span the globe and allow individuals to play a role unheard of prior to the Internet age.

## Two-Level Negotiations

As is clear from the previous section, the traditional conception of high- and low-politics issues as they apply to negotiation stakes does not paint a complete picture. Thus far, this chapter has argued that issue salience provides an alternate basis and that salience varies depending on how a series of factors impact the situation—including cost-benefit calculations, the levels of commitment by top leaders and interested domestic parties, the nature of the situation (i.e., crisis or not), and the amount of international media attention focused on the negotiations. The central theme underlying the presentation of these factors is that the perceptions of various domestic subgroups can heavily impact the overall salience of an issue for political leadership.

On a theoretical level, examination of the interplay between domestic and international politics addresses an age-old question in political science and international relations: what influence does domestic politics have on international relations and vice versa? The remainder of this chapter attempts to address this important question as it relates to international negotiation.

### The Impact of Domestic Politics

One way to assess the interplay between domestic and international politics is to place the discussion of issues into the context of what Robert Putnam calls a two-level game. This term suggests that the international negotiation process has two basic components (Evans, Jacobson, and Putnam 1993; Putnam 1988, 436):

- Level 1: International—bargaining between negotiators leading to a tentative agreement.
- Level 2: Domestic—separate discussions within each group of constituents about whether to ratify the agreement.

Putnam's main objective is to show that there can be a sequence to negotiations, with international negotiations being followed by related domestic negotiations on such matters as ratification. It is important to note, however, that the interaction between the domestic and international negotiation components can also be reciprocal, with the level-two dialogue often beginning during the level-one negotiations. At times in the negotiation process, international negotiators will consult with domestic political actors to make sure that what is being discussed at the bargaining table will be acceptable to them during the ratification phase. In addition to making sure that prospective outcomes will be acceptable later on, domestic pressure may also influence the stance a negotiator takes during the negotiations (Yong 2003). In other words, particularly when the negotiations are well publicized, the negotiator wants to look good to his or her constituents back home and may adopt a hard-line stance to satisfy groups that desire an outcome that narrowly favors their own interests.

Trade negotiations often exhibit the highest degree of domestic involvement in international negotiations because of the impact trade policy has

> **KEY TERM**
>
> **Two-Level Game**  A term used to characterize the double set of negotiations that must be carried out both at the domestic level and at the international level.

on jobs and the general everyday economic existence of many sectors and individuals within a country (see the box on NAFTA). In the United States, the Constitution gives both houses of Congress a role in trade negotiations. Called non-self-executing congressional-executive agreements, trade agreements require congressional approval by each house after the president signs them. What this means in simple political terms is that many more actors and interests are involved before, during, and after trade negotiations.

The so-called fast-track authorization process in American trade legislation and associated trade negotiations is designed to ensure that consultation takes place between the executive branch and members of Congress throughout the bargaining process, not just at the very end. Assuming consultation takes place, the agreements are to be speedily approved by Congress. If the executive unit fails to engage in this periodic consultation, Congress can revoke the fast-track authorization and make the trade negotiation process more cumbersome for the president's negotiating team by requiring a much more difficult evaluation and approval process throughout the negotiations.

---

**KEY TERM**

**Fast Track** Authorization that assures the U.S. president of a congressional vote without amendments on trade negotiations if Congress has been consulted throughout the process.

---

At other times, domestic actors will have sufficient influence to lay out bargaining guidelines prior to negotiations, limiting those directly involved to the pursuit of only certain options during the talks. For example, during the intermediate-range nuclear forces (INF) negotiations under the Reagan administration, other political players in the United States—particularly in the Pentagon—prevented the primary American INF negotiator, Paul Nitze, from cementing the gentlemen's agreement he had made with his Soviet counterpart during their now famous "walk in the woods." Even though the overall force levels they had agreed to would have given the Americans a numerical advantage in total INF warheads over the Soviets in the European theater, Nitze was not able to sell the agreement to hawks in the Reagan administration. The Pentagon insisted that some Pershing II ballistic missiles with quick strike times remain deployed as part of the agreement—no matter what the ultimate warhead advantage for the United States would otherwise be. The "walk in the woods" agreement allowed the United States to deploy only slower-flying ground-launched cruise missiles (GLCMs) in Europe. Once it was clear that the Reagan administration would not accept the proposal, the Soviets publicly rejected it as well.

One could also argue that the Bush administration's repeated assertions that Saddam Hussein's Iraq possessed weapons of mass destruction (WMD) foreclosed a set of more peaceful conflict resolution options in 2002–2003. In fact, by the time that Secretary of State Colin Powell, a moderate voice within the early Bush team, made his now famous February 5, 2003, speech at the United Nations, few options other than military force were still being seriously discussed (at least in the United States). Thus, by laying out the case that Iraq possessed substantial WMD and that Iraq was linked to the al-Qaeda terrorist network, the Bush administration was able to convince enough members of Congress that the use of force was the only real option in dealing with Saddam Hussein and Iraq.

Within the two-level game framework, Putnam explains that the success or failure of negotiations depends on the existence of overlap between perceptions of acceptable outcomes at both levels of negotiation. He calls this overlap a win-set. The boundaries of a win-set are conditioned by the distribution of power, the preferences, and the possible coalitions among level-two constituents. Of course, the influence of these level-two actors on the negotiations will vary depending on the type of political system in which they are operating. Decision makers from authoritarian political systems, for instance, have more power to pursue certain negotiation objectives unilaterally than do decision makers from democratic ones. It is also possible that the negotiators operating at level one may manipulate the outcome to try to appease their international negotiation partners, as well as domestic pressure subgroups, even when the interests of each seem diametrically opposed. In the Kyoto negotiations, one explanation for why the United States signed the pact, despite the opposition of many powerful domestic forces, may have been a Clinton administration calculation that the agreement was unrealistic in its targets and that therefore no attempt would ever be made to implement it anyway. The Clinton team knew other countries would also confront this fact, so by signing the pact, the administration was thus able to look as though it supported the accord, even though that may not have been the case.

> **KEY TERM**
>
> **Win-Set** The existence of overlap between perceptions of acceptable outcomes at both levels of a two-level negotiation.

Put simply, for international agreements to be achieved, some overlap must exist between the set of outcomes acceptable to the international negotiators at level one and those preferred by the groups involved at level two. Without overlap, no final international agreement is possible, either because the domestic constituency will not approve the agreement made at the international level or because what is acceptable as defined by the involved domestic actors proves unacceptable to the other involved country or countries.

It is also worth noting that the open pursuit of international negotiation may constrain the ability of negotiators to derive agreement. That is one reason why secrecy is often viewed as an important part of the negotiation process, as negotiators work to develop creative solutions free from domestic influences that may constrain creativity and the open discussion of interesting options for conflict resolution. Lieberfeld (2008), for instance, argues that the 1993 Oslo accord between Israel and the PLO was possible only because of secrecy. In addition, the failure to implement a final outcome from that accord was partly due to the fact that the latter part of the process was negotiated in the open—where pressure could be brought to bear on the negotiating parties.

## NAFTA Negotiations in the United States: A Two-Level Game

Few cases of international negotiation offer more evidence of the impact of domestic politics on the process and outcome of international negotiations than the negotiations and subsequent debate in the United States over the signing and passage in 1992 of the North American Free Trade Agreement (NAFTA), which allows the free flow of goods and services among Canada, Mexico, and the United States. Creating the world's largest open market, NAFTA appeared to be one more milestone in a long foreign policy career for President George H. W. Bush. From a political perspective, however, the pursuit of NAFTA just prior to an election year provided the opposing candidates, Bill Clinton and Ross Perot, with just the issue to hit home on Bush's apparent lack of concern for domestic affairs. Negatively affected industries lobbied hard against the agreement. Even though econometric analysis showed a net increase in jobs for the U.S. economy, many sectors would still be severely impacted by shifts in production facilities and lower-cost competition from south of the border.

In the United States, concerns over NAFTA focused on three main areas—all related in some way to the effects of the agreement on American jobs—demonstrating the strong domestic character of the issue: low Mexican wages, weak Mexican labor standards, and weak Mexican environmental regulations. Labor unions were concerned about the weaker labor laws in Mexico and how that might lead to the export of American jobs by firms looking to establish lower-cost production facilities while still enjoying tariff-free access to the American market. This position was echoed by environmentalists, who feared that firms might relocate production facilities south of the border to take advantage of weaker environmental restrictions.

Thus, when the 1992 presidential campaign rolled around, Bush's opponents were able to latch on to his support of NAFTA as an exploitable political issue. Ross Perot, running as an independent candidate for president, spoke of the "giant sucking sound" that could be heard as American jobs were siphoned to the south. He hit this point hard and rallied significant public opposition to NAFTA through his flamboyant, populist approach to economic matters. While not denouncing NAFTA outright, candidate Bill Clinton pointed to its deficiencies and promised to negotiate a series of side agreements, aimed squarely at assuaging the concerns of crucial domestic political interests that would help win approval for NAFTA in Congress.

After Clinton's election victory, the worker rights and environmental side agreements were negotiated and ultimately signed at a ceremony attended by former presidents Carter, Ford, and Bush. Later that fall, President Clinton held off the opposition—still led by Perot and many Democratic leaders in Congress—to congressional approval of the pact and narrowly won its passage. In many ways, the conglomeration of political actors that supported and opposed NAFTA was a testament to the old adage "politics makes strange bedfellows."

## The Involvement of Domestic Actors

Earlier in the chapter, it was noted that different international issues are important to different actors or subgroups at the domestic political level. Looking at the relationship of issue salience to the number and types of political actors that get involved in an international negotiation provides another layer of complexity for the salience framework built throughout this chapter.

Referring back to the NAFTA example (see box earlier in the chapter), those negotiations present a good example of what can be called a mixed domestic-international outcome. Perceived national salience in America was very high, leading a wide array of domestic groups to enter the fray. Negotiators for the United States worked to achieve the win-set discussed earlier, trying to find outcomes that would be acceptable to legislators, labor unions, and environmental interest groups, as well as to Canada and Mexico. This extensive domestic-input factor can be a help or a hindrance to negotiators (Mo 1994, 1995). Obviously, it complicates the process by adding another layer of complexity, but it can also provide leverage with the international parties. If a proposal is not acceptable back home, a negotiator can use the threat of domestic objections to try to squeeze more concessions out of a negotiation partner, particularly when that partner is especially anxious for a quick agreement.

The classic negotiation case in U.S. foreign policy annals is that of the Cuban missile crisis. The stakes have arguably never been higher than during this thirteen-day period, when American and Soviet citizens awaited the outcome, perched on the precipice of nuclear war. Yet at the decision-making level, it presents a case of what could be termed a chief of government model—decision making very much under the control of high-level leaders on both sides of the table (Trumbore and Boyer 2000). As is often the case in crisis situations, other domestic actors backed away from or were excluded from the negotiation arena, leaving the positioning to the national leaders in the White House and the Kremlin. Ahmer (2005) also shows at a theoretical level that the degree of chief of government control over policy in two-level settings will vary depending on the type of electoral structure and constituencies that the leader must serve. Thus, leaders in parliamentary systems are likely more constrained in their decision making and negotiation leeway than are leaders who are elected from national constituencies.

The NAFTA case, then, exemplifies an issue that is highly salient for a broad range of domestic actors, whereas the Cuban missile crisis, which was also highly salient for domestic interests, included only a small circle of involved actors—although admittedly very high-level attention. The relationship of salience to domestic involvement can play out in other ways as well. When a broad cross section of citizens does not perceive the negotiations to be very important—as in noncrisis environments with such economic matters as currency valuations—negotiation policies and progress are often in the hands of small groups, far removed from the upper echelons of political leadership. Often, these matters are very routine or highly specialized.

Among the great number of negotiations in the international arena that capture the attention of neither broad cross sections of society nor top leadership are the many routine matters that administrators or bureaucrats handle on a day-to-day basis. Negotiations over the implementation of foreign aid between donor bureaucrats and recipient country officials almost always fit squarely here. Normally, the relative lack of attention paid means that the narrow group making the decisions ends up with a wide degree of policy-making autonomy and operates largely outside the purview of the public and most other political actors.

In international monetary policy, the interplay that exists among central banks, commercial banks, and legislators in many financial capitals of the world provides a good example of an exclusive club working on a highly specialized issue. In Germany, Japan, and the United States, individuals from these various influential posts negotiate among themselves first at the domestic level and then at the international level. Thus, the stakes may be highly salient for that small group of bankers, but monetary policies have historically been issues of low salience for the general public. It should be noted, however, that low salience for monetary policy may be changing in the aftermath of the 2008–2009 global economic crisis. Given the irresponsible bank policies that played a central role in creating the financial turmoil and the number of people around the world who saw their retirement savings decline in 2008, monetary policy has been launched into higher salience—at least for the short-term.

## Summary

It should be very clear that the answer to the question of who gets involved in negotiations at both the domestic and international levels is determined by how salient the central issue is for political actors. In negotiations among Canada, the United States, and Mexico over the environmental area of NAFTA, the logical actors, based on the domestic salience of the issue, were representatives of the respective governments, of environmental groups—domestic and transnational—of organized labor, and of business groups. The "green" groups worried about lax environmental standards spreading northward, labor groups worried that jobs would move to where the standards are lowest, and business groups wanted to make sure that environmental restrictions would not be made more stringent by virtue of the pact. Returning to the concepts presented at the beginning of this chapter, it is difficult to classify environmental legislation according to the high/low politics scheme, as it is certainly of high political importance to the actors just listed, even if of little interest to many others. More precisely, it is the salience of an issue—its resonance in the domestic arena—that determines the nature and number of actors that become involved.

In addition, the relative power of the domestic actors involved in negotiations on the issue must be taken into account. Some issues that are not broadly salient across an entire political system can gain high-level attention because of the action of a small group of domestic actors. The change in travel plans by Vice President Gore regarding the Kyoto meetings illustrates this point by revealing the relative power held by environmental groups in the United States. Moreover, President George W. Bush's speech in 2005 that labeled killing in Darfur "genocide" is widely viewed as the president's bowing to intense political pressure from some lawmakers and human rights groups to speak out on the issue. This speech also allowed Bush to diffuse some of that pressure by making a rhetorical shift, even if not a real one with demonstrative action ("In Break with UN, Bush Calls Sudan Killings Genocide," 6/2/05, washingtonpost.com).

What the examples in this chapter have shown is that no simple classification guidelines exist for understanding how issues affect negotiations. The argument is made for a more complex approach to understanding how issues define negotiations in terms of actor involvement, the intensity of the negotiations themselves, and the possibility for compromise or conflict throughout the negotiation process. The next chapter defines negotiations even further by examining the strategy and tactics used by negotiating parties to achieve their goals.

\*   \*   \*

*For a list of related web resources for this chapter, consult*
*www.icons.umd.edu/negotiating/links.htm.*

# 5

# The Moves

Negotiation is a game of strategy. As with most games, making the right strategic choices is sometimes the result of luck, but more often it is the result of the expert movement of the game pieces around the board. Having explored the board, the players, and the stakes in earlier chapters, it is now time to examine the range of possible moves in the game of negotiation—strategies and tactics used in the international arena.

Making moves that will further negotiation goals involves first devising a plan and then choosing tactics to implement it. In the recurrent phases of the North Korean nuclear crisis highlighted in chapter 1, for example, U.S. administrations from Clinton to Obama have worked to force the North Korean leaders to back down, discontinue their nuclear program, and allow inspections. The tactics used by both sides have included the following: talks of preemptive strike and other strong rhetoric, North Korean incursions into the demilitarized zone, missile tests, nuclear weapons tests, and the push for negotiations (in different forms) from both sides.

Although it sometimes appears that a particular negotiation outcome was obvious from the beginning, in fact a range of choices is available to each party at any point in a negotiation. This chapter will explore strategic choices, first by representing them through a number of simple games and then by examining the layers of complexity associated with real-world decision making. The chapter concludes with a comparative analysis of the primary strategic approaches to international negotiation and the tactics associated with each approach.

## Modeling Strategic Choices

Negotiation models based in game theory illustrate the array of choices one actor has at any given moment, as well as how outcomes are dependent on the choices both or all of the negotiating parties make. Thus, the modeling of strategy and strategic choices is a good way to begin to understand this most critical of negotiation tasks. Because game models presume perfect or full information about the other parties' preferences (see figures 5.1 and 5.2), they are by nature abstractions and simplifications of the real world, but they do help isolate the most important components of negotiation situations. The chapter begins by presenting simple constructions of available choices and then moves on to include additional factors to bring the models closer to real-world complexity.

| KEY TERM |
| --- |
| **Sequential Game**   A game modeled so that each player makes a decision at a different point in time. |

Since it is important to develop an understanding of negotiation through game theory in a relatively straightforward way, the examples presented here focus on two main types of negotiation games: simultaneous games, which illustrate the interdependence of each choice on the choices the other players make, and sequential games, which reveal the mounting complexities inherent in action-reaction decision making. The intention is to get at basic mechanisms of choice as a means of explaining strategy.

### Simultaneous Games

In all games, the decisions one player makes are affected by the possible decisions others will make. This issue is a very acute problem for decision makers who find themselves in simultaneous-game situations. It is also a problem, as illustrated later, in sequential games as actors move along the limbs of a decision tree, though not to quite the same extent or in quite the same way as in simultaneous games. This is why decision making in simultaneous games is called interdependent decision making. When decisions are made in an interdependent setting, high levels of uncertainty exist, and that uncertainty becomes the defining characteristic of the decision-making process during the negotiations. This section focuses on two simultaneous games—the prisoner's dilemma game and the game of chicken—that have been widely applied to international relations situations.

| KEY TERM |
| --- |
| **Simultaneous Game**   A game modeled so that the players must make their decisions at the same time. |

*Prisoner's Dilemma*

In the classic story of the prisoner's dilemma, the police arrest two suspects for a crime they are alleged to have committed together. The prisoners are held in separate cells and are unable to communicate with each other. They are then individually presented with an offer by the police detectives who are interrogating them about the crime. If one prisoner turns over evidence and testifies against the other prisoner, then the one providing the testimony will go free and enjoy the full proceeds of the crime. Both prisoners realize, however, that if each remains silent, the prosecutors will not be able to make a case against them, and both will go free. Being thieves in the first place, both also know that their collaborator is not entirely trustworthy. Thus, there is a risk that the other prisoner will be the one to squeal, sending his or her colleague straight to prison.

Figure 5.1 illustrates the choices and respective numerical payoffs associated with each option available to the prisoners. Each prisoner is presented with two choices: remain silent or squeal on the other prisoner. If both prisoners remain silent, they both go free and ultimately split the proceeds from their crime (the payoff of +5 for each). If they both choose to squeal on the other, then both get a prison sentence of two years (represented by the payoff of –2). Each prisoner confronts the possibility that the other prisoner will squeal and produce a five-year prison sentence for the partner (the –5 payoff). Squealing may also yield personal freedom and the ability to lay sole claim to any hidden loot. Faced with this dilemma, the suspects squeal on each other, and both end up in prison for the crime in the classic ending to this story. This is an outcome both suspects could have avoided if they had trusted each other and kept silent. The problem is, however, that each prisoner can see that squealing is the better option, whether the other prisoner squeals or remains silent. In other words, it is the dominant strategy—better for the individual under both possible situations. Herein lies the difficulty: individually dominant strategies can lead to worse group outcomes—hence the conflict between individual and group rationality.

Many international negotiations, from various global environmental concerns to disputes over markets and free-trade agreements, have been modeled as prisoner's dilemma situations (Lazano 2007; Kaul et al. 2003; Barrett 2003; Conybeare 1986; Sandler 1997). With environmental issues, for example, the comparison to the prisoner's dilemma rests in the fact that each country involved in the negotiations wishes to promote global environmental quality—in theory. However, no country entirely trusts the other countries involved in the negotiations or wants to bear the cost of implementing and enforcing environmental regulations within its borders. In addition, as discussed in chapter 4, there may also be powerful domestic

**Figure 5.1   The Prisoner's Dilemma Game**

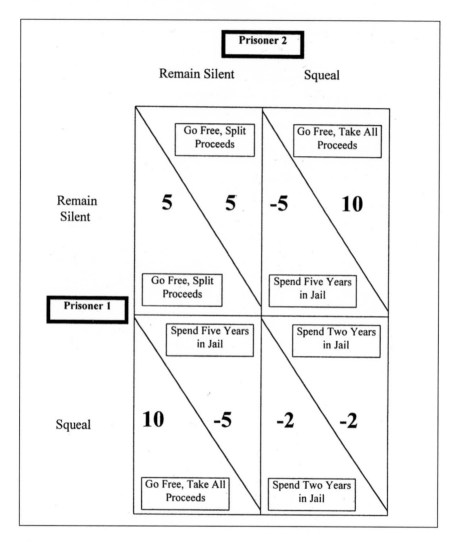

groups pushing for the adoption of policy that favors their own commercial interests at the expense of environmental quality. For example, when focusing on climate change, many business interests oppose strict limits on carbon emissions because such a policy change will make it more costly for them to produce their products. It is worth noting, though, that some companies have made the strategic decision in recent years to adopt methods of production that are consciously environmentally friendly and more carbon neutral. For instance, Subaru, the Japanese automobile manufacturer that has recently sited American production facilities in Indiana, has waged a high-profile advertising campaign touting its zero-landfill output at that facility.

But even though most of us have a basic desire for a healthy environment, many do not wish to bear the cost of environmental regulation and in effect choose to squeal on the others by polluting. This collective squealing results in a negative outcome for the world community that might have been avoided if the game and its choices were structured differently and if the actors trusted each other to a higher degree. The possibility for cooperation in such instances will be discussed later in this chapter, especially as it relates to recent developments surrounding the two primary case studies.

### Chicken

The drama of the second simultaneous game, chicken, unfolds as follows: late at night, two drivers sit in cars facing each other from a distance of about half a mile. Someone on the side of the road swings a flashlight to signal both drivers to start driving toward one another as fast as they can. As they get closer, each driver hopes the other will swerve off the road and become the chicken in this test of wills. If neither swerves, the cars crash head-on and both drivers are killed in the high-speed collision. But, in a perverse way, a crash shows both drivers as strong willed and as winners. If one of them swerves, that driver is branded the chicken, humiliated in front of the onlookers, and seen as the loser, even though in a very real sense the chicken is the driver who spared the lives of both players in this game of survival, will, and humiliation.

Figure 5.2 lays out the logic of chicken, illustrating the possible choices and payoffs for each driver. The potential for disaster is manifest when both players drive straight, ending in death for both (–30 payoffs for both). Each player is faced with the decision to risk embarrassment and loss of the game, which, if experienced individually, has a negative payoff (–10). Alternatively, a player can choose to risk his or her life (payoff of –30) for the win (payoff of 10). Unlike the players in the prisoner's dilemma, the players in chicken do not have dominant strategies (those better for the individual under both possible situations), so the outcome is not as predictable. In order to win, both players must calculate how strong willed the other player is and try to push the game one moment beyond where they think the other will take it.

Chicken is often used as a model for negotiations during international crises (Snyder and Deising 1977). Two or more states involved in an international crisis are engaged in a spiraling game of chicken that may escalate to war and ultimately threaten the survival of some or all of the actors.

**Figure 5.2   The Game of Chicken**

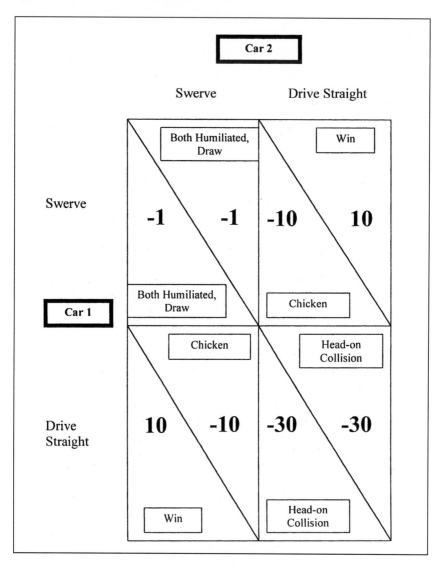

During a crisis, diplomats raise the ante by threatening the use of military force, imposing economic sanctions, and bringing many other tools of state-craft to bear to try to force the other nations to swerve off the chosen road of international affairs that formed the basis of the crisis in the first place.

The classic example of this type of brinkmanship is the 1962 Cuban missile crisis between the United States and the Soviet Union. In the early fall of 1962, when American U-2 spy planes photographed evidence of the installation of Soviet intermediate-range ballistic missiles on the island of Cuba, U.S. decision makers—under the leadership of President John F. Kennedy—engaged in a course of action that ultimately forced the Soviets to withdraw the missiles from the island. Tension between the superpowers was extremely high during this crisis, and Robert Kennedy, the president's brother and the U.S. attorney general at the time, later recalled that "the noose was tightening on all of us, on Americans, on mankind, and that the bridges of escape were crumbling" (1969, 97). In the end, after a series of transglobal negotiations between the White House and the Kremlin, the implementation of a U.S. naval blockade around Cuba, and a pledge by President Kennedy to remove American missiles from Turkey, the Soviets swerved and agreed to remove their missiles from the island. The eventual resolution required that an additional issue—the U.S. missiles based in Turkey—be put on the table to defuse the crisis and give the Soviet Union an opportunity to save face and avoid the complete-humiliation payoff of the chicken matrix. This is issue linkage, as described in chapter 2.

The recurrent North Korean crises can also be modeled as a chicken game. Clearly, much of the anxiety surrounding the North Korean nuclear program is caused by the perception that Kim Jong Il is not a rational leader with whom others can reason. Thus, diplomats worry that his chosen course of action, whatever that might be, is not one that can be deterred. These worries were fueled when North Korea twice tested nuclear weapons in spring 2009. Although this drama has not yet played out, the fear is that North Korea will not veer off and instead continue on the road to direct nuclear confrontation—possibly even using those weapons. To follow through with the chicken analogy, the opportunity for the crisis participants to crash into each other has been averted thus far, with either or both sides veering off before catastrophe.

In simultaneous games such as those described here, each side must make choices at the same time as the other. This simultaneous decision-making setting means that an understanding of the preferences held by the other side is extremely important, even if information is difficult to obtain in any kind of definitive way. That is why research, intelligence gathering, and analysis have become such important parts of the negotiation process, as all parties to negotiations work diligently to understand the incentives and disincentives (game payoffs) that negotiating counterparts perceive when they enter the negotiation arena. The problem of understanding an actor's negotiation preferences in more detail will be covered later in this chapter. Next, the discussion turns to sequential games and the different negotiation dynamics they present.

## Sequential Games

If prisoner's dilemma and chicken represent freeze-frame snapshots of the choices available to negotiators at any particular moment, sequential games illustrate how a series of choices plays out over time. Sequential games model action-reaction processes to reveal the ways international actors react to problems and other stimuli from international affairs. They also demonstrate how those reactions lead to other reactions by even more actors throughout the system.

Traditionally, arms races (Downs, Rocke, and Siverson 1986) and many conflict processes (Brecher and Wilkenfeld 2000; Wilkenfeld 1991) have been modeled in this way. Arms races, for instance, usually begin when one country feels threatened by the actions or military might of another country. The threatened country decides to buy or build new weapons to increase its own sense of security. But as this country becomes more secure through a weapons buildup, the country that provided the initial threat will likely begin to feel less secure and in turn will want to build up its armed forces. So as both sides respond to the military threats their counterpart poses, neither side becomes more secure over the long term, and both sides engage in a conflict spiral.

In 2008, the planned U.S. deployment of its missile defense in Poland was perceived by Russia as upsetting the military balance in Europe. Some even suggested that this deployment might spawn a preemptive strike against the missile system by Russia, though this worst-case scenario was avoided. The 1998 detonations of nuclear weapons first by India and then by Pakistan also reflect the rejuvenation of a conflict spiral that had long been dormant. And given the tensions in the region centering on the war in Afghanistan, keeping India and Pakistan from open hostilities is an important international security goal.

These types of arms-race cycles have traditionally been termed a security dilemma. Negotiation can play a part in changing the dynamics of an escalating process as both sides seek to reduce tensions—and expenditures on weapons—through negotiating limits to weapons buildups or reductions in weapons stockpiles. SALT and START between the United States and the Soviet Union during the Cold War resulted from their joint understanding of the folly of this spiraling arms race.

Sequential choices can be graphically depicted in a decision tree that lays out the options available to negotiators on both sides of the bargaining table at particular points in time. Figure 5.3 depicts a decision tree that models very simply the choices available to the United States and its allies versus North Korean decision makers during the series of nuclear crises that began in the 1990s and continue until the present day. Clearly, it is not possible to present all the available options and decision points in the process,

**Figure 5.3  Hypothetical North Korean Nuclear Crisis Decision Tree**

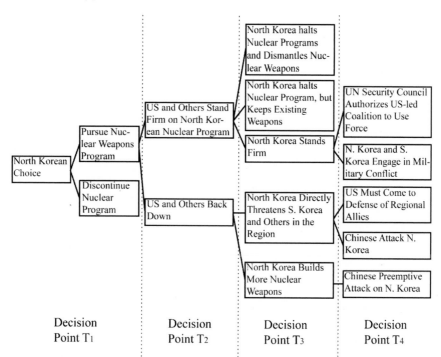

but this figure shows how a choice made at the first decision-making point, T1, constrains the choices available for the other countries' decision makers at the second decision-making point, T2, and beyond.

This decision tree displays at time T1 the choices that the North Korean leaders faced in the early 1990s: 1) continue to pursue the nuclear weapons program, or 2) discontinue it under Western pressure. As the tree shows, if they had chosen to stop the program at that decision point, the crisis would have terminated at the end of T1 and would not have become a protracted crisis.

As detailed in chapter 1, however, North Korea chose to continue its program and presented American and other Western countries with two basic choices at T2: 1) to stand firm on the position that North Korea should halt its nuclear program, or 2) to back down and allow North Korea to continue to threaten countries in the region with its nuclear arsenal in a strategically important region of the world. Repeatedly, the stand-firm approach was chosen, leaving North Korea with (at least) the three possible options listed on the top tree branches at T3. The exact outcome at T3 or T4 has not yet been determined, and negotiations continue toward the resolution of this recurrent crisis. More than likely, when all the negotiations are finished on this issue, a choice not laid out in figure 5.3 will be adopted as the final outcome. It is to be hoped that it will be an outcome that averts the use of force by all parties and especially the use of nuclear weapons by North Korea against one of its neighbors.

From the standpoint of negotiation strategy, decision-tree mapping of the options available to the negotiators provides a way to understand the progression of choices that might emerge from an initial decision. This type of strategic decision making can be done by evaluating a decision tree in the reverse direction. This method has been described as the "look ahead and reason back" approach to strategy in sequential games (Dixit and Nalebuff 1991, 34). In the context of the decision tree in figure 5.3 and the hypothetical options it displays, the negotiator must first look at the possible outcomes at T3 and T4 and rank those outcomes from best to worst. During the North Korean crises, American decision makers—and probably most others on the UN Security Council—would have ranked the options producing an end to the crisis in T3 as the most favorable to American and UN interests. Those outcomes are, in rank order of preference:

1. North Korea halts its nuclear program and dismantles its weapons.
2. North Korea halts its nuclear program and keeps its existing weapons.

The third option in the top half of the decision tree at T3 (North Korea stands firm) is a decidedly less desirable outcome. Nonetheless, when looking at the set of possible outcomes in T3 and T4, the choices for the United States at T2 prompt the United States to choose the upper option, as it has a greater likelihood of producing a desirable solution to the series of crises. If the lower option (United States and others back down) is selected, the crisis is more likely to persist, and a variety of undesirable outcomes is possible.

For the North Koreans, the desirable options would likely push their decision makers in opposite directions from the U.S. choices. As each side examines the potential outcomes and their preferences, negotiators try to make choices that push the other side in the direction of their own preferences. At T1, North Korea chooses to continue its nuclear program because that choice at least gives it some chance of winning the crisis. At T2, however, the United States chooses to stand firm against the North Korean program, as this moves toward choices that are less likely to benefit North Korea and more likely to produce acceptable outcomes for the United States and its partners. Thus, by looking ahead to the set of possible endings to the negotiation episode as shown in T4, negotiators are able to make informed "backward looking" choices and adopt bargaining strategies that have the greatest likelihood of providing an optimal outcome for them.

As a result, it is necessary to gain enough information (or intelligence) about the preferences of one's counterpart to be able to predict with a fair degree of accuracy what choice that opponent will make when faced with the options at any point on the tree. Both simultaneous and sequential games allow for the analysis of negotiation strategies. Figuring out how to resolve the game in a way favorable for one's side depends on how well each side is able to manage the degree of uncertainty that exists during the playing of the game. The following section presents an examination of the strategies negotiation actors can adopt to manage uncertainty.

### Weighing Strategic Choices

A variety of factors exert an impact on an actor's choice when weighing the relative merits of a particular course of action during a negotiation. These factors include (1) how the actor defines the interests he or she represents; (2) the complexities of the negotiation situation and the ways it influences other relationships; and (3) the degree to which these complexities are linked to one another in ways that either provide opportunities to cooperate or sow the seeds of conflict.

### Defining Interests

At the heart of all the games described earlier is the assumption that individuals act in accordance with their own rational interests. An actor is expected to make decisions based on what are perceived to be the best choices vis-à-vis needs for welfare, satisfaction, security, and other key values. To act otherwise would be irrational and run counter to many traditional conceptions of human behavior. To put this point in the context of this book, negotiators and policy makers are assumed to make decisions on the basis of the interests and values held by their constituents, whether those interests are based in the nation-state or in the membership of some nonstate entity, such as Greenpeace. Making this assumption about the relationship between rationality and interests provides social scientists with a way of understanding the logic of choice.

It is common in social science to utilize a rough dichotomy when conceptualizing interests: a narrow view of national (or actor) interest and a broader, or enlightened, view of national interest (Bobrow and Boyer 2004; Lumsdaine 1993). A narrow definition of interest usually occurs when decision makers and negotiators are most concerned with how a particular situation affects political and economic forces at home. For example, at the 1992 Rio Earth Summit, President Bush declined to sign the biodiversity and global warming pacts developed at that meeting. His decision was based on the impact that these two accords were expected to have on American domestic business interests; in other words, the Bush administration was concerned primarily about the costs American companies would have to bear in the form of pollution control and abatement, as well as other environment-friendly practices, to abide by the agreements. This decision not to sign, while rational from a domestic point of view, was very unpopular in the international community. It was a strong blow against international efforts to act on collective interests regarding global environmental quality. Similar reasoning underlies the continued reluctance of many developed countries to pursue the Kyoto restrictions actively, as they may hurt their countries' ability to compete commercially. As noted earlier, though, some businesses are deciding to "go green" as a strategic choice to win over customers through their environmental awareness (Esty and Winston 2006). Whether this trend will continue and generate profits for these firms is yet to be determined.

To return to the prisoner's dilemma game, it is usually argued that conceptions of narrow interests explain why the equilibrium—or natural—outcomes in the game are negative or suboptimal ones (prison for both suspects in the prisoner's dilemma). In the traditional conceptions of the games, both players are out to safeguard their own narrow interests and thus make their decisions based on individual calculations. But if those interests are somehow transformed from narrow ones to broader ones, then greater opportunity for mutual benefit and positive outcomes becomes possible. This means ending up in the upper-left-hand cell of the game, as displayed in figure 5.1. In the prisoner's dilemma, both would escape punishment for the crime. (The box provides a contemporary example of these kinds of choices, with their associated risks and potential payoffs.)

## A Climate Change Dilemma: An Economics-Environment Tradeoff?

It is commonplace for environmental politics and negotiations, specifically, to be placed within a prisoner's dilemma framework. In most global environmental negotiations, decision makers are faced with the choice of pursuing policies that maximize their countries' short-term economic self-interest versus policies that will help improve the global environment over the longer term. In the short term, states must absorb the economic costs of environmentally friendly policies (such as restrictions on $CO_2$ emissions from fossil fuel consumption) while they are trying to compete with other countries for markets and other economic opportunities. This is the apparent dilemma facing decision makers as they consider the implications of global climate change. Why should one country impose restrictions on $CO_2$ emissions if others might not?

Wouldn't such a choice put that country at a disadvantage economically? Certainly, the 2001 decision by the Bush administration not to submit the Kyoto protocol to the Senate for approval was based largely on this set of choices. As this book goes to press, the verdict is still out on whether the Obama administration will be fully able to reverse Bush policy on climate change.

The basic choices and possible outcomes of this prisoner's dilemma–type quandary are as follows. We use the United States as the primary "prisoner" because it has played the most central "defection" roles in recent years on climate change (see the payoffs and matrix references in figure 5.1).

- Sucker payoff for the United States (the –5 payoff value): the United States decides to abide by Kyoto targets and few others do so; thus, the United States is left in a noncompetitive position internationally by having to absorb higher energy and production costs for nonfossil fuel reliance.
- Sucker payoff for the other countries (like the EU in recent statements) (the –5 payoff value): the EU decides to abide by Kyoto targets, the United States does not; the EU is left at a competitive disadvantage economically.
- Temptation payoff for the United States (the +10 payoff value): the United States sees the chance to pursue economic gains while others abide by Kyoto targets.
- Temptation payoff for the other countries (the +10 payoff value): the EU and others see a chance for short-term economic gain and exceed Kyoto targets.
- Optimal theoretic game outcome (upper-left-hand cell): the United States and others abide by Kyoto targets; all compete economically on a similar footing, and gains are made on the global cimate change front.
- Suboptimal equilibrium outcome (lower-right-hand cell): the United States and others all decide to continue at current carbon emission levels; they can then compete on a similar economic footing, but environmental quality suffers now and into the future.

It is interesting to note that, for the moment, the world has landed in a policy situation where the United States is getting the temptation payoff and others may be getting the sucker payoff. This situation could change if the Obama administration is able to follow its campaign rhetoric and undertake a dramatic shift in U.S. climate change policy. But it is worth remembering from our discussion in chapter 4 that domestic politics plays a significant role in shaping the negotiation options available to decision makers. Thus, Obama and other industrialized country leaders will be required to continue to build domestic coalitions that will support more progressive climate change policies.

A number of forces prompt the development of broader conceptions of interest among negotiation actors. Some of these factors depend on the ways actors identify with others involved in the same game. For instance, it is easy to imagine that members of an alliance that has endured over many years will be able to define collective interests far more easily than will newer groups of countries that have not had similar long-term relationships. Along these lines, constructivists (see, for instance, Mattern 2005) argue that commonality of interest and identity are constructed over time through common experiences and processes. Thus, it follows that countries with long-term relationships (e.g., alliances or other organizational memberships) will have higher levels of common interest when confronted with the need for collective international problem-solving.

Broad conceptions of interest have also been positively influenced by the creation of international institutions and the development of international norms that govern behavior in some issue areas, as discussed in more detail in chapter 3. The identification of collective interest in relation to nuclear nonproliferation is one such example. The norms and procedures developed since the 1968 signing of the Nuclear Non-Proliferation Treaty show evidence that narrow national conceptions of interest have increasingly become subordinate—for most states—to the desire to safeguard humankind from the proliferation of weapons of mass destruction. The international outcry in response to India's testing of four nuclear weapons in May 1998—and Pakistan's subsequent detonation of five—demonstrates the degree to which international sentiment has turned against the national right to possess such weapons. There is, of course, still a great deal of tension between the narrow and broad interests in this case and others like it. The continued furor over the North Korean nuclear crises is another case in point. Many leaders, including North Korea, still argue stridently for national interpretations of defense, prosperity, and other key values, but no one can deny that interdependence has grown in the international system over the last century and, with it, so have institutions for collective problem solving.

Finally, the determination of narrow or broad interests can also be influenced by the time frame that is considered to be important to decision makers and negotiators. Distinctions between short-term and long-term perspectives are constant factors in international environmental negotiations (e.g., Rio in 1992, Kyoto in 1997, and other ongoing activities of the Intergovermental Panel on Climate Change [IPCC]). Put simply, short-term interests lead decision makers to pursue agreements that address the immediate economic impact environmental restrictions would have on commercial interests. The comments by American business groups, cited in chapter 4, regarding the impact of the Kyoto Protocol on global warming are a case in point. Because many environmental issues do not have direct contemporary effects and because they will become an observable problem only in the future, it is difficult for negotiators to trade their immediate interests for others that are far more abstract. There is a broad, long-term interest in stemming the tide of global warming and the climatic effects it will have, but it is difficult to take this view at the expense of profits and jobs for domestic firms and workers in the shorter term.

### Factoring in Complexities

The logic of decision making, as conveyed through game theory, helps illustrate the interdependence of decisions in the negotiation arena. In addition, a number of characteristics or variables at work in a negotiation situation can play out in ways that complicate the negotiations. The following factors—some of which were introduced in the negotiation checklist in chapter 2—complicate negotiations and impact their success. Negotiation or bargaining environments become more complex under these conditions:

- Actors and issues are added to the negotiations, or coalitions form.
- Additional issues are linked to an original issue.
- There is a lack of domestic or constituent consensus about the negotiation goals and/or approach.
- The negotiators themselves do not have decision-making latitude but must check back with superiors throughout the negotiations.
- The goals and preferences of the negotiation team change during the negotiations due to domestic or international pressure.
- Negotiations involve a mixture of conflictual and cooperative motives or goals.
- Information about other parties' goals and preferences is lacking.
- The situation is perceived as a crisis, thereby increasing the pressure on negotiators.

These factors of complexity illustrate that even when negotiation goals are clearly articulated—and this is not always the case for international actors—a number of forces can thwart their realization. To assume that actor interests are ordered, stable, and prioritized is often unrealistic. The two-level game shows that domestic political factors can heavily impact the international negotiation process. The game of chicken shows that actors are also at times confronted with high levels of uncertainty about what choices their negotiation counterparts will make. Interdependent decision making implies that the decisions negotiation actors make are intertwined with each other, but it also means that change by one party makes decisions for others more difficult and outcomes more indeterminate.

## Accounting for Long-Term Relationships

Any single negotiation dialogue takes place within the context of the larger relationship between the actors involved. This is part of what we called in chapter 2 the legacy of negotiations. This connection can be useful in a strategic context when negotiators are having trouble seeing ways to resolve conflicting interests at the negotiation table. Negotiators can get a sense of the bigger picture by adding issues (and even actors) from another common negotiation arena to the one in progress (Kremenyuk 2002; Sebenius 1984) and by considering the longer-term impact of current decisions (Axelrod 1984).

A historical example of the addition of issues can be found in what were called the offset agreements reached by the United States and West Germany during the 1960s over military basing rights. While the United States was providing the dominant share of alliance defense in Europe, West Germany agreed to make offset payments to the United States to help defray the cost of the stationing and maintenance of American forces on German soil. In game theory terms, these are often referred to as side payments. In this way, the American and German negotiators agreed to link the issue of defense of the European central front directly with financial issues. Even though Defense Department officials had been willing to bear the military burden, members of Congress were not as willing, so continuation of the U.S. security role in the region was at least partly sustained by linking defense with finance. Put simply, the Germans made payments so that members of Congress would not put up as much of a fuss over the deployment of American forces in Germany during the Cold War.

In game theory, awareness of the impact of repeated play has been called the "shadow of the future" (Axelrod and Keohane 1986, 232–234). Much work has been done on the degree to which negotiators' expectations about future dealings with their counterparts will influence negotiation behavior (Oye 1986). Findings suggest that where the expectation of repeated play is high, the likelihood of cooperative moves becomes greater.

---

**KEY TERM**

**Reciprocity** The practice by countries of making in-kind concessions to each other.

The various rounds of trade negotiations under the General Agreement on Tariffs and Trade (GATT)—established after World War II—provide an example of this dynamic. The GATT rounds progressively led to lower tariff barriers to international trade and were based on reciprocity on the part of the countries participating in the negotiations. The success in those negotiations is striking, with tariff barriers to trade reduced from an average of 57 percent in 1947 to an average of about 7 percent in the 1990s (Spero and Hart 2009). This long-term commitment to free trade on the part of GATT participants ultimately pushed the negotiators to create the World Trade Organization (WTO), which superseded GATT on January 1, 1995, as the primary international institution charged with monitoring and promoting free-trade practices around the globe. These negotiations are ongoing under the Doha round of talks, but have stalled on issues of agricultural subsidies and other non-tariff barriers to trade.

Awareness of this larger long-term relationship, however, can also produce an element of fear. Axelrod (1984, 127) calls this the impact of "tit-for-tat strategies." Again, in the game theory context, the threat that a negotiating partner might reciprocate a squeal payoff sometime in the future provides a negative incentive for such zero-sum strategizing. This can bolster the search for cooperative outcomes on the part of all involved.

## Implementing Strategy

The exploration of why decision making and strategy in the negotiation arena are so complex leads to the question of what it means to win in international negotiation. Most situations lend themselves either to zero-sum or non-zero-sum calculations of interest. Where collective interests are clear—for example, in regard to many environmental problems—the game is usually seen as non-zero-sum. Conversely, where military security is involved, the inclination is toward zero-sum interpretations. This leads negotiators to think, "I won't win here unless you lose." But as discussed previously, even some military-security situations are in reality non-zero-sum because of the problems identified in the security dilemma. As one actor builds arms, it produces short-term security for itself, short-term insecurity for its counterpart, and possibly long-term insecurity for all. In other words, since both parties ultimately lose, the arms buildup creates only the illusion of an "I win, you lose" outcome.

It is important to understand what kind of strategic approach makes sense in a negotiation situation. The concept of a zone of agreement helps with this process (Raiffa 1982; Raiffa et al. 2002). As figure 5.4 depicts, each party to a negotiation starts with a minimum position. Visualizing this position in monetary terms shows how convergence becomes possible during the course of a dialogue (Raiffa et al. 2002, 113). The car-lot transaction is a commonly used example. The seller opens with a price of $7,000 (a1), while the buyer opens with an offer of $2,500 (b1). They then trade concessions and make second offers of $5,000 and $3,500. Their final offers to one another are $4,500 (a3) and $4,000 (b3). Not surprisingly, when they are this close to making a deal, they decide to split the difference and close the deal at $4,250. It is important to note, however, that there is a zone of agreement only if the lowest price the seller will accept (his reservation price) is less than the highest price the buyer will pay (her reservation price).

| KEY TERM |
| --- |
| **Zone of Agreement** The overlapping area of acceptable outcomes for both or all negotiating parties. |

But if this notion is converted to the world of international negotiation—where the currency is national interests, however they are defined—finding any clear zone of agreement can be difficult. This is particularly true when actor preferences along a negotiation continuum, such as that displayed in figure 5.4, are intensely held. That is, while it might seem obvious that the rational solution is to split the difference between initial bargaining positions—such as those depicted by A1 and B1—one or both actors may be strongly wedded to the initial positions and not wish to move much from them. In such cases, where it is difficult for negotiators to identify common interests or a possibility of movement, there may be no zone of agreement. Negotiators will then tend to adopt a more competitive negotiation strategy, pursued through various "hard" negotiating tactics.

**Figure 5.4   Zone of Agreement**

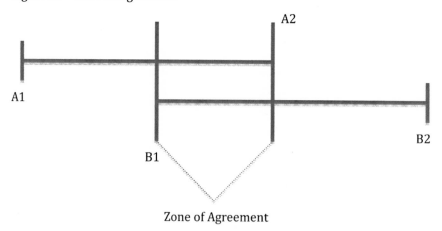

Zone of Agreement

If there are common interests or a possibility of movement away from initial positions, or if there is a will to try to find—or create—a zone of agreement through the use of linkage or a broadening of conceptions of interests, negotiators will engage in collaborative negotiation, using interest-based bargaining techniques. This section is structured around the basic dichotomy between competitive and collaborative approaches to negotiation, including various examples of each.

It should be noted that underlying the discussion is an examination of the use of power by negotiators. As discussed in chapter 2, the successful use of power to achieve goals depends on the situation, the relative balance of capabilities between the involved actors, and changes in the structure of the international system itself. Power, after all, is situational, multidimensional, relative, and dynamic, and, as a result, negotiators must gauge how and when to use their power in overt and covert ways. Power tactics are generally used overtly in competitive situations and used covertly in collaborative ones. In collaborative situations, however, power is used more to persuade than to coerce a negotiation counterpart into an agreement.

## Competitive Negotiation

Although it would be a cheerier world if only positive incentives (or "carrots") were needed to induce cooperation and agreement, it is clear that negotiations often take a negative turn and a variety of sticks—lethal and otherwise—are used to achieve desired goals. As realists have often reminded us in the political science literature, it is naive to assume that everyone will play by the rules of the game. Similarly, it can be foolish to believe that all actors are persuaded by the notion of collective interests. It is often determined, therefore, that the rational approach to an international negotiation situation is a competitive one. Positional bargaining and adversarial and coercive diplomacy are all examples of competitive strategy in negotiation situations.

### Positional Bargaining

As mentioned earlier, sometimes a negotiator represents an international actor that has identified only one desirable outcome to a situation and, as a result, puts that outcome forward and refuses to move away from it. For example, in the zone of agreement case, what if the seller did not back away from his opening position and said instead, "I'll only accept $7,000 for the car"? In international negotiations, it may be the case that the negotiator's domestic constituents will accept only that outcome, or it may be that legal or other constraints rule out other agreements. During the 1962 Cuban missile crisis, President Kennedy reasoned that a zero-tolerance stand—no

| KEY TERM |
| --- |
| **Positional Bargaining**<br>Negotiating stance where an actor identifies only one desirable outcome and refuses to move away from it or consider any other options. |

Soviet missiles in Cuba—was the only stand that would allow him to keep the White House in the 1964 election. Given the vehemence of American anticommunism during the 1950s and 1960s, any concession that the U.S. public and Kennedy's political opponents might perceive as soft on communism would have been political suicide. As a result, hard positional bargaining was the only real option available to the president regarding the missile deployment. Although Kennedy did find ways to introduce flexibility into the negotiations, he never backed down from his bottom-line demand: the missiles had to go.

*Adversarial Diplomacy*

Adversarial diplomacy occurs when the interests of two or more countries clash, but there is little or no chance of armed conflict. Negotiations over economic issues—market shares, methods for dealing with trade imbalances—and, more recently, negotiations over intellectual property rights (e.g., CDs and software) have produced the most prominent examples of adversarial diplomacy in recent years.

| KEY TERM |
| --- |
| **Adversarial Diplomacy**<br>Negotiating stance when the interests of two or more countries clash, but there is little or no chance of armed conflict. |

During much of the 1990s, for example, the United States and Japan were at odds over America's efforts to penetrate Japan's domestic economic market. The dispute became particularly tense in June 1996 during a series of negotiations over U.S. access to the Japanese automobile market. Ultimately, the Clinton administration threatened the imposition of a 100 percent import surcharge on Japanese luxury cars. On the brink of this potentially devastating blow to some key manufacturers (which actually had operations in both countries), the two sides relented and returned to the negotiation table. Cowed by the degree to which their automobile sectors had become interdependent and aware that their larger cooperative relationship in the world was at stake, both parties quickly accepted a face-saving agreement.

The practice of adversarial diplomacy often involves significant threats of sanctions, such as those the United States utilized in the automobile case. Other tactics or tools associated with this form of diplomacy range from imposing strict deadlines on negotiations to threatening the cessation of diplomatic contact. There is a continuum of such tactics, ranging from symbolic measures aimed at the arena of public opinion to those more activist in nature, where threats are actually translated into concrete actions. These tactics can include the actual imposing of economic and political sanctions or the pulling of an ambassador from a foreign capital.

### Coercive Diplomacy

Despite the end of the Cold War, the use of military force in the international system is still common. Instability in Asia in the wake of the Indian and Pakistani nuclear detonations of 1998 and North Korea's continuing threats, problems of terrorism and its impact around the world, ethnopolitical strife in Africa, and conflict in Europe over post-communist state-building efforts all point to the continued existence of a nonpacific world in the current unipolar international system. It is clear that many international actors continue to view military force as a primary way of achieving their goals in contemporary international affairs. Thus, the

> **KEY TERM**
>
> **Coercive Diplomacy**
> Negotiating stance involving the threat of force or limited use of force as a tool at the negotiation table.

threat of military force—and its ultimate use, if deemed necessary—remains a requisite tool of international affairs (see, for instance, discussions by Haass 1997; George 1997; E. Cohen 1997). Clearly, the actions taken by the United States and a small group of supporting countries in both Iraq and Afghanistan are testimony to the perception that military force is still a viable tool for achieving desirable diplomatic results. Later discussion focuses on understanding how force can be used as a tool at the negotiation table.

A good example of coercive diplomacy is the North Korea case referred to throughout this book. During the recurrent crises, the atmosphere has been extremely hostile, and the threat of military force overt on the parts of both the Americans and the North Koreans. Whether through nuclear weapons and missile testing or incursions into the demilitarized zone that divides North and South Korea, the North Korean regime showed ample evidence that it believed military force can be used effectively to achieve its foreign policy goals. From the American side, too, military commitments made to allies in the region (especially South Korea and Japan) and the continued presence of American forces were strong symbols of the U.S. commitment to what it viewed as a favorable outcome to the crises and their underlying issues.

But the use of military force or its threatened use can also have a more subtle impact on negotiations. At the 1945 Potsdam Conference attended by U.S. president Harry S Truman, Soviet premier Joseph Stalin, and British prime minister Winston Churchill, Truman mentioned to Stalin that the

United States had just developed a new weapon of mass destruction: the first atomic bomb. Though the bomb was used only against Japanese forces in the Pacific, the mention of its development to Stalin was also a signal of U.S. power and political desires for the postwar period. In this way, the bomb was meant to keep the Soviets in their place, particularly as the victorious powers wrangled over the postwar European political landscape. It also gave birth to the U.S.-Soviet nuclear arms race that would define East-West relations for the next forty-five years.

## Collaborative Negotiation

When negotiators are able to identify common interests and use them as the basis for a dialogue, the approach is described as collaborative negotiation or problem solving. The strategy is to emphasize common ground while downplaying areas of contention. To a great extent, this approach necessitates a willful change of the character of the negotiation game. The anarchic nature of the international system has traditionally lent itself to relative gains or "beggar thy neighbor" outlooks. This is why a competitive stance in the negotiation arena is more natural to nation-states in particular. Nonetheless, collaboration does frequently emerge, especially among actors exhibiting high levels of interdependence and some sense of long-term, collective interest.

Changing the game so that the focus is on broad rather than narrow conceptions of interest and directing it toward mutually acceptable negotiation outcomes rather than clear-cut victories involves the enhancement of communication between the parties and the construction of trusting relationships. As Winston Churchill once remarked, "To jaw-jaw is always better than to war-war" (as quoted in Freeman 1997). Churchill was alluding to the need to keep the lines of communication open between opposing parties—a crucial part of the negotiation process.

Effective communication is particularly important during crisis negotiations. This was evidenced after the Cuban missile crisis by the superpowers' creation of a hot line. Frightened by the communication mishaps that characterized the crisis at critical junctures, the White House and the Kremlin signed the Hot-Line Agreement of 1963 to ensure a permanent link between them. Often depicted in films as a red phone (although originally merely a Teletype machine), it boosted confidence in Washington and Moscow about the reduced possibility of deadly misunderstandings by allowing direct intercontinental communication between the leaders of each superpower.

Interest-based bargaining, informal track-two diplomatic approaches, and the injection of new insights through mediation provide three alternatives to the tools of the competitive negotiator.

*Interest-Based Bargaining*

When one conjures up images of negotiators, it is easy to think of them as being soft or hard in their approaches. For example, U.S. president Franklin Roosevelt has often been characterized as being too soft a negotiator at the Yalta Conference in 1945. His conciliatory approach to negotiating with Soviet premier Joseph Stalin is commonly construed as one of the reasons why the Soviets were able to consolidate power in eastern Europe after World War II and establish a political-military hold on the region until 1989. By contrast, the hard stance of George H. W. Bush in refusing to back down and allow Saddam Hussein a face-saving retreat after his ill-conceived 1990 invasion of Kuwait effectively closed off the

| KEY TERM |
| --- |
| **Interest-Based Bargaining** Negotiating stance that focuses on trying to understand the needs of the other party and finding areas of common interest. |

negotiation channel in that case. Although the United States was triumphant on the battlefield, critics of the Bush strategy lamented the loss of civilian life on the Iraqi side and argued that negotiations with the Iraqi leader should have been given more of a chance. Very similar criticisms were heard regarding George W. Bush's approach to Saddam and Iraq, especially as the toll of human lives mounted during 2004.

In the well-known book *Getting to Yes* (1991), Roger Fisher and William Ury of the Harvard Negotiation Project argue that neither soft nor hard negotiating positions are likely to produce good outcomes. They call their take on interest-based bargaining "principled negotiation" and argue that the focus must be taken off of positional negotiating and put instead on efforts to find areas of common interest among the actors.

To move beyond the problems of positional bargaining, Fisher and Ury suggest four specific moves:

- Separate the people from the problem.
- Focus on interests, not positions.
- Invent options for mutual gain.
- Insist on using objective criteria to judge the merits of possible solutions.

These are all measures that can be used to build trust among negotiation adversaries and boost their confidence in the negotiation process.

The idea of separating the people from the problem suggests that negative emotions and perceptions of the "other" (see chapter 3) be removed from the negotiation table to the greatest extent possible. Instead of looking at one's counterparts as enemies, it is better to perceive them as mere representatives of interests—maybe even interests that do not oppose your own. By getting to know one's counterparts on a personal level, an under-standing of those interests and the needs underlying them becomes possible. Indeed, the centerpiece of principled negotiation is a focus on interests and needs rather than on positions. An excellent real-world example of this approach is the Israeli-Egyptian negotiations over the Sinai Peninsula. The positions of the two states were diametrically opposed—Israel insisting on keeping the territory it had won in the 1967 Six-Day War and Egypt demanding the territory's return. Progress was achieved during the Camp David negotiations in 1978 only when the American mediator, President Jimmy Carter, got the negotiating teams to focus on underlying interests. Ultimately, it was determined that Israel's need was for security in the form of a buffer zone, while Egypt's need was to reassert its sovereignty, for the benefit of domestic and regional concerns, by regaining lost territory. Framing the problem in this way allowed an eventual solution to present itself. Ultimately, it was clear that the needs of both sides could be met by making the Sinai a totally demilitarized zone, under the control of Egypt but closely monitored by the UN.

The idea of the demilitarized zone is an excellent example of what Fisher and Ury call an "option invented for mutual gain" (1991, 56). Brain-storming about the needs and interests of both sides and the nature of the problem itself allowed the negotiators to find ways to harmonize their interests, despite their seemingly total divergence. This solution allowed both sides to achieve their goals, while still saving face in regard to the compromise they had made.

Finally, demilitarization in this case represented an objective standard or criterion—from the security lexicon—upon which agreement could be based. Although such standards cannot be found for all areas of international negotiation, in many cases they can be found and used. In the human rights arena, the twin covenants on civil/political and economic/social rights fulfill this need. In the environmental arena, scientific judgments and definitions, as well as international laws and legal traditions, provide guidelines for states seeking fair solutions to international disputes.

*Track-Two Diplomacy*

One of the most innovative methods for building trust among negotia-tors is the growing use of track-two, or unofficial, diplomacy in a variety of international conflict settings (Byrne 2007; Davies and Kaufman 2002). This type of negotiation usually involves nontraditional diplomats and nontraditional settings. The strength of the track-two approach on conflict resolution is based on the idea that informal negotiations allow the parties "to come together more easily to explore mutual fears, grievances and demands" (Rasmussen 1997, 44). Track-two diplomacy also provides the opportunity for tentative negotiation offers to be floated, policy linkages to be explored, and other barriers to successful negotiations to be broached in ways that formal negotiations might preclude. A variety of actors can participate in these informal negotiations as well. Examples range from third parties, such as scientists exploring hypothetical issues and engaging in dialogues about them, to networks of low-level officials from conflicting parties whose participation in negotiations is much less controversial than that of their national political leaders. The so-called Oslo negotiations between the Israelis and the Palestinians in the early 1990s quickly became a classic example of track-two diplomacy and are discussed in detail in the accompanying box.

### Track-Two Diplomacy: The Oslo Agreement

One of the most notable successes of the track-two approach was the breakthrough in Israeli-Palestinian negotiations from 1992 to 1993. As has so often been the case in the protracted Israeli-Palestinian conflict, the momentum in the peace process by the end of the 1990–1991 Persian Gulf War had given way to stalemate by late 1992. Through the intervention of Norwegian diplomats, however, the talks were jump-started in September of that year. The mediation of Norway's foreign minister, Johan Jørgen Holst, facilitated this approach. The track-two talks, held near Oslo, created opportunities for close relationships to develop between Israeli and Palestinian representatives in these secret, unofficial negotiations. The atmosphere was deliberately kept intimate in an effort to increase the chances for a breakthrough. Israelis and Palestinians "shared plates of Norwegian salmon and wandered together in nearby woods" (Fedarko 1993, 51). The model developed by the Norwegians represented a stark contrast to the traditional one then being applied in the U.S.-sponsored Madrid negotiations.

It was within this informal environment that the details of a peace agreement between the two parties were examined and finalized. After the process became public, videotape even showed negotiators from both sides lightheartedly playing with Holst's toddler son during some of the sessions. From this relaxed environment, agreements emerged that accomplished the following:

- Israel recognized the PLO as "the representative of the Palestinian people."
- The PLO denounced violence and recognized Israel's right to exist.
- Both sides agreed to a five-year plan, to culminate in 1998 with the creation of Palestinian self-rule in the West Bank and Gaza.

Although the assassination of Israeli prime minister Yitzhak Rabin in October 1995 and the subsequent election of a series of more conservative prime ministers has sidetracked progress toward completely fulfilling these agreements, the achievements of this track-two approach are nonetheless striking in the context of the long-term hatred and distrust that have characterized the conflict for nearly fifty years. It is worth noting, however, that the 2003 Roadmap for Peace was based on many of the same tenets as Oslo and was at least partly the result of continuing two-track processes that persist in the region, even if at lower levels of attention than during the workup to Oslo.

Other examples of confidence-building measures and informal diplomacy have also had notable effects on the reduction of tensions among negotiating parties and have helped to move talks from stalemate to agreement. Confidence-building measures were employed for years during the Cold War as ways of reducing superpower tensions in Europe. Both sides made a habit of informing the other of military exercises and would often use only blanks in weapons during such exercises. Moreover, military officers were routinely exchanged as ways of personalizing the forces of the other side in an effort to pull the countries away from the faceless stereotypes and xenophobia that at times cause international tensions to flare.

## *Mediation*

A last option under the heading of collaborative approaches is the use of mediation to help negotiators find a zone of agreement (Beardsley et al. 2006; Butler 2007; Hansen, Mitchell, and Nemeth 2008). This form of third-party intervention (as discussed in chapter 2) often succeeds when a negotiation has reached a point of deadlock. An outside perspective or "new blood" may be needed to find ways to resolve the conflict of the moment (Princen 1992). In this vein, mediation is undertaken at a point during the negotiation when the parties desire some form of progress but find it beyond their capabilities to create that progress or to make it occur within the necessary time frame. Along these lines, former UN secretary general Kofi Annan argued for the value of mediation as follows, "The process of negotiations is not a football match; it

> **KEY TERM**
>
> **Mediation** An outside perspective brought in to help find ways to resolve a deadlocked conflict when parties desire progress but cannot resolve issues themselves.

is not a question of keeping score of goals or winners and losers. Rather, we [try] to accommodate the expressed concerns of both sides, so as to create a win-win situation" ("Annan Announces Cyprus Plan," 3/31/04, cnn.com).

To achieve success in deadlocked negotiations, mediators have a number of tactics at their disposal. These mediation tactics can be divided into three broad categories: communication, formulation, and manipulation (Bercovitch 1997, 137–138). Communication strategies, or what Wilkenfeld et al. (2005) call facilitative mediation, deal with the perception that all parties to the negotiation are able to speak freely and be heard by the other parties. Thus, a mediator will need to build trust among the actors to reestablish a working relationship among parties that may have become hostile and unwilling to talk. Moreover, a mediator must also create a forum for the discussion of new and innovative ideas regarding the problems at hand. The role of President Carter in the Camp David negotiations discussed earlier is a good example of how a mediator can facilitate communication and the exploration of new options for conflict resolution.

A mediator can also shape the process and substance or the formulation of the negotiation. This is done by encouraging the parties to deal with simple issues first and then work toward the more difficult and complicated ones. It also means identifying potential common interests and compromises that may serve the purposes of all involved, including assuring the secrecy of negotiations to protect the parties' reputations. As mentioned previously and in the box on track-two diplomacy, the Oslo mediation by Norway's foreign minister, Johan Jørgen Holst, exhibited many of these approaches. Before addressing the major issues, the negotiations first had to proceed to a point where the Israeli Knesset would make it legal to negotiate with the Palestinians. The secret talks also served the purpose of highlighting the high costs that both sides would continue to incur if the intifada protests and the Israeli responses to the uprising continued into the foreseeable future.

Finally, a mediator's ability to use his or her position to obtain an agreeable outcome to the problem represents the third tactic: manipulation. The mediator can take personal responsibility for the concessions made so that the parties' constituents can "blame" someone else aside from their own negotiators; use threats, promises, and other incentives to promote cooperation and agreement; and press parties to show flexibility on certain issues. In many ways, this set of tactics depends quite heavily on the reputation of the mediator in the international arena and, more specifically, within the current set of negotiations.

What all this means is that, at times, successful mediation is dependent on the role of the mediator within world affairs. Sometimes, intervention by a representative of a great power is required to push a resolution to the final stages. The role of the United States as the dominant political-military power in the world today most certainly had an impact on the success of the Dayton Peace Accords toward resolving the problems in Bosnia in the late 1990s. American initiatives prompted these negotiations after other international interventions had proven unsuccessful. Without the muscle of the United States, it is unlikely that an agreement could have been achieved at that point in time. As this implies, even in collaborative negotiation settings, power relationships have an impact on helping some negotiation actors move toward compromise and the exploration of new options to conflict resolution.

## Summary

Negotiators must account for a variety of factors when they choose their strategies and tactics for use in a particular situation. Negotiations among friends differ greatly from those among adversaries; negotiations (and their resulting choices) exhibiting limited opportunities for communication among parties differ from negotiations where the parties regularly and easily communicate with one another; and negotiations involving a mediator differ from those where only the main parties are involved. In each setting, negotiators, decision makers, and the constituents who give them their authority must make different calculations.

In many ways, this chapter has attempted to provide an appreciation of the complexity inherent in determining and understanding the choices made within negotiations. In particular, the interdependence of decision making that develops during negotiations means that a decision a particular negotiation actor makes is seldom singular or discrete; instead, it is only part of the process that produces an outcome, woven into a fabric comprising the decisions other parties make at a variety of points along the way. As a result, negotiators must choose their strategies and tactics carefully and weigh their choices in an environment fraught with uncertainty and ambiguity. Then again, it is this ambiguity, when combined with the skill of the negotiator, that makes international negotiation and diplomacy the interesting and often unpredictable "game of kings."

*  *  *

*For a list of related web resources for this chapter, consult*
*www.icons.umd.edu/negotiating/links.htm.*

# 6

# Outcomes

One of the aims of this book is to show that in some respects the diplomatic arena is a far different place today than it was a generation ago. Many important catalysts for change have occurred at the international system level, including the end of the Cold War, the ethnic fragmentation of some previously strong states, and a proliferation of issues now part of the negotiation dialogue among states. International negotiations are further complicated by the existence of two additional levels of analysis—the global and the domestic. Processes closely related to negotiation, including mobilization and issue definition, can greatly affect action on issues such as climate change and international trade agreements. Citizen diplomats do sometimes respond to transnational calls for action on issues such as these, and domestic constituencies can be affected in very different ways by the outcomes of the negotiations. The result is a crosscutting, sometimes conflicting array of influences on the state decision-making apparatus.

## Identifying Important Trends

The negotiation landscape is greatly affected by the same large forces that are reshaping all social and political relationships in the contemporary era: the information and communication revolution and its accompanying mass mobilization of citizens. Access to news and knowledge has increased at astonishing rates in every region of the world—including sub-Saharan Africa, which is benefiting from public and private international endeavors designed to catch it up. International media sources provide nearly instantaneous reporting on events around the world, significantly increasing the number of people watching negotiations and, in some cases, the number of people participating. The introduction of non-Western satellite news channels, such as Al Jazeera, and the addition of social-networking sites (Facebook, Twitter) to available means of communication have also "flattened" the news cycle in the global community. The student movement in Iran during the summer of 2009 provided ample illustration of new modes at work.

The calculus of national interest, the foundation of all foreign policy decisions, today resembles more of a labyrinth than the simple high/low policy categorization of a bygone era. The latitude of policy makers at the nation-state level is constrained by the intense two-level negotiation games in which they often find themselves embroiled. Strong domestic input from concerned citizens and, in some cases, substate actors and so-called substitute states has infringed on the diplomatic purview of states. The importance of an issue to national interest is no longer a simple starting point for negotiation decisions, as there is no longer anything simple about the notion of national interest.

As new actors, issues, and forms of interaction are introduced into the diplomatic arena, policy makers must be retrained in the art of negotiation. The results of various strategies have been studied, plotted, and through the game theoretic approach, even modeled. These results show that cooperative approaches can sometimes be used in place of competitive ones to head off destructive standoffs and dangerous escalations (chicken scenarios) and to build opportunities for trust to enhance communication and collective problem solving among parties (prisoner's dilemmas). Longitudinal analyses of conflicts and the negotiations that have attempted to resolve them demonstrate that outcomes satisfactory to both sides, rather than those that represent a win for one and a loss for another, tend to be more long lasting.

This search for non-zero-sum or win-win outcomes is aided by some newer approaches in the diplomatic repertoire, most notably the informal track-two negotiation setting. In its pure form, this is the Oslo-type forum, where nongovernmental parties from opposing sides work to resolve problems. The influence of the trademark informal setting is felt in an adaptation of track-two negotiations as well: a hybrid model, characterized by more traditional negotiators, working in informal nontraditional settings. The Clinton administration used this approach in its mediation attempts at the Dayton Peace Accords on the Bosnian conflict and the Wye River talks and in Camp David II, between the Israelis and the Palestinians. In his adaptation of the approach, George W. Bush held numerous meetings with foreign leaders in the casual setting of his ranch in "cowboy attire."

President Obama seems to favor opening direct lines to the people of other regions, as evidenced by his Cairo and Ghana addresses during the summer of 2009.

Yet for all of these vaunted changes in the diplomatic realm, there are counter-examples of leaders ordering ruthless attacks on internal and external enemies who stand in the way of personal and perceived national aspirations. Such individuals remind us that—to a great extent—the more things change, the more they stay the same. Indeed, traditional diplomacy (high politics, top leaders, competitive negotiation strategies) is a mainstay of the diplomatic toolbox. With this in mind, it is clear that the analytical tools and frameworks applied to the understanding of international negotiation must be broad enough to encompass both new and traditional diplomacy and flexible enough to account for the presence or absence of certain characteristics—media attention, high domestic salience—across cases.

### Analyzing Real-World Cases

The study of diplomacy inevitably leads to a clearer understanding of the key relationships among state and nonstate actors. Regrettably, the opportunity to apply what has been learned is continual, with new conflicts and negotiation cases—or recurring ones—appearing in the news each day. This book has examined a number of particularly high-profile examples—the ongoing international climate negotiations and the North Korean nuclear proliferation talks, among them— to illustrate the key negotiation concepts and the important diplomatic trends discussed earlier. In addition, it offers an organizational metaphor for the sorting of cases: that of a board game, with a board (setup), players (important actors), stakes (issues and their salience for players), and moves (strategies and tactics). Among the key elements of the negotiation process that the analogy helps elucidate are the importance of individual personalities to the proceedings, the extent of domestic-level input into the negotiation positions of the various parties, and the degree to which the negotiation represents a unique encounter among the parties, as opposed to one of many episodes in an unfolding saga.

One way to apply what has been learned in this book is to take a case—current or historical—and plug it into the analytical framework that is presented. (See the appendix for a discussion of alternative applications of this framework.) We do so in this chapter by exploring the role of negotiation in the protracted conflict involving Iraq, the United States, other powers, alliances, and international and regional organizations, a conflict that has been center stage in the international system since 1990. Protracted conflicts are "hostile interactions which extend over long periods of time with sporadic outbreaks of open warfare fluctuating in frequency and intensity. . . . [The] stakes are very high. . . . [They] linger on in time. . . . [They] are processes" (Azar et al. 1978). While some protracted conflicts have continued for decades—Arab-Israel, India-Pakistan, Greece-Turkey, Taiwan Strait, Korean Peninsula—others have been resolved after long periods of struggle—the Cold War, Indochina, Ecuador-Peru. All are typified by the alternating use of force and diplomacy/negotiation, and they often constitute the most dangerous situations facing individual actors and the international community as a whole. The example that follows—the 1990–1991 Gulf War, better known as Desert Storm—is organized using the board framework. Its main characteristics are noted and then reexamined in light of the significant failures of the subsequent decade, including the return to war in 2003–2004.

## The U.S.-Iraq Protracted Conflict:
## Balancing Force and Diplomacy

### Phase I: The 1991 Gulf War and Its Aftermath

*Background*

During the forty-five-year Cold War, the United States and the Soviet Union were engaged in a policy of mutual containment, an ideological struggle that saw them face off against one another in every region of the international system at one time or another. One of the most complex arenas was the Middle East. The underlying security framework was an Arab-Israeli balance, with the United States committed to the survival and strengthening of Israel, while the Soviet Union invested in Egypt, Syria, and Iraq. Later, in the 1970s, the United States buttressed its position with a "twin pillar" policy of close security relationships with Iran and Saudi Arabia. The fall of the shah of Iran in 1979 and the replacement of the monarchy with an Islamic republic dealt the first heavy blow to this sensitive security structure. The resulting uncertainty and perceived challenges to sovereignty and stability gave rise to war between Iraq and Iran. During that eight-year war (1980–1988), the superpowers pursued a balancing strategy, tilting at times toward Tehran or Baghdad, whenever the other seemed to have gained a meaningful advantage. This was especially evident in the area of arms trade. Following the 1988 cease-fire between Iraq and Iran, however, the United States suddenly changed the game from a balancing act to one of dual containment (Ahrari and Starkey 1997). The resulting uncertainty was compounded in 1989 when the Berlin Wall fell, the Soviet Union began to fragment, and Moscow ceased to be able to play the role of patron to Arab states.

## Setup

In August 1990, in the wake of all of these changes to the global and regional security landscape, Iraqi leader Saddam Hussein decided to test the waters and attempted to assert his own and Iraq's preeminence in the Arab world. The war with Iran had put his regime $80 billion in debt, mostly to neighboring Gulf states. Hussein's position was that these debts should be forgiven, in return for his regime's efforts to tame Khomeinist Iran for them. During the spring and summer of 1990, Kuwait became the focus of Hussein's resentment. In addition to refusing to forgive Baghdad's debts, Kuwait was also exceeding its OPEC-induced oil production quota, thereby contributing to low oil prices on the world market. This further inhibited Iraq's efforts at postwar reconstruction.

Perhaps thinking the United States would look the other way after contributing to his vast military buildup, Hussein revived a claim about the illegitimacy of the Iraq-Kuwait border (dating back to British colonialism) and asserted Iraq's rights to the Rumaila oilfield, from which Kuwait had been pumping vast amounts of oil. When little was done in response to his complaints, he invaded neighboring Kuwait on August 2, 1990. Saddam Hussein's invasion and subsequent annexation of Kuwait was met by much initial indecision in the Arab world. There was a week of confusion, after which the Arab League finally convened in Cairo. However, the delayed regional action had encouraged Saudi Arabia to fashion its own response. After viewing American satellite intelligence of the Saudi-Iraqi border, King Fahd made the decision to invite the United States to deploy troops to Saudi Arabia. This eclipsed any chance of a unified Arab reaction to the crisis. After some initial confusion in Washington—related to whether U.S. ambassador April Glaspie had given a "yellow light" to Hussein in a meeting prior to the invasion—President George H. W. Bush declared that the invasion was a terrible affront to international principles and would not be allowed to stand. He responded to the Saudi request for assistance—termed by then chairman of the Joint Chiefs of Staff Colin Powell as Saudi Arabia's "911 call." The Bush administration immediately and simultaneously opened up diplomatic and military channels to respond to the threat.

## Players

Given the boldness of the invasion, the salience of the Persian Gulf region to Middle Eastern security, and the importance of the oil sector to so many states around the world, the impact of the Iraqi incursion into Kuwait was major. The United States, now alone on the superpower stage, still had to consider the likely moves to be made by Russia, Iran, and Jordan in the aftermath of the invasion. The anxieties of the neighboring Gulf countries, ostensibly part of a collective security arrangement of their own (the Gulf Cooperation Council) had to be taken into account. Efforts to bring the reactions of Israel, Britain, France, Japan, and other close allies into step with that of the United States were also placed high on the diplomatic agenda. Personal diplomacy by President Bush and Secretary of State James Baker was intense during the initial Desert Shield period (a time during which the mission was defined as stopping any further Iraqi incursions into neighboring countries). On the Iraqi side, Saddam Hussein had his foreign minister, Tariq Aziz, display the public face of the regime. Aziz shuttled between Arab capitals and the United Nations and made most of the public statements on Iraqi positions. Other important actors during the unfolding of the crisis included Egyptian president Hosni Mubarak, well positioned in the Arab world and vis-à-vis the West to play the role of a de facto mediator, and UN secretary-general Javier Perez de Cuellar, who ultimately traveled to Baghdad in January 1991 in a last-ditch attempt to get Hussein to withdraw from Kuwaiti territory.

*Stakes*

Assessments of the national interests at stake in this standoff have never been easy to make. Indeed, they have been the subject of political punditry since 1990. What is clear is that the first President Bush found himself at a critical juncture for the definition of what he had called the dawn of a "new world order." Whether the favored U.S. policy of the day in the Gulf was balance of power (tilting toward Iraq or Iran) or dual containment of both states, Saddam Hussein's affront to the most basic principle of national sovereignty was a watershed point for Bush and the post–Cold War United States. Had Hussein succeeded in his bold move to take over strategically important oil fields, there is also no doubt that the economic repercussions on the United States and its Western allies and Japan would have been highly significant as well. The economic stakes were rarely mentioned by the Bush administration, however, during the vast military buildup of coalition forces. Other states in the now even-more-dangerous neighborhood clearly felt the threat to their own territorial integrity emanating from Iraq. Two of these states, Israel and Saudi Arabia, considered themselves to be under a U.S. security blanket and watched carefully as the U.S.-led response was formulated.

*Moves*

The first order of business for the United States, in response to Iraq's August 1990 announcement that it was annexing Kuwait, was to make a strong military countermove. By the third week of August, working with Britain and several other countries, the United States had assembled naval and air forces in the Persian Gulf region that were superior to those of Iraq. Amid questions at home and abroad about the legality of its actions, the Bush administration then went to both the United Nations Security Council and the U.S. Congress to seek sanctioning of the possible use of this force against Iraq. The resulting Resolution 678 at the UN, passed in November 1990, authorized force but mandated a six-week period first, during which diplomacy had to be tried in an effort to oust Hussein from Kuwait. International opinion in favor of trying to deal diplomatically with Saddam Hussein waned, however, when he took and held Westerners stranded in his country as hostages. His "human shield" strategy only heightened international resolve against him and greatly helped American efforts to win support for the multinational coalition. The vote in Congress in January 1991 to authorize force was actually quite close, but even those who voted against it (a 52–47 vote for the use of force in the Senate) quickly closed ranks behind Bush, giving him a mandate to take the action he deemed fit.

General international agreement that Hussein had to be stopped characterized the proceedings at the UN Security Council during this time, resulting in the passage of twelve resolutions. On the domestic front, George H. W. Bush used his trademark "Rolodex diplomacy" (personally telephoning heads of state in every region of the world) to assemble what would ultimately be a thirty-seven-member multinational coalition against Iraq's action. At what point the diplomatic channel was effectively abandoned by the United States has also been the subject of much debate. Clearly, the march to war was on by late 1990, so a last-minute meeting between Aziz and Secretary of State Baker in Geneva on January 9, 1991, was never considered a true negotiation. Indeed, Bush had already stated that any meeting at that point would not be for negotiating but would be an opportunity to convince Hussein to withdraw from Kuwait.

Fatefully then, Desert Shield was followed by the massive military operation, Desert Storm, launched on January 17, 1991. Iraq was soundly and quickly defeated in this war by the coalition and forced to surrender. As part of the formal cease-fire of February 1991, which Hussein had to sign before U.S. forces would withdraw from southern Iraq, Hussein stayed in power but agreed to allow UN weapons inspectors to ensure that his weapons of mass destruction programs were dismantled (*Washington Post* 1998). Herein lay the twin seeds of future conflict—Hussein's continued presence at the helm in Baghdad and his subsequent refusal to allow the UN inspectors to do their jobs, eventually even throwing them out of the country. What followed was a series of crises during the next decade ultimately leading to a second U.S.-Iraq Gulf War. It is important to ask why one of history's most successful coalition operations was followed by such a series of disasters on the diplomatic front. Clearly, the nature of Saddam Hussein's regime made true negotiation between the opposing parties difficult and even fruitless (witness Kofi Annan's mediation attempt of 1998 that ultimately failed). The breakdown of the vast coalition against Hussein, however, suggests deeper difficulties with the follow-up to the war.

Following the cease-fire of February 1991, reluctantly accepted by Saddam Hussein, there was a steady succession of crises between the United States and Iraq. George H. W. Bush left office amid criticism that he had failed to see the war through to a proper conclusion—the ouster of Saddam Hussein. His successor, Bill Clinton, then faced many of the same problems in trying to force Hussein to live up to the terms of the cease-fire. Collectively, the many crises that broke out between 1991 and the next U.S.-led invasion of Iraq in 2003 can be grouped into two broad categories: the post-cease-fire attacks on minority populations inside Iraq (the Shiites and the Kurds) and a series of inspections crises involving the United Nations Special Commission on Iraq (UNSCOM), sent to inspect sites for possible weapons of mass destruction.

While there was little doubt that Saddam Hussein was not living up to his end of the cease-fire agreement, a shift in international public opinion was readily discernible by late 1997. The Clinton administration, fed up with Hussein's transgressions, threatened an air campaign against Baghdad. Much to its surprise, international and even domestic support for the policy was weak. Faced with a wave of "wag the dog" criticism at home, and given the breaking scandal over Clinton's relationship with White House intern Monica Lewinsky, the administration realized that the thirty-seven-member coalition from 1990 had lost some prominent supporters, including Egypt, China, France, Pakistan, Spain, Russia, Turkey, and even the Gulf countries of Bahrain, Oman, Qatar, Saudi Arabia, and the United Arab Emirates! There was clearly a good deal of sympathy for the Iraqi people, who were suffering under both Hussein and the economic sanctions imposed on their country during the war. Moreover, led by Jordan's foreign minister, Fayez Tarawneh, many regional actors began to draw parallels between Iraqi noncompliance with UN resolutions and what they deemed similar actions by Israel over time. There was also some feeling that the United States risked becoming an international bully if it continued to threaten force at every turn with Baghdad.

Eventually, though still threatening Hussein with harsh rhetoric and sporadic air strikes, the Clinton administration backed down from the notion of renewing the war. The UNSCOM inspectors left Baghdad in 1999, complaining that Hussein was not allowing them to do their jobs. The small window, utilized by the world to witness Hussein's treatment of his own people and to watch his development of weapons of war, was shut. It took a new president and the dramatic events of September 11, 2001, to reopen it. And this time, the diplomatic environment was even more changed.

## Phase 2: Gulf War 2003—New System, New Strategy

During the decade following the end of the 1991 Gulf War, two major changes took place in the international system. The end of the Cold War and the dissolution of the Soviet Union had reinforced the unipolarity that typified the decade of the 1990s. But what had begun as an international system with a hegemonic power (the United States) attempting to find its proper role in a new world order of diffuse power and authority had devolved by the end of the decade into a system in which the United States took on more of a classic power-politics role. Certainly the second circumstance, the attack on the United States by al Qaeda on September 11, 2001, and the subsequent and continuing U.S.-led military operations in Afghanistan played a large role in redefining how the United States viewed its relationship with the rest of the international system. The new U.S. administration under President George W. Bush, already committed to a more unilateral and traditional force-oriented approach to foreign policy, found itself in a very different environment from that faced by the elder Bush in the 1990–1991 Gulf crisis. That earlier war had failed to bring about regime change in Iraq, much to the dismay of many of the more conservative policy advisers—Vice President Dick Cheney, Secretary of Defense Donald Rumsfeld, Deputy Secretary of Defense Paul Wolfowitz—who had served in the first Bush administration and had now joined the second. The UNSCOM crises of the 1990s, which had resulted in the complete cessation of weapons inspections in Iraq, fed fears that weapons of mass destruction were being developed inside Iraq and could be proliferated to other potentially dangerous users, including terrorist groups such as al Qaeda. The events of September 11, 2001, led to a sense of urgency and to the development of the Bush doctrine that justified unilateral actions against rogue states.

In the aftermath of 9/11, the Bush administration made clear that it would not distinguish between terrorists and supporters of terrorism. According to some reports (Suskind 2004; Woodward 2004), Iraq was discussed as a potential target at a war council meeting as early as September 15, 2001. By November of that year, Bush had instructed Secretary of Defense Rumsfeld to begin planning a war in Iraq; Bush identified Iraq as one of the three members of the "axis of evil" in his January 2002 State of the Union address, along with Iran and North Korea. Military preparations began in early 2002 for a war in Iraq, and by March British prime minister Tony Blair had pledged his government's support for a war.

While the critical players in the development of this second major Iraq crisis were much the same as in 1991, both the circumstances of the international system and the strategy employed by the United States were fundamentally different. The elder Bush was a pragmatic internationalist with a real sense of noblesse oblige toward the rest of the world (Sewall 2004). This allowed other members of the international community, and the United Nations, to feel comfortable in joining the U.S.-led coalition. Yet, while the players in 2002–2003 had remained largely the same, circumstances and approach had changed drastically. The younger Bush, less experienced in foreign policy, adopted an approach "brimming with missionary conviction and grand design" (Sewall 2004). While the United States could count on Great Britain and an array of other European states, including Spain, Portugal, Italy, Hungary, Poland, Denmark, and the Czech Republic, a powerful group of detractors continued to include France, Germany, Russia, and all of the Gulf states, with the exception of Kuwait. Turkey also refused critical logistical support. Perhaps most important, UN secretary-general Kofi Annan stood firmly against the United States and its allies in many of the maneuvers and negotiations that followed.

Both U.S. and British intelligence in late 2002 and early 2003 suggested that Saddam Hussein had developed chemical and biological weapons stockpiles, as well as a potential nuclear weapons program. The Bush administration initially justified its call for action against Iraq in terms of preventing WMD proliferation, in addition to citing Iraqi support for al Qaeda, noncompliance with prior UN resolutions, and the liberation of the Iraqi people as reasons for the need for regime change. These issues were dramatically presented to the world in a speech by Secretary of State Colin Powell to the UN Security Council on February 5, 2003. Other considerations weighing heavily on the minds of policy planners in the international community included that Iraq had the second largest crude oil reserves in the world, that Iraq had been impoverished during the period of UN sanctions and had become reliant on the UN oil-for-food program, and the risk of civil war in Iraq if the authoritarian regime of Saddam Hussein were to be removed.

As noted, the United States began military planning long before it sought diplomatic solutions. At the urging of Britain and other members of the international community, the United States attempted to build support against Iraq through the United Nations. It successfully negotiated the unanimous adoption of UN Resolution 1441 on November 8, 2002, which established a return of weapons inspectors to Iraq. But at perhaps the most critical point of prewar negotiations, the United States failed to convince critical states, including Security Council members France, Russia, and Germany, that containment of Saddam Hussein had failed and that preemption was necessary. In the face of a probable negative vote in the Security Council, the United States and Britain withdrew a draft resolution seeking UN authority for war in Iraq on March 18, 2003. Instead, the United States relied on a "coalition of the willing" that operated outside of the purview of both the UN and NATO. This coalition initiated war against Iraq on March 20, 2003.

While the strategy of the first Bush administration had been to seek a wide coalition to reinforce the legitimacy of possible military force through burden sharing, both military and financial, the second Bush administration focused more on the ability of its military to dictate facts on the ground. It adopted a go-it-alone strategy—even Britain's contribution of troops was more symbolic than crucial militarily. The ensuing breakdown of multilateralism, and the shunting aside of the United Nations and its institutions, has made the task of recovery and nation-building more difficult to achieve.

A focus on the critical negotiations involving key members of the international community, in the fateful days between perception of crisis and the ultimate decision to use force, reveals that conceptions of the relationship between force and negotiation in the 1990–1991 march to war were very different from those of 2002–2003. In the first case (1990–1991) there is evidence that force was to be used as a last resort, after diplomatic avenues had been exhausted. This allowed the international community, through the institutions of the United Nations, to exercise collective security in defense of the principle of sovereignty for one of its member states. In the second instance, while the United States and Britain labored hard to convey a similar sense of urgency and imminent threat to the security of the international community, the facts on the ground were not persuasive to key international actors, nor were the tactics used by the United States and Britain conducive to harmony and a joint sense of mission. This latter set of circumstances resulted in a narrow coalition, an unpopular military action, and deep divisions among traditional allies. While negotiations were pursued in both instances, the manner in which these negotiations were carried out and concluded led to very different outcomes.

## Looking Forward

The post–Cold War era presents negotiators everywhere with new rules and new players. The exploration of traditional and recent trends in diplomacy has shown that many of the main parameters of negotiation have remained fairly constant through the transition (crisis, coalition building, mediation, issue linkage, and so on). So, what are the new developments in the negotiation arena? Manifestations are in evidence everywhere, from the prominence of environmental issues on the diplomatic agenda to the citizen diplomats who negotiate them in a new kind of international forum. The determination of national interest has been greatly complicated for governments, democratic and nondemocratic alike. For the democracies of the world, diplomatic agenda setting is highly subject to strong domestic pulls; for the nondemocracies, deliberations are clearly influenced by international and public opinion. In the contemporary process, it is also clear that culture and identity play greater roles in shaping negotiation positions and moves, as manifested in the application of new techniques such as culture-based mediation and track-two facilitation.

Nonetheless, as the new century dawns, it is not possible to foresee all of the forces that will shape its international relations. The larger role now afforded nonstate entities bodes both well and ill: for all of the citizen groups now at work on health and development issues, crime and drug syndicates are also making greater inroads. Yet, there is good reason to believe that the broadening or democratization of the diplomatic arena will continue at a rapid pace. Moreover, it is clear that technology will play a prominent role. The process of connecting people around the world to one another will undoubtedly have far-reaching implications for the diplomatic agenda and the negotiation process.

*   *   *

*For a list of related web resources for this chapter, consult*
*www.icons.umd.edu/negotiating/links.htm.*

# Appendix: Students as Diplomats

The framework presented in the preceding chapters creates a context for thinking about the range of factors that influence international negotiations and their outcomes. This framework not only provides students and observers of international relations with a model for analyzing specific negotiations but also offers insights into the negotiation process itself. But without the opportunity to see international negotiations "in action," a true understanding of the intricacies of international diplomacy may prove elusive for many students. Participation in simulations of international negotiations can provide students with an insider's view that allows them to explore more deeply the complex nature of negotiations.

The ICONS Project at the University of Maryland has developed a series of simulation activities designed to reinforce some of these lessons learned about international negotiation by allowing students to experience first-hand the processes of international negotiations. These simulations place students in the roles of diplomats or decision makers in the international arena. Working in teams, students try their hands at developing policy positions and pursuing them in a simulated international negotiation that includes actors with different—often conflicting—interests and priorities. The material on the following pages describes the structure of ICONS simulations and the way that ICONS' unique web-based interface provides students with opportunities to understand better the dynamics of international negotiations and to develop relevant negotiation skills.

## Simulation as Active Learning in International Relations

Simulations place participants in specific roles and require that they overcome a host of obstacles in their pursuit of goals (Walcott 1980). In international relations simulations, the underlying idea is that students should walk a mile in the shoes of real-world decision makers, thus gaining insight into and appreciation for the tremendous complexities of the international system. In addition, international relations simulations promote a freer exchange of ideas and foster critical thinking and curiosity among participating students (Shaw 2004). Some of the more popular international relations exercises include Model UN and various regional spin-offs, such as the Model Organization of American States (Dent and Sondrol 1998). These exercises, in which students shape policies in rapidly changing political environments, grew out of older, more theoretical exercises, such as Harold Guetzkow's Inter-Nation Simulation (Guetzkow and Cherryholmes 1966). These simulation exercises share the aim of representing decision-making environments for participants, who then attempt to navigate the complex international terrain themselves.

Simulations that focus on negotiation have also grown in popularity as more and more colleges and universities introduce courses that deal specifically with this topic. A special volume of the journal *International Negotiation* (1998, vol. 3) provides an overview of some of these exercises, which include, in addition to ICONS, the Global Problems Summit, an issue-focused simulation. Simulation exercises provide students with active learning opportunities that can have lasting impact. Long after lecture notes have been lost and professors' names forgotten, few learners will forget the time they averted war for all Kenyans by forging a last-minute border agreement with neighboring Uganda!

Great advances in technology in the late twentieth century sparked several efforts to use computer technology to enhance student experiences in international relations simulations. In the early 1970s Robert Noel worked with colleagues from the University of California, Santa Barbara, to develop the POLIS Foreign Policy simulation that allowed students at different locations to participate jointly in an exercise by using ARPANET technology (Wilkenfeld and Kaufman 1993). The ICONS Project, which emerged in the early 1980s, built upon the simulation model first developed by Noel and has continued to grow and evolve as technology has improved and access to computer technology has spread around the world (Starkey and Wilkenfeld 1996). The degree to which simulations have proven to be effective teaching tools in the field of negotiation and diplomacy has been heightened by simulation designers' willingness to use interactive technologies. Software applications, Internet-based programs, and video teleconferencing have allowed for the creation of increasingly complex—and realistic—negotiation simulations (Thiessen and McMahon 1999; Ross et al. 2001; Elliot et al. 2002; Friedman 2002).

Online simulations present unique learning opportunities, as they expand the possibilities of when, where, and how students can participate in a simulation. They can facilitate discussions among student teams based in widely ranging time zones who cannot always be on a computer simultaneously. The online negotiation environment also provides participating students with a venue for honing their writing skills, especially their ability to construct persuasive arguments. In the case of ICONS simulations, which use a custom-built interface called ICONSnet, all online activity during the course of a negotiation is archived, providing faculty and students with an accessible transcript of the exercise upon its completion. This transcript is an invaluable resource for examining why a negotiation evolved in a certain way and identifying trends and turning points in a simulation—all of which deepen student understanding of negotiation processes in general.

### Participation in ICONS Exercises: Understanding the Process

All three authors of this book have worked with ICONS simulation exercises for many years as part of their efforts to enhance student learning about international relations, foreign policy, and negotiation, and they regard simulations as an especially useful tool for putting negotiation theory into practice. Via its customized online interface, ICONSnet, ICONS provides to instructors and their students background information on the context of the negotiation for each simulation (i.e., the board), the actors involved in the simulated negotiation (i.e., the players), and the issues to be explored in a particular exercise (i.e., the stakes). The remainder of this chapter will be devoted to an explanation of the ways that ICONS simulations can be used to supplement the material presented in earlier chapters of *International Negotiation in a Complex World*.

While ICONS provides background material and a structure for conducting a simulation, it is the participating students who determine how the process unfolds (i.e., the moves). Students must set priorities for the actors that they represent in the simulation and develop strategies for pursuing these priorities within the context of the exercise. Throughout the exercise, students utilize ICONSnet's online communication tools to negotiate with the various parties in the simulation. The decisions and actions made by students during the course of a simulation determine the overall result of a given exercise—be it unanimous agreement on a comprehensive proposal, a stalemate among parties, or something in between. As in the "real world," the negotiators in an ICONS simulation direct the outcome of the exercise.

### Student Participants: One Class or Multiple Schools?

ICONSnet can be accessed twenty-four hours a day, seven days a week, from any computer with Internet access. As a result, it can allow students from geographically dispersed schools to participate in a simulation exercise together. Each semester, ICONS organizes such distributed simulations, which involve students from across the United States and from all around the world. These distributed exercises provide students with the chance to work with and learn from students with whom they would not otherwise have contact. Students from non-English-speaking countries can even participate with the assistance of translation teams (staffed by foreign-language students practicing their translation skills). It is not unusual to have schools in four or five countries participating in a simulation together. These distributed simulations run for three weeks, with the start date set months in advance by ICONS Project staff. The schedule is available at the ICONS Project website: www.icons.umd.edu (see figure A.1).

While participation in a multiple-school simulation brings exposure to peers in other locations, it can also present scheduling challenges and time commitments beyond the scope of some courses. To address these concerns, ICONS also offers shorter, more flexible simulations that professors can use with their own class. These popular single-class simulations are available on a variety of topics, from regional affairs to crisis events, and ulitize the same online tools as the multiple-school simulations. (A listing of selected

**Figure A.1   ICONS Project Website: www.icons.umd.edu/highered**

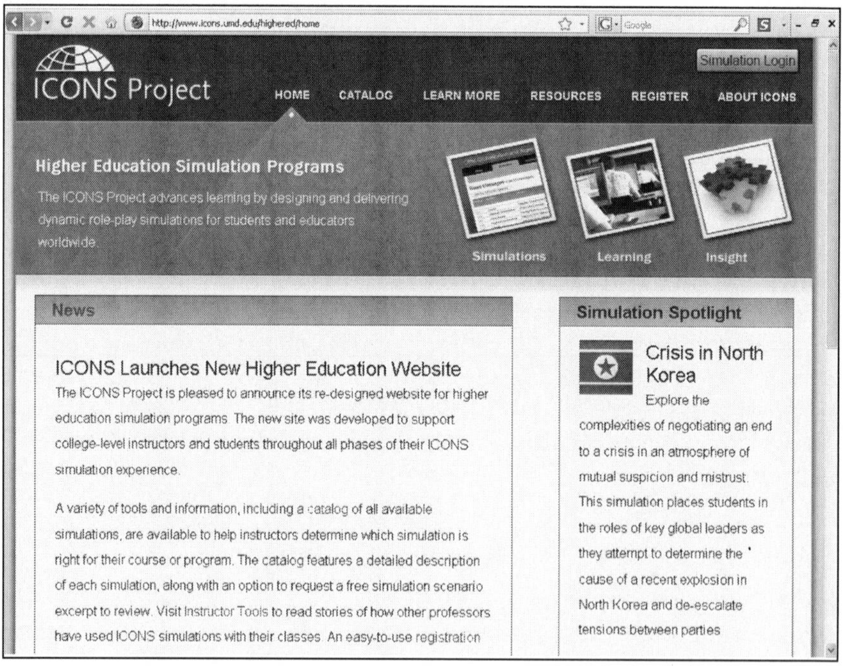

## Examples of ICONS Simulation Offerings

**DISTRIBUTED SIMULATIONS:** Bring together students from classes around the country and the world in ICONS-coordinated online exercises.

- International System: Negotiations focused on international security concerns, the global environment, world health, human rights, and debt.

**SINGLE-CLASS SIMULATIONS:** Involve students from just one class or campus in instructor-coordinated online exercises.

- Crisis in North Korea: A mysterious explosion in North Korea triggers a crisis negotiation among the Six-Party Talks members.
- Globalization and Nigerian Oil: Negotiations between state and nongovernment actors on oil rights and regional conflict resolution.
- International Whaling Commission: Multilateral negotiations designed to help students develop problem-solving skills and to learn about the dynamics of international environmental regimes.
- Borders, Environment, and Trade in the Americas: Key regional issues are explored as countries decide whether to pursue hemispheric or subregional cooperation.

A full list of simulations is available at www.icons.umd.edu.

exercises is provided in the accompanying box.) The web-based system provides students with a means of continuing negotiations outside of class time, thereby enhancing the quality of the simulation experience.

### Getting Started

Student preparation is essential to the success of a simulation. As in any negotiation, the ability of an actor to achieve its goals will rely in large part on the effort put into preparing for the negotiation. Once a faculty member decides to include an ICONS exercise in class and has completed online registration for a specific exercise, both instructor and students will have access to a variety of online resources to assist in the preparation phase of the simulation. They will also be provided with individual log-ins, which allow them to access these online resources. Faculty also receive access to an online facilitator guide, sample assignments, and supplemental instructional resources.

As part of the preparation process, every participating student must read through the simulation scenario, which outlines the primary issues to be discussed and defines the context and scope of the upcoming negotiations. The ICONSnet interface also provides students with information on the roles they will be playing in the negotiation. (See figure A.2 for an example.) Some ICONS simulations contain detailed role sheets clearly outlining a party's interests, while others require that students conduct extensive research using the online ICONS Research Library to determine their party's interests. Time frame and learning goals should determine which type of ICONS simulation faculty choose to meet their curricular needs.

## Developing a Strategy

Strategy is an important consideration during the negotiation phase, as each team tries to make progress on the critical issues while protecting its own interests. Balancing these two tasks involves significant effort; it requires that participants carefully consider how they present themselves in a negotiation and how they plan to work with other parties in the simulation.

**Figure A.2   Sample Information on Simulation Actors**

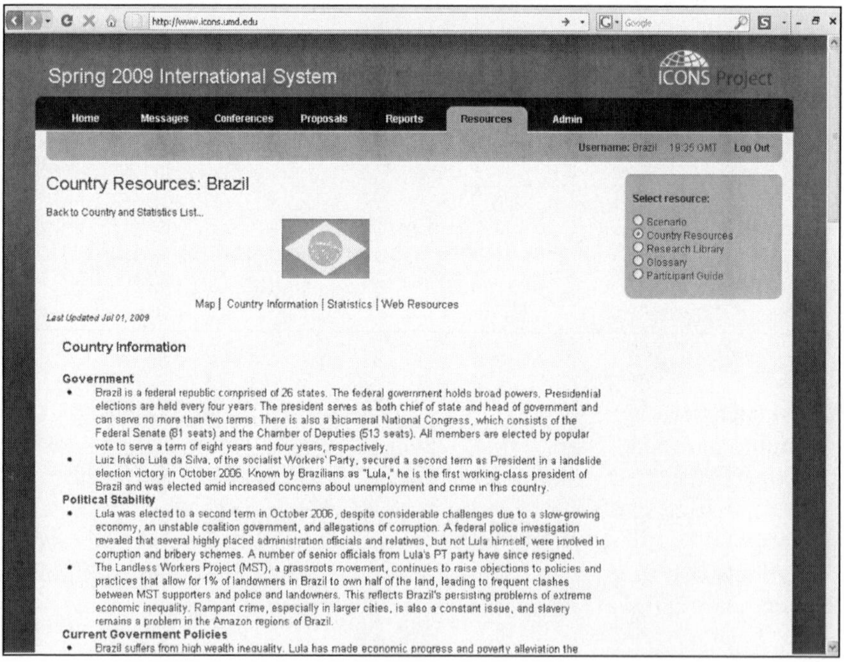

As discussed in chapter 5, creating a collaborative or problem-solving negotiation approach takes work. If a team strives to achieve only its own goals, it is unlikely that others will make concessions. Without such concessions, progress toward a mutually acceptable outcome is unlikely.

## Working Effectively in Teams

As discussed in chapter 4, international negotiations are two-level games, and ICONS encourages faculty to have students work in teams to re-create this dynamic, such that negotiations take place not only among the different teams in each simulation but also within each team as student team members work to come to agreement about goals, strategies, and tactics. In simulations focusing on multiple issue areas, teams frequently divide themselves into subgroups according to the issues outlined in the simulation scenario. This division of labor often leads to internal disputes within the team about priorities and about how to move ahead (e.g., as when human rights and security specialists are concerned with achieving different, possibly conflicting, goals). Each team must determine ways to resolve these disputes and work together effectively to bring coherent policies to the negotiation table. Faculty members can encourage intrateam collaboration by requiring the joint creation of a team position paper or negotiation brief.

## Negotiating with Counterparts

After students have completed their preparation, the next step in an ICONS simulation is the online negotiation phase, during which the teams in a simulation interact with one another using the web-based ICONSnet communication interface. Teams start the interactive phase of the simulation by logging on to the negotiation community and sending initial policy statements on the relevant negotiation issues to their counterparts. The simulation itself really picks up momentum when teams respond to each others' statements with questions, suggestions, clarifications, and requests. As the simulation continues, it is important to keep in mind that, as in the real world, the negotiators themselves determine the course and the outcome of these negotiations.

During this phase, the instructor typically plays the role of the facilitator, known within the simulation as the Simulation Control (Simcon). In this role, an instructor will be able to access all communication that takes place among participants within the simulation and easily identify the individual responsible for each piece of the communication. ICONS provides a variety of tools and resources to help instructors facilitate a simulation, and instructors can shape the role of Simcon to be as hands-off or involved as they would like. For ICONS' multischool simulations, ICONS staff play the role of Simcon, thus allowing instructors to serve as advisers to their own teams.

## Sending Simulation Messages

Participants in ICONS negotiations communicate in two ways; these are intended to mirror the kinds of interactions that negotiators have with each other in the real world. The first involves sending statements, or simulation messages. In general, these messages convey positions on the various issues under negotiation and respond to the communications received from the other country teams. (See figure A.3 for a sample message.) They can be sent to an individual team or simultaneously to a group of teams. Teams can send these messages at any time of the day or night, and they are posted to the negotiation community to be picked up when the recipient signs on to the system. In this way, the ICONS message area is similar to an e-mail system, providing a space for asynchronous communication with messages arriving in character (i.e., from Japan or Germany rather than John Doe or Jane Smith). Members of each team are encouraged, whenever possible, to construct statements jointly and work out policy responses together. To assist with this coordination, ICONS provides an online space (My Team Area) where teammates can communicate internally throughout the exercise to organize efforts and plan strategy before exchanging official statements with other country teams in the simulation.

**Figure A.3   Sample Message**

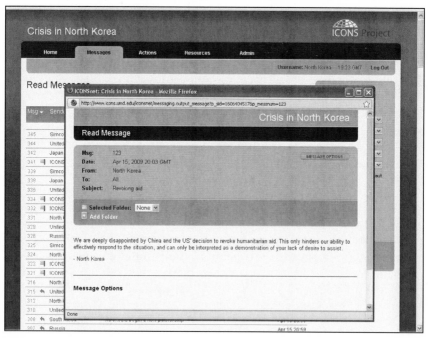

## Participating in Real-Time Conferences

The second kind of communication that occurs during some ICONS simulations is the real-time conference. Conferences are held at prescheduled times, and typically focus on one of the specific issues of the simulation. Representatives from each team assemble virtually via ICONSnet at a predetermined time and work through items on an agenda, with Simcon acting as the chairperson. The conferences allow a real-time dialogue to focus on a particular aspect of the negotiation. They can provide an opportunity to sharpen ideas and solidify relationships that have already been developing via message exchange.

## Submitting and Evaluating Proposals

Through messages and conferences, teams are often able to make great strides toward reaching some agreement or settlements among the relevant parties on the issues of the negotiation. In some ICONS exercises, teams build on that progress by submitting formal proposals to be considered and voted on by other teams. Through ICONSnet, each team can submit proposals that reflect their plans for how the international community will address a specific issue. (See figure A.4 for a portion of a sample proposal.)

**Figure A.4   Sample Proposal (excerpt)**

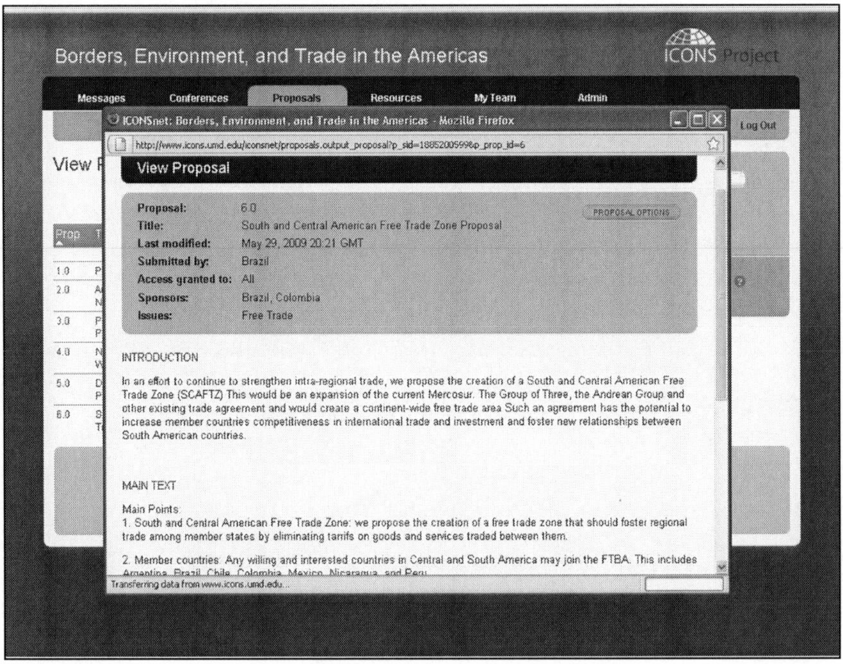

Teams then exchange messages exploring the merits and shortcomings of the proposal; the authoring team can then amend the proposal in order to secure support from other teams. As the simulation comes to an end, teams have the opportunity to cast a vote in favor of or in opposition to those proposals finalized during the course of the negotiations.

## Assessing Outcomes

Since ICONS simulations are short in duration, they can provide only a snapshot of the negotiation process. Participants are sometimes frustrated by the lack of apparent progress in the negotiations as they come to a close. They must be reminded that a simulation is not meant to replicate the entire negotiation process. To do so, the negotiations would have to run for months or even years! Instead, the intention is that participants will learn firsthand about the complexities of the negotiation arena and how challenging that arena can be to navigate. The best way to determine the success of a simulation is to look not at specific outcomes but at what progress was made in negotiating each of the issues and to explore the degree to which each team was able to pursue or achieve its individual interests. The simulation participants themselves, however, are the best judges of what was actually accomplished. One way to encourage student reflection and self-assessment throughout the simulation process is to include a journal-writing activity during the exercise (Young 2006).

Instructors are encouraged to build into the simulation experience time for a "debriefing" at the conclusion of the exercise. The simulation offers significant lessons both in terms of content knowledge (deeper understanding of the negotiation issues and the relevant actors) and procedural knowledge about how international negotiations unfold and evolve, as well as about individual negotiation, communication, and collaboration skills (Torney-Purta 1998). The online Faculty Area for each simulation provides resources and sample assignments to assist with the debriefing phase. Faculty can focus discussions and written reflection assignments to emphasize those learning objectives most relevant to an individual course. Including a robust debriefing phase ensures that the simulation was not only engaging and entertaining for students but also a meaningful learning experience that reinforces theoretical curriculum goals.

# References

AbiNader, Jean. 1998. "The Gulf between the Arabs and America." *Washington Post*, March 1, C1, C5.

Ahmer, Tarar. 2005. "Constituencies and Preferences in International Bargaining." *Journal of Conflict Resolution* 49, no. 3: 383–407.

Ahrari, M. E., and Brigid Starkey. 1997. "Polarity and Stability in the Post–Cold War Persian Gulf." *Fletcher Forum of World Affairs* 21, no. 1 (Winter/Spring): 133–151.

Albin, Cecelia. 2001. *Justice and Fairness in International Negotiations.* Cambridge, UK: Cambridge University Press.

Alliance of Small Island States. 1997. "A NGO Perspective on the United Nations Barbados Plan of Action for Small Island Developing States."November 10–14. www.aosis.org/meeting.htm.

Anderson, Dean. 1995. "Rapporteur's Report of Workshop Presentations and Discussions." In *The Emerging International Regime for Climate Change: Structures and Options after Berlin*, ed. Michael Grubb and Dean Anderson. London: Royal Institute of International Affairs: 7–44.

*An Inconvenient Truth.* 2006. Paramount Pictures. Documentary film. Produced by Laurie David, Lawrence Bender, and Scott Z. Burns.

*Asia Report.* 2003. "North Korea: A Phased Negotiation Strategy." No. 61 (August 1). The DPRK Briefing Book: Policy Area: Multilateral Talks. www.nautilus.org/DPRKBriefingBook/multilateralTalks/negotiationStrategy.html

Axelrod, Robert M. 1984. *The Evolution of Cooperation.* New York: Basic.

Axelrod, Robert M., and Robert Keohane. 1986. "Achieving Cooperation under Anarchy: Strategies and Institutions." In *Cooperation under Anarchy*, ed. Kenneth E. Oye. Princeton, N.J.: Princeton University Press: 226–254.

Azar, Edward E., Paul Jureidini, and Ronald McLaurin. 1978. "Protracted Social Conflict: Theory and Practice in the Middle East." *Journal of Palestine Studies* 8, no. 1: 41–60.

Barr, Cameron, and Lawrence J. Goodrich. 1997. "The Future of the Kyoto Climate Accord Is Still Up in the Air." *Christian Science Monitor*, December 12. www.csmonitor.com/durable/1997/12/12/intl/intl.6.html.

Barrett, Scott. 2003. *Environment and Statecraft: The Strategy of Environmental Treaty-Making.* New York: Oxford University Press.

BBC News. 1997. "Agreement at Kyoto Climate Conference." December 10. http://news2.thdo.bbc.co.uk/hi/english/despatches/newsid%5F38000/38374.stm.

———. 1999. "America's Richard Holbrooke: The Balkans' Bulldozer." August 5. http://news.bbc.co.uk/2/hi/americas/413122.stm.

———. 2009. "North Korea 'Defiant' Amid Warnings." May 27. http://news.bbc.co.uk/2/hi/asia-pacific/8068619.stm.

Beardsley, Kyle C., David M. Quinn, Bidisha Biswas, and Jonathan Wilkenfeld. 2006. "Mediation Style and Crisis Outcome." *Journal of Conflcit Resolution* 50, no. 1: 58–86.

Ben-Yehuda, Hemda. 1999. "Opportunity Crises: Frameworks and Findings, 1918–1994." *Conflict Management and Peace Studies* 17, no. 1: 69–102.

Bercovitch, Jacob. 1997. "Mediation in International Conflict: An Overview of Theory, a Review of Practice." In *Peacemaking in International Conflict: Methods and Techniques,* ed. I. William Zartman and J. Lewis Rasmussen. Washington, D.C.: United States Institute of Peace Press: 125–153.

Bernstein, Thomas. 1995. "Muted Differences: The Negotiations to Normalize U.S.-Chinese Relations." Institute for the Study of Diplomacy, Case Number 426. Pew Case Studies in International Affairs. Washington, D.C.: Georgetown University.

Bobrow, Davis B. 1981. "The Perspective of Great Power Foreign Policy." In *Dynamics of Third Party Intervention: Kissinger and the Middle East,* ed. Jeffrey Z. Rubin. New York: Praeger: 171–196.

Bobrow, Davis B., and Mark A. Boyer. 2004. *Defensive Internationalism.* Ann Arbor: University of Michigan Press.

Bondansky, Daniel. 2001. "Bonn Voyage: Kyoto's Uncertain Revival." *National Interest* 65 (Fall): 45–56.

*Boston Globe.* 2001. "The Stakes in North Korea." June 30, A14.

Boyer, Mark A. 2000. "Issue Definition and Two-Level Games: An Application to the American Foreign Policy Process." *Diplomacy and Statecraft* 11, no. 2: 185–212.

Brams, Steven J., and Jeffrey M. Togman. 1998. "Cooperation through Threats: The Northern Ireland Case." *PS: Political Science and Politics* 31, no. 1 (March): 32–39.

Brecher, Michael, and Jonathan Wilkenfeld. 2000. *A Study of Crisis,* 2nd ed. Ann Arbor: University of Michigan Press.

Butler, Michael J. 2007. "Crisis Bargaining and Third-Party Mediation: Bridging the Gap." *International Negotiation* 12, no. 2: 249–274.

Butler, Michael J., and Mark A. Boyer. 2003. "Bosnian Peacekeeping and EU Tax Harmony: Evolving Policy Frames and Changing Policy Processes." *International Journal* 58, no. 2: 389–416.

———. 2009 "Diplomacy and Negotiation in a Foreign Policy Context." *International Studies Compendium.* Hoboken, N.J.: Wiley-Blackwell.

Byrne, Sean J. 2007. "The Roles of External Ethnoguarantors and Primary Mediators in Cyprus and Northern Ireland." *Conflict Resolution Quarterly* 24, no. 2: 149–172.

Carnegie Endowment for International Peace. 2007. "A Closer Japan-US Economic Relationship." February 22. www.policyinnovations.org/calendar/data/000011.

Carter, Jimmy. 1982. *Keeping Faith: Memoirs of a President*. New York: Bantam.

CBS News. 2008. "Schwarzenegger's Green Challenge." *60 Minutes*. December 12. www.cbsnews.com/stories/2008/12/18/60minutes/main4677334.shtml.

CNN.com. 2004. "Annan Announces Cyprus Plan." March 31.

———. 2004. "Celebrations as EU Grows to 25." June 14.

———. 2009. "Iran 101: Understanding the Unrest." June 18.

———. 2009. "Iran Bans International Journalists from Covering Rallies." June 16.

Cha, Victor. 2009. "Up Close and Personal, Here's What I Learned." *Washington Post*, June 14, B1.

Cohen, Eliot A. 1997. "Military Power and International Order." In *Managing Global Chaos: Sources of and Responses to International Conflict*, ed. Chester Crocker, Fen Osler Hampson, and Pamela Aall. Washington, D.C.: United States Institute of Peace Press: 223–236.

Cohen, Raymond. 1997. *Negotiating across Cultures*, 2nd ed. Washington, D.C.: United States Institute of Peace Press.

Colosi, Thomas R. 1986. "The Iceberg Principle: Secrecy in Negotiation." In *Perspectives on Negotiation: Four Case Studies and Interpretations*, ed. Diane B. Bendahmane and John W. McDonald Jr. Washington, D.C.: Center for the Study of Foreign Affairs.

Conybeare, John. 1986. "Trade Wars: A Comparative Study of Anglo-Hanse, Franco-Italian, and Smoot-Hawley Conflicts." In *Cooperation under Anarchy*, ed. Kenneth E. Oye. Princeton, N.J.: Princeton University Press: 147–172.

Cooper, Richard N. 1998. "Toward a Real Global Warming Treaty." *Foreign Affairs* 77, no. 2 (March/April): 66–79.

CRI News. 2008. "Barosso: Interdependence and Reform Are Needed to Solve Global Financial Crisis." October 24. http://english.cri.cn/4026/2008/10/24/1241s417627.htm.

Cumings, Bruce. 2003. "Wrong Again." *London Review of Books* 25, no. 23 (October 31). www.lrb.co.uk/v25/n23/cumi01_.html.

Davies, John, and Edward Kaufman, eds. 2002. *Second Track/Citizens' Diplomacy: Concepts and Techniques for Conflict Transformation*. Lanham, Md.: Rowman & Littlefield.

Debt and Development Coalition Ireland. "Crisis in the Global Economy—Reform Must Be Democratic and People-Centered." www.debtireland.org/campaigns/DDCI_financial_crisis_briefing.pdf.

Dent, David W., and Paul Sondrol. 1998. "Teaching through Simulation: The Model OAS." *LASA Forum* 27, no. 4 (Winter): 8–14.

Dixit, Avinash K., and Barry Nalebuff. 1991. *Thinking Strategically: The Competitive Edge in Business, Politics, and Everyday Life*. New York: Norton.

Donahue, Thomas R. 1991. "The Case against NAFTA." *Columbia Journal of World Business* 26: 91–95.

Downs, George W., David M. Rocke, and Randolph M. Siverson. 1986. "Arms Race and Cooperation." In *Cooperation under Anarchy*, ed. Kenneth E. Oye. Princeton, N.J.: Princeton University Press: 118–146.

Drezner, Daniel W., ed. 2003. *Locating the Proper Authorities: The Interaction of Domestic and International Institutions*. Ann Arbor: University of Michigan Press.

Driscoll, David D. 1997. "What Is the International Monetary Fund?" July. www.imf.org/external/pubs/ft/exrp/what.htm.

Druckman, Daniel. 1994. "Nationalism, Patriotism, and Group Loyalty: A Social Psychological Perspective." *Mershon International Studies Review* 38, no. 1 (April): 43–68.

Druckman, Daniel, and Benjamin Broome. 1991. "Value Differences and Conflict Resolution: Familiarity or Liking?" *Journal of Conflict Resolution* 35, no. 4 (December): 571–593.

Druckman, Daniel, and James N. Druckman. 1996. "Visibility and Negotiating Flexibility." *Journal of Social Psychology* 136, no. 1 (February): 117–120.

Edwards, Michael. 2001. "Introduction." In *Global Citizen Action*, ed. Michael Edwards and John Gaventa. Boulder, Colo.: Rienner: 1–16.

Eilperin, Juliet. 2008. "Interim Climate Pact Approved." *Washington Post*, December 13, A2.

Elliot, Guy, et al. 2002. "Teaching Conflict Assessment and Frame Analysis Through Interactive Web-based Simulations." *Interactive Journal of Conflict Management* 13, no. 4: 320–340.

Environmental News Network. 1997. "Kyoto Pact Reached, No Promise of Ratification." December 11. www.enn.com/specialreports/climate/news/kyotoends.asp.

Esty, Daniel C., and Andrew S. Winston. 2006. *Green to Gold: How Smart Companies Use Environmental Strategy to Innovate, Create Value, and Build Competitive Advantage*. New Haven, Conn.: Yale University Press.

EU Digest. 2007. "France Leads Backlash Against Euro, Monetary Union." January 13. www.eu-digest.com/2007/01/globeandmailcom-france-leads-backlash.html.

EurActiv. 2008. "EU Plays 'Good Cop, Bad Cop' with Turkey." April 22. www.euractiv.com/en/enlargement/eu-plays-good-cop-bad-cop-turkey/article-171814.

Eurofound. Eironline. 2008. "Industrial Relations in the Airline Sector." March 5. www.eurofound.europa.eu/eiro/2005/08/study/tn0508101s.htm.

Evans, Peter B., Harold K. Jacobson, and Robert D. Putnam, eds. 1993. *Double-Edged Diplomacy: International Bargaining and Domestic Politics*. Berkeley: University of California Press.

Fahrenthold, David A. 2009. "Warming Skeptics Get Heard on the Hill." *Washington Post*, May 19, A4.

Fedarko, Kevin. 1993. "Swimming the Oslo Channel." *Time*, September 13, 50–51.

Fisher, Roger, and William Ury. 1991. *Getting to Yes: Negotiating Agreements without Giving In*, 2nd ed. New York: Penguin.

Fisher, Roger, et al. 1997. *Coping with International Conflict*. Upper Saddle River, N.J.: Prentice Hall.

Florini, Ann M. 2001. "Transnational Civil Society." In *Global Citizen Action*, ed. Michael Edwards and John Gaventa. Boulder, Colo.: Rienner.

Freeman, Chas. W., Jr. 1997. *The Diplomat's Dictionary*, rev. ed. Washington, D.C.: United States Institute of Peace Press.

Friedman, Raymond. 2002. "New Perspectives on Teaching about Conflict: Simulations, Cases, and Exercises." *International Journal of Conflict Management* 13, no. 4: 318–320.

Friedman, Thomas. 2008. *Hot, Flat and Crowded*. New York: Macmillan.

Ganguli, Sumit, and Devin T. Hagerty. 2006. *Fearful Symmetry: India-Pakistan Crises in the Shadow of Nuclear Weapons*. Seattle: University of Washington Press.

George, Alexander L. 1997. *Forceful Persuasion: Coercive Diplomacy as an Alternative to War*. Washington, D.C.: United States Institute of Peace Press.

Gilboa, Eytan. 2001. "Diplomacy in the Media Age: Three Models of Uses and Effects." *Diplomacy and Statecraft* 12, no. 2: 1–28.

Guetzkow, Harold, and Cleo H. Cherryholmes. 1966. *Inter-Nation Simulation Kit*. Chicago: Science Research Associates.

Haas, Peter M. 1992. "Introduction: Epistemic Communities and International Policy Coordination." *International Organization* 46, no. 1 (Winter): 1–36.

Haass, Richard N. 1997. "Using Force: Lessons and Choices for U.S. Foreign Policy." In *Managing Global Chaos: Sources of and Responses to International Conflict*, ed. Chester Crocker, Fen Osler Hampson, and Pamela Aall. Washington, D.C.: United States Institute of Peace Press: 197–208.

Hansen, Holly E., Sara McLaughlin Mitchell, and Stephen Nemeth. 2008. "IO Mediation of Interstate Conflicts." *Journal of Conflict Resolution* 52, no. 2: 295–325.

Hardin, Garrett. 1968. "The Tragedy of the Commons." *Science* 162 (December 13): 1243–1248.

Hazard, Leah. 2008. "Mexico's War on Drugs: A War on the Economy?" *Global Envision*, September 8. www.globalenvision.org/tags/drug-trafficking.

Herskovitz, Jon. 2009. "North Korea Threatens South, Restarts Plutonium Plant." Reuters, May 27. www.reuters.com/article/topNews/idUSSEO14165620090527.

Herzog, Michael. 2006. "Can Hamas Be Tamed?" *Foreign Affairs* 88, no. 2 (March/April): 83–94.

Hewitt, J. Joseph, Jonathan Wilkenfeld, and Ted Robert Gurr. 2009. *Peace and Conflict 2010*. Boulder, Colo.: Paradigm.

Hill, Christopher. 2005. "The Beijing Accord and the Future of the Six-Party Talks." United States Institute of Peace. Current Issues Briefing. September 28. www.usip.org/events/beijing-accord-and-future-six-party-talks.

Holbrooke, Richard. 1999. *To End a War*. New York: Modern Library.

*Hong Kong Economic Journal*. 2003. "Hu Jintao Writes to Kim Jong-Il to Open Door to Six-Party Talks." The Nautilus Institute. DPRK Briefing Book, Policy Area: Multilateral Talks. August 28. www.nautilus.org/DPRKBriefingBook/multilateralTalks/index.html.

Hook, Steven W. 1995. *National Interest and Foreign Aid*. Boulder, Colo.: Rienner.

Hopmann, P. Terrence. 1996. *The Negotiation Process and the Resolution of International Conflicts*. Columbia: University of South Carolina Press.

Houghton, John T., G. J. Jenkins, and J. J. Ephraums. 1990. *Climate Change: The IPCC Scientific Assessment 1990*. Cambridge, UK: Cambridge University Press.

Huntington, Samuel P. 1993. "The Clash of Civilizations?" *Foreign Affairs* 73, no. 3 (Summer): 22–49.

Ingraham, Jesson. 1999. "The Irish Peace Process." February 2. cain.ulst.ac.uk/events/peace/talks.htm.

Jarman, Neil. 1997. *Material Conflicts: Parades and Visual Displays in Northern Ireland.* Oxford, UK: Berg.

Jeffrey, Charles, ed. 1997. *The Regional Dimension of the European Union.* London: Frank Cass.

Kaul, Inge, Pedro Conceicao, Katell Le Goulven, and Ronald U. Mendoza. 2003. *Providing Global Public Goods: Managing Globalization.* New York: Oxford University Press.

Kennan, George. 1997. "Diplomacy without Diplomats?" *Foreign Affairs* 76, no. 5 (September/October): 198–212.

Kennedy, Robert F. 1969. *Thirteen Days: A Memoir of the Cuban Missile Crisis.* New York: Norton.

Kerrigan, Karen. 1997. "Viewpoint: Global Warming Treaty Damages U.S." *Business News*, October 27. www.amcity.com/dayton/stories/102797/editorial4.html.

Kessler, Glenn. 2004. "North Korea Still Denies Enriching Uranium." *Washington Post*, January 13, A12.

Kissinger, Henry. 2009. "Reining in Pyongyang." *Washington Post*, June 8, A15.

Kleiner, Juergen. 2005. "The Bush Administration and the Nuclear Challenges by North Korea." *Diplomacy and Statecraft* 16, no. 2 (June): 203–226.

Kratochwil, Friedrich. 1984. "Thrasymmachos Revisited: On the Relevance of Norms and the Study of Law for International Relations." *Journal of International Affairs* 37, no. 2 (Winter): 343–356.

Krauss, Carolin. 2009. "Drug Trade in Colombia." International Relations and Security Center (ISN) ETH Zurich. www.isn.ethz.ch/isn/Current-Affairs/Special-Reports/Drug-Trade-in-Colombia/Editorial.

Kremenyuk, Victor, ed. 2002. *International Negotiation: Analysis, Approaches, Issues.* San Francisco: Jossey-Bass.

Kuekeleire, Stephen. 2003. "The European Union as a Diplomatic Actor: Internal, Traditional, and Structural Diplomacy." *Diplomacy and Statecraft* 14, no. 3 (September): 31–56.

Kumar, Chetan. 2004. "Conflict Prevention in South Asia." In *Conflict Prevention: From Rhetoric to Reality*, ed. Albrecht Schnabel and David Carment. Lanham, Md.: Lexington: 103–126.

Larkin, John. 2003. "Mission Impossible?" *Time*. May 5. www.time.com/time/magazine/article/0,9171,449514,00.html.

Langhorne, Richard. 1997. "Current Developments in Diplomacy: Who Are the Diplomats Now?" *Diplomacy and Statecraft* 8, no. 2 (July): 1–15.

———. 2005. "The Diplomacy of Nonstate Actors." *Diplomacy and Statecraft* 16, no. 2 (June): 331–339.

Lehti, Mark, and David J. Smith. 2003. *Post-Cold War Identity Politics: Northern and Baltic Experiences.* London: Frank Cass.

Lewis, John L. 2004. "Hope on North Korea." *Washington Post*, January 27, A17.

Lewis, Richard D. 2000. *When Cultures Collide: Managing Successfully across Cultures.* Sonoma, Calif.: Nicholas Brealy.

Lieberfeld, Daniel. 2008. "Secrecy and 'Two-Level Games' in the Oslo Accord: What the Primary Sources Tell Us." *International Negotiation* 13, no. 1: 133–146.

Lisowski, Michael. 2005. "How NGOs Use Their Facilitative Negotiating Power and Bargaining Assets to Affect International Environmental Negotiations." *Diplomacy and Statecraft* 16, no. 2 (June): 361–383.

Lozano, Rodrigo. 2007. "Collaboration as a Pathway for Sustainability." *Sustainable Development* 15, no. 6: 370–381.

Lumsdaine, David H. 1993. *Moral Vision in International Politics: The Foreign Aid Regime, 1949–1989.* Princeton, N.J.: Princeton University Press.

Mansbach, Richard. 1997. *The Global Puzzle*, 2nd ed. New York: Houghton Mifflin.

Mathews, Jessica. 1997. "Power Shift." *Foreign Affairs* 76, no. 1 (January/February): 50–67.

Mattern, Janice Bialy. 2005. *Ordering International Politics: Identity, Crisis, and Representational Force.* London: Routledge.

Mazarr, Michael J. 1995. "Going Just a Little Nuclear: Nonproliferation Lessons from North Korea." *International Security* 20, no. 2 (Autumn): 92–122.

McDonald, John W., ed. 1996. "Defining a U.S. Negotiating Style." *Special Issue of International Negotiation* 1, no. 2: 181–346.

Media Reality Check. 1997. "Media Research Center Cyberalert: Full Gore on Kyoto." December 15. www.mrc.org/news/cyberalert/1997/cyb19971215.html.

Mo, Jongryn. 1994. "The Logic of Two-Level Games with Endogenous Domestic Coalitions." *Journal of Conflict Resolution* 38, no. 3: 402–422.

———. 1995. "Domestic Institutions and International Bargaining: The Role of Agent Veto in Two-Level Games." *American Political Science Review* 89, no. 4: 914–924.

Moore, Thomas Gale. 1998. *Climate of Fear: Why We Shouldn't Worry about Global Warming.* Washington, D.C.: Cato Institute.

Mott, Richard N. 1997. "Can Gore's Actions Match His Lofty Words?" *Japan Times Online.* December 5. www.japantimes.co.jp/cop3/indepth/mott.html.

Mufson, Steven, and Juliet Eilperin. 2007. "Bush Steps Out Front on Climate Issue; But No Policy Shift Is Planned as Nations Begin Debate on Post-Kyoto Accord." *Washington Post,* September 23, A14.

Murray, John S. 1986. "Understanding Competing Theories of Negotiation." *Negotiation Journal* 2, no. 2 (April): 179–186.

Mushakoji, Kinhide. 1976. "The Cultural Premises of Japanese Diplomacy." In *The Silent Power: Japan's Identity and World Role*, ed. Japan Center for International Exchange. Tokyo: Simul Press: 35–49.

Northern Ireland Monitoring Commission. 2009. Twenty-First Report. May 7. cain.ulst.ac.uk/issues/politics/docs/imc/imcreports.htm.

Official Documentation and Information from Norway. Ministry of Fisheries Homepage. http://odin.dep.no/fid/eng.

Oh, Kangdon, and Ralph C. Hassig. 2003. "North Korea: The Hardest Nut." *Foreign Policy* 139 (November/December): 44–46.

Oka, Takashi. 1992. "Tools for a U.S.-Japan Partnership." *Christian Science Monitor*, November 27, 18A.

Olsen, Edward A. 2003. "U.S.-North Korea: From Brinkmanship to Dialogue." Strategic Insight (April 1). Center for Contemporary Conflict, National Security Affairs Department. www.ccc.nps.nav.mil/rsepResources/si/apr03/eastAsia.asp.

Otterman, Sharon. 2003. "Iraq: The Role of Tribes." Council on Foreign Relations. Backgrounder. November 14. www.cfr.org/publication/7681.

Pigman, Geoffrey Allen. 2005. "Making Room at the Negotiating Table: The Growth of Diplomacy Between Nation-State Governments and Non-State Economic Entities." *Diplomacy and Statecraft* 16, no. 2 (June): 385–401.

Pletka, Danielle. 2009. "Negotiating for the Other Side." *Washington Post*, June 5, A17.

Ponce, Mercedes M., ed. 1997. "The Florida Connection: Florida's Position on the Free Trade Area of the Americas." May. http://americas.fiu.edu/americas/americas-frames-noblue.html.

Price-Smith, Andrew T. 2002. *The Health of Nations*. Cambridge, Mass.: MIT Press.

Princen, Thomas. 1992. *Intermediaries in International Conflict*. Princeton, N.J.: Princeton University Press.

Purvis, Nigel. 2003. "Climate Change Negotiations: A Foreign Policy Perspective." *Resources for the Future*. March 28. www.brookings.org/views/articles/fellows/purvis20030328.htm.

Putnam, Robert D. 1988. "Diplomacy and Domestic Politics: The Logic of Two-Level Games." *International Organization* 42, no. 3: 427–460.

Raiffa, Howard. 1982. *The Art and Science of Negotiation*. Cambridge, Mass.: Harvard University Press.

Raiffa, Howard, et al. 2002. *Negotiation Analysis*. Cambridge, Mass.: Harvard University Press.

Rasmussen, J. Lewis. 1997. "Peacemaking in the Twenty-First Century: New Rules, New Roles, New Actors." In *Peacemaking in International Conflict: Methods and Techniques*, ed. I. William Zartman and J. Lewis Rasmussen. Washington, D.C.: United States Institute of Peace Press: 23–50.

Reiner, David M. 2001. "Climate Impasse." *Environment* 43, no. 2 (March): 36–43.

Reno, William. 1996. "Business Conflict and the Shadow State: The Case of West Africa." In *Business and the State in International Relations*, ed. Ronald W. Cox. Boulder, Colo.: Westview: 149–163.

Robinson, Gillian. 1992. "Cross-Community Marriage in Northern Ireland." http://cain.ulst.ac.uk/issues/marriage/ccmni.htm.

Ross, John, Jr., et al. 2001. "Interactive Video Negotiator Training: A Preliminary Evaluation of the McGill Negotiation Simulator." *Simulation and Gaming* 32, no. 4: 451–468.

Rourke, John T., Ralph G. Carter, and Mark A. Boyer. 1996. *Making American Foreign Policy*, 2nd ed. Guilford, Conn.: Brown and Benchmark.

Ruggie, John G. 1975. "International Responses to Technology: Concepts and Trends." *International Organization* 29 (Summer): 552–584.

Sandler, Todd. 1997. *Global Challenges*. Cambridge, UK: Cambridge University Press.

Satter, David. 2003. *Darkness at Dawn: The Rise of the Russian Criminal State*. New Haven, Conn.: Yale University Press.

Sebenius, James K. 1984. *Negotiating the Law of the Sea*. Cambridge, Mass.: Harvard University Press.

———. 2002. "International Negotiation Analysis." In *International Negotiation*, 2nd ed., ed. Victor A. Kremenyuk. San Francisco: Jossey-Bass: 229–255.

Sewall, Sarah. 2004. "Stepping Back, Staying Put." *Washington Post*, June 20, B1.

Shaw, Carolyn M. 2004. "Using Role-Play Scenarios in the IR Classroom: An Examination of Exercises on Peacekeeping Operations and Foreign-Policy Decision Making." *International Studies Perspectives* 5, no. 1: 1–22.

Sick, Gary. 1985. *All Fall Down: America's Fateful Encounter with Iran*. London: I. B. Tauris.

Sigal, Leon. 2003. "Negotiating with the North." Bulletin of the Atomic Scientists (November/December). The Nautilus Institute. DPRK Briefing Book, Policy Area: Multilateral Talks. December 9. www.nautilus.org/DPRKBriefing Book/multilateralTalks/index.html.

Skocpol, Theda. 1988. "The Limits of the New Deal System and the Roots of Contemporary Welfare Dilemmas." In *The Politics of Policy in the United States*, ed. Margaret Weir, Ann Shola Orloft, and Theda Skocpol. Princeton, N.J.: Princeton University Press: 293–311.

Smith, Fred, and Jim Sheehan. 1997. "Kyoto Gets Gored." CEI Update. December 8. www.junkscience.com/news/kyoto6.htm.

Snyder, Glenn, and Paul Deising. 1977. *Conflict among Nations*. Princeton, N.J.: Princeton University Press.

Spero, Joan Edelman, and Jeffrey A. Hart. 2003. *The Politics of International Economic Relations*, 6th ed. Dallas: Thompson Wadsworth.

Starkey, Brigid, and Jonathan Wilkenfeld. 1996. "Project ICONS: Computer-Assisted Negotiations for the IR Classroom." *International Studies Notes* 21, no. 1 (Winter): 25–29.

Summit of the Americas Center. 2005. "Florida Position Paper." www.americas net.net/home/florida_outreach.htm.

Suskind, Ron. 2004. *The Price of Loyalty: George W. Bush, the White House, and the Education of Paul O'Neill*. New York: Simon & Schuster.

Taylor, Philip. 1984. *Nonstate Actors in International Politics: From Transregional to Substate Organizations*. Boulder, Colo.: Westview.

Thiessen, Ernest M., and Joseph P. McMahon, Jr. 1999. "Beyond Win-Win in Cyberspace." November 11. www.jpmcmahon.com/beyond_win.htm.

Tkacik, John J. 2004. "Offer Real Support, Not Excuses, for Taiwan's WHO Bid." The Heritage Foundation Policy Research and Analysis. Executive Memorandum 927. April 29. www.heritage.org/Research/AsiaandthePacific/ em927.cfm.

Torney-Purta, Judith. 1998. "Evaluating Programs Designed to Teach International Content and Negotiation Skills." *International Negotiation* (Special Edition) 3: 77–97.

Trumbore, Peter F., and Mark A. Boyer. 2000. "Two-Level Negotiations in International Crisis: Testing the Impact of Regime Type and Issue Area." *Journal of Peace Research* 37, no. 6: 679–698.

United Nations Environment Programme. "Information Unit for Conventions (IUC)." www.unep.org/dec/support/information_unit.html.

United Nations Framework Convention on Climate Change. www.unfccc.de.

University of Maryland. 2006. Sadat Lecture for Peace. October 24. www.sadat.umd.edu/lecture/lecture/ElBaradei.htm.

Viega, Pedro da Motta. 2005. "Brazil and the G20 Group of Developing Countries." In *Managing the Challenges of WTO Participation: 45 Case Studies*, ed. Peter Gallagher, Patrick Low, and Andrew L. Soler. Cambridge, UK: Cambridge University Press: 109–119.

Villagrasa, Delia. 2002. "Kyoto Protocol Negotiations: Reflections on the Role of Women." *Gender and Development* 10, no. 2: 1–4.

Walcott, Charles, ed. 1980. *Simple Simulations II*. Washington, D.C.: American Political Science Association.

Warrick, Joby. 1997. "Climate Pact Rescued in Final Hours." *Washington Post*, December 13, A1.

*Washington Post*. 1998. "Iraq: Road to the Current Crisis." February 15, A34.

———. 2005. "In Break with UN, Bush Calls Sudan Killings Genocide." June 2. www.washingtonpost.com/wpdyn/content/article/2005/06/01/AR2005060101725.html.

Wilkenfeld, Jonathan. 1991. "Trigger-Response Transitions in Foreign Policy Crises, 1929–1985." *Journal of Conflict Resolution* 35, no. 1 (March): 143–169.

Wilkenfeld, Jonathan, and Joyce Kaufman. 1993. "Political Science: Network Simulation in International Politics." *Social Science Computer Review* 11, no. 4 (Winter): 464–476.

Wilkenfeld, Jonathan, et al. 2005. *Mediating International Crises*. London: Routledge.

Women's International League for Peace and Freedom. NGO Webring. www.peacewomen.org/webring.html.

Woodward, Bob. 2004. *Plan of Attack*. New York: Simon & Schuster.

Yong, Heun An. 2003. "Politicians, Electoral Law and International Bargaining Approaches: A Case Study of Korea-US Agricultural Trade Negotiations." *Pacific Focus* 18, no. 1: 151–173.

Young, Joseph K. 2006. "Simulating Two-Level Negotiations." *International Studies Perspectives* 7, no. 1: 77–82.

Young, Oran. 1968. *The Politics of Force: Bargaining during International Crises*. Princeton, N.J.: Princeton University Press.

Zartman, I. William, and Saadia Touval. 1996. "International Mediation in the Post–Cold War Era." In *Managing Global Chaos: Sources of and Responses to International Conflict*, ed. Chester Crocker, Fen Osler Hampson, and Pamela Aall. Washington, D.C.: United States Institute of Peace Press: 445–461.

Zimmerman, William. 1973. "Issue Area and Foreign Policy Process: A Research Note in Search of a General Theory." *American Political Science Review* 67: 1204–1212.

# Index

# About the Authors

**Dr. Brigid Starkey** is a lecturer in political science at the University of Maryland, Baltimore County (UMBC). She also serves as a research and training consultant to the International Communication and Negotiation Simulations (ICONS) Project. Dr. Starkey teaches in the area of international relations and comparative politics. She publishes in the areas of negotiation and interactive learning for the college classroom. Dr. Starkey's articles have appeared in *Simulation and Gaming, International Studies Notes,* and the *Fletcher Forum of World Affairs.*

**Dr. Mark A. Boyer** is a professor of political science at the University of Connecticut and codirector of the GlobalEd Project. He was Pew Faculty Fellow in International Affairs and an SSRC-MacArthur Fellow in International Peace and Security. Dr. Boyer is the author of *International Cooperation and Public Goods* (1993), coauthor (with Davis B. Bobrow) of *Defensive Internationalism* (2004), and coauthor (with John Rourke) of *World Politics,* 6th ed. (2005), among others. He has published articles in such journals as the *Journal of Conflict Resolution, Review of International Political Economy, International Journal, Social Science Computer Review, Defence Economics,* and *Diplomacy and Statecraft.*

**Dr. Jonathan Wilkenfeld** is a professor in the Department of Government and Politics and director of the Center for International Development and Conflict Management at the University of Maryland. He is also the founder of the International Communication and Negotiation Simulations (ICONS) Project. Dr. Wilkenfeld has published widely in the area of foreign policy analysis, international crisis, negotiation, and simulation. His book *A Study of Crisis* was coauthored with Michael Brecher (2000); his most recent work is *Mediating International Crises* (Wilkenfeld et al. 2005).